CULTURAL ANTAGONISM AND THE CRISIS OF REALITY IN LATIN AMERICA

CULTURAL ANTAGONISM AND THE CRISIS OF REALITY IN LATIN AMERICA

Horacio Legrás

BLOOMSBURY ACADEMIC
NEW YORK • LONDON • OXFORD • NEW DELHI • SYDNEY

BLOOMSBURY ACADEMIC
Bloomsbury Publishing Inc
1385 Broadway, New York, NY 10018, USA
50 Bedford Square, London, WC1B 3DP, UK
29 Earlsfort Terrace, Dublin 2, Ireland

BLOOMSBURY, BLOOMSBURY ACADEMIC and the Diana logo are trademarks of Bloomsbury Publishing Plc

First published in the United States of America 2022
Paperback edition published 2024

Copyright © Horacio Legrás, 2022

Horacio Legrás has asserted his right under the Copyright, Designs and Patents Act, 1988, to be identified as Author of this work.

For legal purposes the Acknowledgments on p. xiv constitute an extension of this copyright page.

Cover design by Eleanor Rose
Cover image © Horacio Legrás

All rights reserved. No part of this publication may be reproduced or transmitted in any form or by any means, electronic or mechanical, including photocopying, recording, or any information storage or retrieval system, without prior permission in writing from the publishers.

Bloomsbury Publishing Inc does not have any control over, or responsibility for, any third-party websites referred to or in this book. All internet addresses given in this book were correct at the time of going to press. The author and publisher regret any inconvenience caused if addresses have changed or sites have ceased to exist, but can accept no responsibility for any such changes.

A catalog record for this book is available from the Library of Congress.

ISBN: HB: 978-1-5013-9294-8
PB: 978-1-5013-9290-0
ePDF: 978-1-5013-9292-4
eBook: 978-1-5013-9293-1

Typeset by Newgen KnowledgeWorks Pvt. Ltd., Chennai, India

To find out more about our authors and books visit www.bloomsbury.com and sign up for our newsletters.

In memory of my mother, Blanca Miriam Legrás

CONTENTS

Preface	ix
Acknowledgments	xiv
Chapter 1 THE NATIVIST AVANT-GARDE	1
Chapter 2 MIGUEL ANGEL ASTURIAS: THE SCIENCE OF LITERATURE	21
Chapter 3 SEEING WOMEN PHOTOGRAPHED IN REVOLUTIONARY MEXICO	51
Chapter 4 DIALECTIC OF DIASPORIC CONSCIOUSNESS: THE AFRO-CUBAN VOICE AND THE HYPOSTASIS OF MEANING	77
Chapter 5 JOSÉ MARÍA ARGUEDAS: CAPITALIST ACCUMULATION AND NOVELISTIC MODE OF PRESENTATION IN THE ANDES	113
Chapter 6 PSYCHOTIC VIOLENCE: CRIME AND CONSUMPTION IN THE APOCALYPTIC PHASE OF CAPITAL	133
Works Cited	157
Index	169

PREFACE

A passage from W. E. B. Du Bois's *Black Reconstruction in America* sets the tone that I want to resonate throughout this book. Du Bois is describing the first century of the US independent life.

> America thus stepped forward in the first blossoming of the modern age and added to the Art of Beauty, gift of the Renaissance, and to Freedom of Belief, gift of Martin Luther and Leo X, a vision of democratic self-government: the domination of political life by the intelligent decision of free and self-sustaining men. What an idea and what an area for its realization— endless land of richest fertility, natural resources such as Earth seldom exhibited before, a population infinite in variety, of universal gift, burned in the fires of poverty and caste, yearning towards the Unknown God; and self-reliant pioneers, unafraid of man or devil. It was the Supreme Adventure, in the last Great Battle of the West, for that human freedom which would release the human spirit from lower lust for mere meat, and set it free to dream and sing.
> And then some unjust God leaned, laughing, over the ramparts of heaven and drop a black man in the midst.[1]

Reality is always organized as a scene. It is in the nature of an antagonism to pierce through its fictional consistency. In the European tradition, the idea of antagonism is associated with Marx's notion of class conflict (*Klassengegensatz*). In Latin America, the situation is more complicated since several identities compete to embody the antagonistic position that in Europe was hegemonized by the working class. However, none of these identities ever managed to embody this position completely. In Europe, the challenge of the working class was immediately recognizable to the dominant block, since this antagonistic position emerged from the very structure of the dominant conditions of production. In Latin America, what becomes antagonistic is never simply an identity. It is an identity that is partially out of place, untimely, unrecognizable, even outright uncanny. Historically, literature and the arts played the role of staging these antagonistic formations for societies often described as hybrid, heterogeneous, or *abiggarradas*. However, since these antagonisms were not

---

1. W. E. B Du Bois, *Black Reconstruction in America. 1860–1880* (New York: Simon & Schuster, 1992), 29–30.

an organic part of the social dynamic of the reproduction of power, their effect on the social imaginary was not so much one of open contestation but rather a pervasive impugnation of the claims of these social forms to incarnate and regulate the sense and the boundaries of reality.[2]

In this book, I map different ways in which a reckoning with antagonism led to a more or less vast reconceptualization of the real in twentieth-century Latin America. (I exclude from consideration the nineteenth century for reasons that will become clear below). Unlike the United States, where a dominant narrative stereotyped the antagonistic element under the heading of race, in Latin America the incarnations of the antagonism are multiple, and break down along the lines of national formations. The reason for this is rather simple. The establishment of what counts as real is the result of the tension between the forces of reproduction (the state, the cultural industry, socialized time) and those phenomena representing dispersion and intractability. The antagonism that belies the idea of social homogeneity is not the same for a Cuban intellectual of the 1930s whose work is framed by the strong presence of Afro-Cuban culture as it might be for a Mexican photographer in the early twentieth century confronted with the rise to social prominence of the figure of women. Likewise, Miguel Angel Asturias uses an ethnographic gesture to cast the peasant as antagonistic in the Guatemala of the 1940s, while an ethnographer like José María Arguedas turns to the temporal contradictions of uneven development to produce his outline of antagonism in the Peru of the 1960s. While each one of these processes answers to a particular and unique genealogy, the standing question is: why should the emergence of an antagonism affect the notion of reality as a whole?

I think that an answer to this question lies in the role that positivism and historicism played in the consolidation of the Latin American nation-states in the nineteenth century. By the 1870s, positivism had acquired the status of an official ideology in the most developed countries of the region. Its official status endowed positivism with a marked dogmatic tone. Positivism could not entertain other relationship to a heterogeneous reality than one of disavowal. The gap created by this disavowal was covered by historicism, which acted as a constant reminder of the irrecusable injunction to join the great current of civilized nations. If positivism could not find its bearings in the real (from which it was somewhat detached), it could always place it in

---

2. The staging of an antagonism is not a prerogative of artistic formations and can also be achieved by some popular performances, although only under certain specific conditions. See Kathleen Wilson, "The Performance of Freedom: Maroons and the Colonial Order in Eighteenth-Century Jamaica and the Atlantic Sound," *William and Mary Quarterly*, vol. 66, no. 1 (2009): 45–86.

the indefinite postponement of the historical.[3] This alliance between positivism and historicism constituted a strong imaginary formation that the twentieth century never completely outgrew.

While it can be argued that the first decades of independent life showed a respite to the drive for imaginarization (for the reduction of history to a field of unified meanings), a process akin to what Marx called "formal subsumption" has accompanied the integration of Latin America into the global flows of capitalism since colonial times. For formal subsumption, I understand the fact that the commodities that flowed from Latin America to England and other industrial centers were not themselves produced under capitalist conditions such as wage labor, the reinvestment of profits, the juridical oversight of production, a unified monetary policy, an ethical conception of the self as either worker or entrepreneur—among others. The local histories embodied in these peripheral products was erased in the process of incorporation into the world of commodities.

Throughout its history, Latin America was subjected not only to a formal subsumption of labor but to a formal subsumption of its symbolic production as well.[4] At the historical point when literature and art became the sites of enunciation of a complex process of modernization, the history of this formal subsumption took on the value of a negation of existence that was itself in need of negation. The project of embodiment inherent to Latin American modernism veers towards the past in a restitutive gesture towards an imaginary dimension ravaged by successive projects of abstraction, to the point that a respite in this process, such as Von Humboldt's 1799 expedition, is lived as a redemption impinging in the dimension of the figural.[5] Like in the case of Freud's hysterics, the cultural forms of the Latin American avant-garde suffered

---

3. This deferral of the present into a projected future history constituted an unwarranted metaphysics which was not perceived as such by its practitioners. The positivists were able to *experience* this metaphysical promise through processes of financial indebtedness that constituted an unbreakable part of the integration of Latin American economies into the world market, but whose "real" effects were far more palpable at the level of state management and its bureaucrats than at the level of those marginalized populations that would soon incarnate the shape of antagonism in its purest form. Joseph Vogl discusses the epistemological ties of capital to cognitive realism Joseph Vogl, *The Specter of Capital,* trans. Joachim Redner and Robert Savage (Stanford: Stanford University Press, 2015).

4. Karl Marx discusses formal and real subsumption in the section "Results of the Immediate Processes of Production," of *Capital* but he left that section out of the published Volume I. The section in question appears reproduced as an appendix in the Penguin edition of *Capital*. Karl Marx, *Capital*, Vol. 1, trans. Ben Fowkes (New York: Penguin, 1992).

5. On Humboldt, see Mary Louise Pratt, *Imperial Eyes: Studies in Travel Writing and Transculturation* (London: Routledge, 2007). See also the more recent and

"mainly from reminiscences." Since the 1920s, literature and art hystericized the cultural history of Latin America and, by doing so, they pried open the possibility of a temporalization no longer subjected to the positivist prejudice of an irreversible flow of historical time.

In conditions of uneven development, the dominance of capital is temporal rather than territorial. Existence is only conferred on what is up-to-date. Insofar as the determinate negation of a Latin American phenomenality was emplaced in the gaze of capital, history proper could not begin. The twentieth century starts when the presence of otherness and others in the constitution of the real becomes irrepressible and, as a consequence, the consistency itself of the world flickers.[6] For such a process to start, the new shape of the antagonism must let itself be encoded in a discourse of universal purchase. Hence the historical significance of art and literature in the evolution of modern social imaginaries in the region. This does not mean that literature and art were always and everywhere at the service of providing shape to the recalcitrance that positivism aimed to suppress. Literature incorporated antagonistic elements into the mantle of a unified national representation in the works of the regionalist of the 1920s and 1930s.[7] Transculturation itself continued the governmental efforts of positivism by other means.[8] However, the development of this cultural apparatus of capture was traversed by a counter-history. This counter-history manifests itself by systematically blocking the solidarity between the order of representation and the order of reality. Through it, the historical becomes the place of repression and the present a time haunted by what a positivist historicism showed itself unable to exorcise. At some point, it became thinkable that the beginning of an effective history should coincide with the destruction of a fictive reality.

Cultural Antagonism and the Crisis of Reality in Latin America is composed of six chapters, which are as case studies in the constitution of a particular negativity whose effect lies in the impugnation of reality as a shared field of experience. Chapter 1, "The Nativist Avant-Garde," brings to light some constitutive conditions for the discourse of literature and the arts in twentieth-century Latin America as such conditions were originally elaborated by a series of writers who in their poetic, narrative, or editorial work, privileged local

---

comprehensive study by Daniela Bleichmar, *Visual Voyages. Images of Latin American Nature from Columbus to Darwin* (New Haven, CT: Yale University Press, 2017).

6. I use the word *other* as a mantle for forms of life that remain irreducible to a capitalist real subsumption of subjectivity at any particular point in time.

7. Carlos Alonso, *The Spanish American Regional Novel. Modernity and Autochthony* (Cambridge: Cambridge University Press, 1989).

8. Alberto Moreiras, "Introduction: The Conflict in Transculturation," in *Literary Cultures of Latin America. A Comparative History*. Vol. III, ed. Mario Valdés and Djelal Kadir (Oxford: Oxford University Press, 2004), 129–37.

themes often connected to indigenous or marginalized populations but dealt with them in a language that included the experimental fervor that characterized the European avant-gardes. In this chapter, I develop the notion of the nowthen as the specific embodiment of the Latin American artists' consciousness of the fragmented nature of his/her reality. Chapter 2, "Miguel Angel Asturias: The Science of Literature," centers on Asturias's *Men of Maize*. This formidable difficult novel has not attracted all the critical attention it deserves, in part because it has not been linked to any of the dominant narratives about Latin American literature. This chapter aims to correct this state of affairs. I read *Men of Maize* as staging the recognizable paradox of all auto-ethnographic writing: how to produce a portrait of popular life without positioning the narrator in the space of an observer alienated from the reality he tries to depict? Asturias reacts to the challenge of auto-ethnography with the tools forged in the confluence of ethnography and the historical avant-gardes. The result is a peculiar "science of literature"—an operation that is simultaneously cognitive and critical. Chapter 3, "Seeing Women Photographed in Revolutionary Mexico," is a historical reconstruction of documentary photography during the Mexican revolution (1910–20). This body of work is not so much "outside the canon," but canonic in its own way—and therefore deserving of its theory. In this chapter, I discuss how the image of women brings a unique tension to the documentary goals of photography and how the hermeneutical purchase of the image feeds from and alters the revolutionary framework that surrounds it. Chapter 4, "Dialectic of Diasporic Consciousness: The Afro-Cuban Voice and the Hypostasis of Meaning," maps the failed attempts by ethnography, *testimonio*, and literature to capture and vindicate the Black voice as an essential supplement to the idea of Cubanness. From Lydia Cabrera's *El Monte* to the novelistic production of Alejo Carpentier, from the Afro-Cuban lexicons of Fernando Ortiz to the meditations of testimonial writers and historians, the Black voice appears as constitutive of a logic of sense irreducible to that of meaning and national signification. Chapter 5, "José María Arguedas: Capitalist Accumulation and Novelistic Mode of Presentation in the Andes," reflects on the reception of José María Arguedas's *Todas las Sangres* (All the Bloods) in 1964. The long-awaited novel by Arguedas ended in turmoil when a selected group of social scientists dismissed the novel as a falsification of reality. In this chapter, I argue that *Todas las sangres* is best understood in terms of a problematic presentation of history under conditions of uneven capitalist development. Closing the book and the configuration of meaning opened by twentieth-century intellectuals, the final chapter, "Psychotic Violence: Crime and Consumption in the Apocalyptic Phase of Capital," takes violence against women in Ciudad Juárez as a site of revelation of how global modernity conditions the subjective formations of the present.

ACKNOWLEDGMENTS

The genre of the acknowledgment forces the writer to look back into the past to discern how this particular thing called "a book" came into being. As I abandon myself to this exercise, I am surprised by the number of people and circumstances that are needed to write a book. Adriana Johnson and Carl Good are the only two people who have read the whole manuscript, and I would not dare to submit it to a publisher (much less to a reader) without their counsel. I thank my friends in Southern California for the informal but formative discussions of some aspects of the book over the years: Freya Schiwy, Alessandro Fornazzari, Marta Hernández Salván, Jorge Marturano, Jacques Lezra. Two of my graduate students, Gwen Pare and George Allen, read several of the chapters and made valuable suggestions. For the final shape of the manuscript, I am also indebted to two anonymous readers whose punctual and friendly advice improved the argument and readability of the book. Finally, I want to acknowledge the professionalism of everyone at Bloomsbury, which made the always difficult task of putting the last touches on the manuscript relatively painless.

I should also thank my colleagues both inside and outside the Spanish and Portuguese department at the University of California-Irvine. As always, the School of Humanities at UCI offered its steady and generous support. I benefited from exchanges with colleagues in a variety of units in which I participate in different capacities, such as the Culture and Theory Program, Latin American Studies, and the Department of Comparative Literature. A special mention is due to Nahum Chandler with whom I shared a number of memorable working groups.

I presented some of the materials that went to constitute *Cultural Antagonism and the Crisis of Reality in Latin America* in a number of venues and invited lectures. I am especially grateful to their organizers who are also friends and partners in the intellectual adventure that we share: Karen Benezra, Jorge Quintana-Navarrete, Mabel Moraña, Juan Poblete, Adam Shellhorse, Mariano Siskind, Erin Graff, and John Kraniauskas.

Lastly, I apologize—to use a phrase from Pedro Henriquez Ureña—to those omitted by the ingratitude of my memory.

Chapter 1

THE NATIVIST AVANT-GARDE

The encounter between the potential universality of the antagonism and the actual universality of art is the defining event of Latin American expression for the twentieth century. By itself, it creates a horizon of intelligibility for arts, politics, and society whose consistency will only begin to waver in the 1990s. In this encounter, art and antagonism are not evenly matched. The antagonism appears in a historical drift from the realm of the subaltern to that of the popular. This is why, even when stenciled in the immediate sphere of the practical, its outlines remain fuzzy and indefinite. The question of the subject of an unscripted history exerted the most lucid minds of revolutionary Mexico and constituted the leitmotif behind José Carlos Mariátegui's extraordinary analytic effort in the *Seven Essays*. As for art, the fact that it achieved actual universality doesn't mean that things are less complicated on its end. Formalism, autonomy, and disinterest remain the constitutive elements of artistic universality, but they realize themselves in ways that are peculiar to Latin America and often difficult to recognize from a metropolitan perspective.

Art and antagonism met in the most consequential way around the avant-gardes of the early twentieth century. The 1920s were imprinted with a holistic attitude that fed on a unique porosity between different disciplines, social discourses, and artistic practices. Academic specialization has erased many of the vital connections that the works of art of the period interwove with their environments.[1] Contrary to this tendency, in *The Mobility of Modernism*, Harper Montgomery takes intersections and displacements as the proper locus of the Latin American avant-garde.[2] What is found at the crossroads is the centrality of José Carlos Mariátegui's *Amauta*, a cultural and symbolic knot in

---

1. For a criticism of the academic compartmentalization of the avant-garde see Harper Montgomery, "Innovators and Iconoclasts: Six Books on Latin American Modern and Contemporary Art," *Latin American Research Review*, vol. 54, no. 4 (2019): 1082–9, doi: http://doi.org/10.25222/larr.675.

2. Harper Montgomery, *The Mobility of Modernism* (Austin: Texas University Press, 2018).

which the always mobile aesthetics of modernity acquired a remarkable level of consistency.³

Through the 1920s and 1930s, a significant number of Latin American artists, writers, and intellectuals embarked on a trip to Europe that substantially recanted their perspectives on their countries of origin. The trip back home became—to evoke the title of Aimé Césaire's iconic poem—a return to the native land. The reflexive movement that dominates Césaire's poem also animates figures like Diego Rivera, Teresa de la Parra or Lydia Cabrera who translated Aimé Césaire's poem into Spanish. For these artists, their return also implied a turn towards local, undervalued motifs in which something of the seductive materiality of modernity seemed to shine through.⁴

I refer to these artists and intellectuals as the nativist avant-garde. The nativist avant-garde artists are neither avant-garde in any recognizable sense nor nativists in any traditional sense either. Their production has always baffled the critics.⁵ They form neither a school nor a movement but rather a disposition that will resonate with particular force in Latin American culture for the rest of the twentieth century. To say it with a formula that I will unpack slowly throughout this chapter, these are writers and artists who apply a modernist sensibility to traditional contents made available by the confluence of the process of archivization and the political solicitations of the early twentieth century.⁶ The list of names that could be included in this group is neither short

---

3. A quick look at the index of *Amauta* provides a glimpse of a pregnant moment dominated by the tripartite figure of the artist, the writer, and the public intellectual. The Archivo José Carlos Mariátegui in Peru contains the 1,100 articles published in *Amauta*, along with an extensive searchable database. See www.mariategui.org.

4. A similar conceptual itinerary is present in artists who never left their native land, as it is the case with the exceptional work of the Afro-Cubist Jose Manuel Acosta, who was an important member of Havana's avant-garde in the 1920s.

5. As late as the 1970s, Brazilian critics used the expression "regional allegory" to underline what they perceived as a dual allegiance in Clarice Lispector's *The Hour of the Star*. The case of José María Arguedas is also telling, since literary criticism had to elaborate a prosthetic notion of "neo-indigenismo" to accommodate his literature.

6. Gordon Brotherston notices that the early twentieth century brings up a "profound shift" in literary production characterized by "increasing concern with representation, in both the political and the literary senses; failing faith in the universality of Western metropolitan values, including orthodox Marxism; and in particular, the exhumation, edition, and translation of classic Indian texts." Gordon Brotherston, "The Latin American Novel and Its Indigenous Sources," in *On Modern Latin American Fiction*, ed. John King (New York: Noonday Press, 1987), 67. The confluence of avant-garde and native forms has been pointed out by a number of authors. Giuseppe Bellini writes: "Indigenous surrealism resurfaces in the *Leyendas* [*de Guatemala*] and alongside it also resurfaces the experience of European surrealism." Giussepe Bellini, "Nota Crítica," in *Tres Obras: Leyendas de Guatemala, El Alhajadito, El señor Presidente*, Miguel Angel

nor inconsequential: Miguel Angel Asturias, Alejo Carpentier, Wifredo Lam, Lydia Cabrera, João Guimarães Rosa, Tarsila do Amaral, Augusto Roa Bastos, Clarice Lispector, José María Arguedas, Diego Rivera, Gamaliel Churata, Juan Rulfo, Carlos Mérida, José Carlos Mariátegui, among others.

The notion of a nativist avant-garde sounds counterintuitive. This is an effect of a historicist politics of time that locates the determinate negation of the present in the future. Against this prejudice stands the fact that important segments of the avant-garde oriented their aesthetic search towards the past. This happened not only in Latin America, but in Europe as well. In the 1930s, a representative of the European avant-garde like Bertolt Brecht could write: "To want the new is old-fashioned. What is new is to want the old."[7] Arguably the reasons for this turn to the past were different in Europe and in Latin America. At any rate, the new orientation made cultural producers more sensitive to the process of formal symbolic subsumption that has plagued the continent from its earliest colonial period. So, the themes of technology, speed, or modernity characteristic of Mexican Estridentismo or of Mário de Andrade's *Pauliceia Desvairada* existed side by side with another tendency that eulogized the obstinacy of the past. We see it not only in the *Macunaíma* of the same de Andrade, but also in the paintings of José Sabogal in Peru and the murals of Diego Rivera in Mexico, in the proto-surrealist writing of Asturias in Guatemala, and the photography of Martin Chambi in the Andes.[8]

At first sight, it seems that the notion of a nativist avant-garde receives its most immediate determination from the sphere of representation. And yet, in the same way that the essence of *Futurismo* does not lie in the multiplication of airplanes and elevators, no amount of gauchos and *compadritos* would ever suffice to turn Borges into a nativist avant-garde. The problem of the nativist avant-garde was the shape of the antagonism insofar as the latter can be thought in terms of what Jacques Lacan called the *real*. And the real cannot be reached through representation.

On the other hand, it is doubtful that relying only on the formal aspects of the work has given us a satisfactory account of the operations that mediate and make possible a novel like Mário de Andrade's *Macunaíma*. What is

---

Asturias (Caracas: Biblioteca Ayacucho, 1977), 6. Elizabeth Monasterios notices the confluence of avant-gardism and indigenous expression in the Andes in "Revisionismos inesperados. La contramarcha vanguardista de Gamaliel Churata y Arturo Borda," *Revista Iberoamericana*, vol. 253 (2015): 989–1013. For a similar treatment see also Mabel Moraña, *Churata Postcolonial* (Lima: Centro de Estudios Literarios Cornejo Polar, 2015).

7. Bertolt Brecht, *Journals 1934–1955* (London: Routledge, 1995): 47.

8. Only recently the work of Chambi has elicited sustained critical interest. See Jorge Coronado, *Portraits in the Andes: Photography and Agency, 1900–1950* (Pittsburgh: University of Pittsburgh Press, 2018).

Macunaíma in the eyes of the modernist artist? Is it a collage—the genre of the total availability of forms as a potential material for art? The collage thrived in a world where the multiplication of techniques of archivization constantly folded the dimension of time into a simultaneity of perception.⁹ In Europe, this thinking of the simultaneous rarely confronted the question of the ethics of its procedure. In Latin America the issue was unavoidable. As soon as the Latin American artist subtracts an object from its original context, the question immediately arises as to the ethics and politics of its incorporation into the poem or the work of art.¹⁰ And if the writer or the artists fails to account for this possibility, he/she will be retrospectively chastised by an alert criticism; this is how Pablo Neruda's "Alturas de Machu Picchu" (included in *Canto General*) became a sort of critical punching bag in the 1990s. Neruda may have overplayed the sovereignty of literature in his poem, but feigning ignorance about the radical autonomy of the archive cannot be said to have constituted the norm for the Latin American artist.¹¹ We have abundant biographical evidence that writers, painters, musicians, and choreographers did not just play around with the materials that overran their modern compositions from the abundance of the past or from a heterogeneous present. Quite often, the incorporation of indigenous or cultural material was presided over by a careful and cautious study of their folkloric and ethnographic valences.

The process of embodiment characteristic of their practice led a substantial number of Latin American artists to disavow their debt to the avant-garde. In his famous prologue to *The Kingdom of this World*, Alejo Carpentier minimized the surrealist influence upon his work and postulated the unbridled nature of the Latin American reality as the definitive origin of his aesthetic quest.¹² For

---

9. James Clifford, "On Ethnographic Surrealism," in *The Predicament of Culture* (Cambridge, MA: Harvard University Press, 1988), 119.

10. Incorporation of other textualities into the work of art is perhaps the fundamental creative trope of modernity. Anxiety regarding the lawfulness of such incorporation does not arise in all cases. One of the interesting points regarding the nativist avant-garde lies precisely in the emergence of such problematic.

11. The criticism that fell upon Neruda was related to issues of cultural borrowing and authority which, having been originally brought about by the nativist avant-garde, reached a political climax in Rigoberta Menchú's testimony. The most authoritative reconstruction of this moment remains. George M. Gugelberger, ed. *The Real Thing. Testimonial Discourse and Latin America* (Durham, NC: Duke University Press, 1996). Strictly speaking, one cannot accuse Neruda of being insensitive toward the material that he brings into his poem, in part, because "Alturas de Machu Picchu" does not bring any such material from an alternate symbolic or discursive register. Neruda's poem closes onto itself and reaches the other of its representation in the ideality of the poem.

12. Alejo Carpentier, *The Kingdom of This World*, trans. Harriet de Onis (New York: Noonday Press, 1957). See also Alejo Carpentier, "On the Marvelous Real in America," in *Magical Realism: Theory, History, Community*, ed. Lois Parkinson Zamora

Carpentier, in Latin America, surrealism realizes itself in the world. According to this logic, the Latin American writer just needs to open his/her eyes and see. And even that example is subjected to the epistemic privilege of the periphery. Let us just recall the patronizing smile with which Carpentier evoked the horror experienced by André Breton at a voodoo session in Haiti: "So little prepared was Breton to receive the full impact of our home-grown surrealism" that in attending a voodoo ritual "the great pope of surrealism almost fainted; horrified, he repeated, 'C'est horrible, C'est horrible.'"[13] The implicit claim contained in this quote is that a regionalist awareness could compensate for and even outweigh the benefits of a merely formal (external) exposition to aesthetic demands for which the avant-garde is but an index. However, this separation between mere aesthetic investment and openness to an exuberant world remains disingenuous.[14]

Artists like André Breton and Antonin Artaud traveled to Mexico seeking the actualization of the aesthetic in the world; and it was on similar grounds Paul Valery urged Asturias to go back to Guatemala to save his aesthetic soul. Ironically, one of the best expressions of the modernist desire to go back to the thing themselves in the terrain of the aesthetic acquired a definite formulation in Martin Heidegger's 1935 "The Origin of the Work of Art."[15] In this lecture, delivered the same year, Walter Benjamin published "The Work of Art in

and Wendy B. Faris, trans. Tanya Huntington and Lois Parkinson Zamora (Durham, NC: Duke University Press, 1995), 89–108.

13. Alejo Carpentier, *Entrevistas*, ed. Virgilio López Vermus (Havana: Letras Cubanas, 1985), 283.

14. As Fernando Rosenberg noticed, the particularization of experience in the direction of the real was already part—and a fundamental one—of the avant-garde credo. A consequential avant-garde has to start by rejecting the very geopolitics that provides the historical avant-garde with its metropolitan prestige. This anti-historicist tendency was rapidly adopted by its Latin American companions who "attempted … to undermine the diffusionist premise altogether." Fernando Rosenberg, "Cultural Theory and the Avant-Garde," in *The Blackwell Companion to Latin American Culture and Literature*, ed. Sara Castro-Klaren (London: Routledge, 2008), 412.

Similarly, while discussing the Brazilian "week of modern art," Randal Johnson notes: "In its attempt to bring Brazilian art into the twentieth century, the initial impulse of modernism was toward aesthetic renewal, but by 1924 the question of the creation of an authentically national art began to dominate literary debates, and artists began searching for proper cultural symbols." Randal Johnson, "Tupy or not Tupy," in *On Modern Latin American Fiction*, ed. John King (New York: Noonday Press, 1987), 43.

15. Martin Heidegger, "The Origin of the Work of Art," in *Heidegger. Basic Writings*, trans. David Farrell Krell (New York: HarpersCollins, 1993). Heidegger's text suffered several revisions after 1935. Farrell Krell's translation represents the latest version of the text. My characterization of Heidegger's position as modern may seem disputable. I think, however, that overall Heidegger's philosophy expresses a definite modern

the Age of Mechanical Reproduction," Heidegger lays out a tension between a grounded principle of negativity (earth) and the formative power of the civilization and the individual (art).¹⁶ Like Heidegger, some Latin American artists found that a certain level of aesthetic negativity was already a property of the world. For them, the happiness of which art could be a vehicle was already located in the midst of things. We see this dialectic operative in the work of Sergei Eisenstein. A man of unimpeachable avant-garde credentials, Eisenstein produced in Mexico his least studied film, ¡Qué Viva Mexico! In this movie, the Russian director ended up locating the promise of art in the cultural and aesthetic traditions of the Mexican popular classes. Although he never completed the film, ¡Qué Viva México! makes Eisenstein one of the first of the nativist avant-garde.¹⁷ Judging by the celebrated "Epilogue" that the Russian director envisioned as a closure to his film, Eisenstein perceived something that was not always easy to grasp for his Latin American counterparts: the political process that interested them so much was one in which the question of individuality (who am I?) is displaced by the question of subjectivity (who may I become?). The epilogue of Eisenstein's movie includes a carnivalesque representation of "many of the social types from the previous episodes plus additional working-class subjects."¹⁸ All actors are wearing masks for the day of the death celebration. In a frantic montage, actors removed their skeleton masks to reveal themselves as either actual people or skeletons that represent the persistence of a doomed class.

The Question of Realism

If Dawn Ades is correct and "the relationship between radical art and revolutionary politics was perhaps an even more crucial issue in Latin America

concern with the re-aestheticization of the world, even if it does so through manifestly anti-modernists and anti-cosmopolitan positions.

16. Heidegger revised this piece for successive conferences. The English translation referred here is the transcription of a lecture delivered in Frankfurt in 1936. The conflict between earth and world recalls Hegel's opposition between matter and spirit. This early Heideggerian theory of art does not include the tension between Gods and men proper of a later period in Heidegger's reflections on poetry.

17. Carpentier met with Eisenstein in Paris and was profoundly impressed by the ideas of the Russian director. Martin Lienhard observed that ¡Qué Viva México! was one of the sources for Asturias's construction of a multi-temporal perspective in *Men of Maize*. See Martin Lienhard, *La voz y su huella* (Lima: Horizonte, 1992), 260.

18. Paul Schroeder, *Latin American Cinema. A Comparative History* (Oakland: University of California Press, 2016), 54.

than it was in Europe,"¹⁹ the alignment of politics and art also implied fathoming the type of subjectivity in which these two forms could converge. While the figure of the indigenous (and the primitive) represented an immediate embodiment of antagonism for the political vocation of many artists and intellectuals, the blurred nature of those subjectivities meant a formidable conceptual obstacle to the articulation of the aesthetic and the political vocation. In practical terms, if modernity and subalternity were to be thought together and their antagonism conceived, realism was not a viable rhetorical modality for this task. Georg Lukacs believed that the realist style was the ideal form of politically engaged representation. The paradox of Latin American expression is that many of its artists and writers ventured into irrealism for the same reason.²⁰ Irrealism is not the fantastic (or the magical as some people like to think) but the untimely. In an essay titled *Critical Irrealism* ("L'irréalisme critique,") Michael Löwy links irrealism to a politics of time. After dismissing the idea that realism is "the only acceptable form for an art that shows a critical edge toward existing reality," Löwy considers the political expediency of aesthetic strategies grounded on a principled rejection of historicism: "Nostalgia for an idealized past can certainly take reactionary and conservative shapes [formes régressives], but it can also take a revolutionary shape when what is at stake is not a return to a premodern past but instead a detour through the past as a way toward a utopian future."²¹

19. Dawn Ades, *Art in Latin America. The Modern Era. 1820–1980* (New Haven, CT: Yale University Press, 1989), 125. The Latin American artists who in the 1920s and 1930s flocked to France, Spain, and Italy did not simply encounter industrial modernity and a nonconformist art; they also had a taste of a political dimension colored by mass movements and class struggles. The avant-garde itself was a deeply politicized space. Many French surrealists were involved with the French Communist party just as some muralists in Mexico, and adherents of *antropofagia* in Brazil were also involved in their respective countries' communist parties. However, the clear-cut political identities of Europe were mostly unavailable in Latin America; and even in those cases in which these subjectivities enjoyed a relative centrality they existed against the background of a cultural dynamic that made any closure of the political field in terms of traditional liberal identities impossible.

20. In *Aesthetic Theory*, Theodore Adorno sees this paradox as constitutive of modern art: "By virtue of its rejection of the empirical world—a rejection that inherits in art's concept and thus is not mere escape, but a law immanent to it—art sanctions the primacy of reality." Theodore W. Adorno, *Aesthetic Theory,* trans. Robert Hullot-Kentor (Minneapolis: University of Minnesota Press, 1997), 2.

21. Michael Löwy, "L'irréalisme critique," *Actuel Marx*, vol. 45, no. 1 (2009): 52–65. The word *irrealismo* appears in Latin American criticism before Löwy's essay. Significantly, it was used several times in the discussions that followed the publication of José María Arguedas's *Todas las Sangres* around. See for instance, Winston Orillo, "*Todas las Sangres*, gigantesco esfuerzo novelistico de José María Arguedas" (*Correo de Lima*, February 25, 1965).

It has been noticed that the rise to prominence of literary realism seems to be inextricable from the increasing centralization and bureaucratization of life in modern societies.[22] The rhetoric of realism was, first and foremost, the rhetoric of emerging governmentality. The problem with realism is simple enough: it wanted to remain ideologically critical of a world that it had already confirmed aesthetically. This historical declension of realism as fundamentally dependent on the needs of social reproduction helps to explain why, in a recent work, Fredric Jameson speaks of realism as having "a vested interest, an ontological stake, in the solidity of social reality, on the resistance of bourgeois society to history and to change."[23]

We find Jameson's critical stance toward realism anticipated by José Carlos Mariátegui in a programmatic essay published in *Amauta* and titled "Literary Populism and Capitalist Stabilization." In this essay, Mariátegui dismisses realism as a bourgeois "naturalist enchantment of its own traditions." In Mariátegui's famous formulation, James Joyce "will always be preferable to the Zolas of this century."[24] In his quest for arriving at a more authentic and more operational notion of the present, Mariátegui enlists myth, poetry, emotion, and, as we saw, a decisive refusal of realism. Reality itself is not sacrificed in the operation. Once disclosure becomes the measure of truth, the whole game of representation is stacked differently. Following Jameson's locution, we can say that the local avant-garde writer too has a vested interest in the real, although not "an ontological stake in the solidity of social reality."[25]

This thesis is not easy to sustain, and it may even be self-contradictory. For Kant, art has the function of constituting the field of experience as open to all.[26] Art performs this task a priori and not as a result of a conscious decision of the artist.[27] Artistic production is the ultimate vehicle in the confirmation of reality and it is difficult to see how it can carry the opposite effect. We confront here

---

22. Warwick Research Collective, *Combined and Uneven Development: Towards a New Theory of World-Literature* (Liverpool: Liverpool University Press, 2015), 74.

23. Fredric Jameson, *The Antinomies of Realism* (London: Verso, 2013), 5. Similarly, Lilian R. Furst observes: "The bourgeois were the primary readers of realist writing, whose tone and content were geared to appeal to an audience convinced of its capacity to master the physical world." Lilian R. Furst, *Realism* (London: Longman, 1992), 3.

24. José Carlos Mariátegui, "Populismo literario y estabilización capitalista" (Literary Populism and Capitalist Stabilization) Amauta, no. 28 (1930): 6–9.

25. Mariátegui, "Literary," 7.

26. I refer to the argument about taste presupposing a *sensus communis*, developed by Immanuel Kant in his *Critique of Judgment*, trans. W. S. Pluhar (Indianapolis, IN: Hackett, 1987), 88–9.

27. For a development of this argument see David Lloyd and Paul Thomas, *Culture and the State* (New York: Routledge, 1998), 101–4.

what Nahum Chandler calls "the paradoxical centrality of marginal examples … to any theoretical formulation of a general problematic."²⁸

The centrality of the marginal example carries additional risks. A literature or an art bent on a certain vindication of the past lives in constant danger of plunging into stereotype. At this point, it becomes clear that not only did the forms of the avant-garde (that Kant did not know) require the native as a ground, but the native too required the avant-garde as its own guarantee of truth. Essentialism was prevented (in the measure that there are safeguards for that risk) through the problematization of the relationship between political positionality and the disclosing force of the aesthetic. The antagonism can only be registered through breaks, allusions, and the general destabilization of the perceptual hegemon of the time. The only proof we possess of the political vocation of so-called magical realism is its style insofar as this style testifies to the irrevocable distance between the undisclosable ethos of its subaltern material and the modalities of unveiling proper of its necessarily hegemonic form of expression. Irrealism is the scar of the ethical commitment on the skin of the literary text.

The Temporal Structure of the Nativist Avant-Garde

In the work of the nativist avant-garde, the negativities which a hegemonic version of history had enclosed in a web of in-actuality acquired a remarkable vitality, and their mere resurfacing began to wreak havoc on the present. The politics of temporality that emerged had far less to do with a utopian imagination grounded on the illusory notion of the progressive and irreversible nature of time (a possibility already co-opted by historicism) than with the truly revolutionary idea that cultural intervention puts the very fabric of the temporal in question.

This new articulation of the temporal gave origin to a form of apprehension that I call the "now-then." In his exegesis of Heidegger, Paul Ricouer points to a possibility in the German language of which Heidegger avails himself: using the conjugated form of the verb *to be* as an auxiliary verb: "One can say in German, *Ich bin gewesen*. 'I-am-as-having-been.'"²⁹ This *Ich bin gewesen* could constitute a good illustration of the temporal structure of the now-then. It is, however, far easier to intellectually agree with this idea than to grasp it in its fundamental and operational sense.

---

28. Nahum Chandler, *The Problem of the Negro as a Problem for Thought* (New York: Fordham University Press, 2014), 133.

29. The German expression is almost untranslatable. The addition of an "as" inexistent in the original indicates the absence of a similar structure in English, French, or Spanish. A more literal translation would be "I am having been."

The now-then is a temporal structure inherent in modernity's own de-distancing attitude, but it informs the novel form with particular tenacity, as one of its historical missions was perhaps to alert us to the fact that, as Ian Baucom put it, the present is "invested by a range of pasts which are not, in fact, pasts."[30] Far from indicating just a temporal overlap, the logic of the now-then impinges on the perception of the present itself. When Heidegger denounces the present as "the temporal category least apt to open up an originary and authentic inquiry into the nature of the real," he is emphasizing the many ways in which ideologies of the historical dictate the shape of the existent.[31]

Insofar as the past is brought into the purview of what, at this moment, *is*, the now-then appears as a prisoner of the tyranny of the present. (Strictly speaking, the tyranny belongs to subjectivism: to the idea that there is presence—reality—only for and because of the perceiving, constituting subject.) Only the dimension of truth formation can sustain the present along with all the pasts which no longer are, but without which the present would not be as such, or simply not-be. An inquiry informed by an ethics of the now-then produces an ontological interrogation because it suggests the bases of the present may themselves not be present. In this line of reasoning the question becomes: what type of consequences should be drawn from developmentalism's failure to rewrite, subsume, or even annihilate the auratic surplus of the past?

The creation of the now-then, the revelation of the unintegrated and yet operative past in the present, announced a disposition that imprinted Latin American expression for most of the twentieth century. It confronted state-driven forms of modernization firmly grounded (not without tremendous, vacillating efforts) in the absolute primacy of the now, and therefore in the merely formal subsumption and disavowal of what needed to be welcomed into the fold of recognition.

In seminar VII, *The Ethics of Psychoanalysis*, Lacan formulated his idea that only the real in its indetermination can be the point of origin of a truly ethical exploration.[32] A calculated decision is not a decision. There is decision only in

---

30. Ian Baucom, *Specters of the Atlantic. Finance Capital, Slavery, and the Philosophy of History* (Durham, NC: Duke University Press, 2011), 20. I take the notion of de-distancing from Martin Heidegger's *Being and Time*. The original German expression is rendered as de-severance by John Macqauire and Edward Robinson and as de-distancing in the most recent translation by Joan Stambaugh. Throughout this book, I quote Heidegger from both translations.

31. Paul Ricouer. *Time and Narrative*, trans. Kathleen McLaughlin and David Pellauer (Chicago: University of Chicago Press, 1984), 64.

32. The real in question is the subject's desire insofar as that desire impinges on the other. Like Levinas, Lacan thinks that a true ethical relationship is only possible respect to the absolutely other. Unlike Levinas, he believes that this other is inside each individual. In *Seminar VII*, it is called *Das Ding*. Jacques Lacan, *The Seminar of Jacques Lacan, Book VII. The Ethics of Psychoanalysis* (New York: W. W. Norton, 1992), 20.

the face of the unfathomable. A particularly salient example of this necessary correlation between ethics and indetermination can be found in a 1928 poem by Carlos Drummond de Andrade which would stick with unshakable but also mysterious force to the memory of Brazilian literature: "No meio do caminho." I quote some of its best-known lines:

> No meio do caminho tinha uma pedra
> tinha uma pedra no meio do caminho
> tinha uma pedra
> No meio do caminho tinha uma pedra
> Nunca me esquecerei desse acontecimento
> na vida de minhas retinas tão fatigadas.[33]

In this poem, the stone signifies itself, without metaphor, without replacement. (The real, Lacan says, is what always return to the same place.) Is not the history of the readings of this poem—which is, as a matter of fact, the history of its misreadings—the best proof that nothing can (or should) come in place of the stone? The sheer irreducibility of the stone contrasts quite clearly with the matter-of-factness of the road. The road is simply another name for the program that under the form of absolute necessity (destiny, nation, civilization) has dominated the imaginary of the previous century. This is not to say that the stone stands for the transcendental or even the ahistorical.[34] The stone stands for nothing because every question about the meaning of the stone is formulated from the perspective of the road. If anything, the stone represents the encounter with something that was until very recently circumvented, ignored, jumped over, or perhaps merely incomprehensible in the framework of the road. The stone is the center of the ethical encounter in the poem, not because it says something but rather because it interrupts that communicational possibility. Treating de Andrade's stone as a figure of the real means separating it from any final or conclusive signification. It means that responsibility only arises in the face of the incalculable.

Written ten years before Drummond de Andrade's poem, César Vallejo's "Los heraldos negros," works as a counterpart to "No meio do caminho," since this time it is the subject rather than the object that bears the full blow of the encounter.

---

33. In the middle of the road there was a stone/there was a stone in the middle of the road/there was a stone/in the middle of the road there was a stone/I will never forget this event/in the whole life of my fatigued retinas. Carlos Drummond de Andrade, *Alguma Poesía* (Rio de Janeiro: Pindorama, 1930), 37.

34. The expression *No meio do caminho* is also a quote of the opening line of Dante's *Inferno* (volume 1 of the *Divine Comedy*) whose cadence De Andrade evokes in his own poem.

> Y el hombre ... ¡Pobre ... pobre! Vuelve los ojos, como
> cuando por sobre el hombro nos llama una palmada;
> vuelve los ojos locos, y todo lo vivido
> se empoza, como charco de culpa, en la mirada.[35]

The turn here takes the form of a recoding of an oversight. The call reaches the writer from behind, from what was left out, from what was not paid its due. In the poem, only the head, only the eyes of the man turn. If the writer turns, it is because he/she has almost passed by; the writer regrets this inertia retrospectively: hence his/her guilt. This almost-passing-by is a persistent, essential trait of the Latin American turn. (It is how the turn inscribes the reality of the uneven development of Latin American societies.) The motif of the face-to-face relation that dominates Levinas's figuration of the ethical is mostly absent here. It is, as a matter of fact, structurally impossible. That the turn answers to a call—that it is actually a call and not an awakening—is sufficiently indicated by the use of the word "palmada" (tap) in Vallejo's poem.

Although the writer is the one who turns, the agency of the turn belongs to him/her only secondarily. The turn is a function, even a subset, of the vast social mobilizations that multiplied, in the wake of the massive incorporation of Latin America into the world market, a series of figures that could no longer be contained inside the traditional framework of the patriarchal-oligarchic legacies of the nineteenth century.

The fact that I characterized the artist's turn as ethical and its origination as already political seem to establish a priority of the political over the ethical. It is not clear, however, that notions like ethical or political can delimit precise regions of being. A conceptual deficit is inherent to these notions. A turn obeying a purely political causality is perhaps unthinkable. For a turn to be possible, there must be a complication in the mapping performed by the political. On the other hand, the ethical notation of the world that arises in the suspension of the political trajectory cannot sustain its force of indetermination indefinitely. The desire to actualize its potential inheres in the ethical as its particular passion. Duty is the first step by which the logic of the unconditional leads the ethical to take a step into the political. At this point the risk emerges of a sinister fall of the ethical into an ideology of the ethical. The ethical may become a vogue and lose its ethical status altogether. Rescuing ethics from its permanent co-optation in a discourse of rights is one of the conceptual battles of our time, an ethical as much as a political battle.[36] Ethics and politics can only break this deadlock

---

35. "And man ... Poor ... Poor! He turns his eyes, as/when the slap in the shoulder summons us;/turns his crazed eyes, and everything lived/wells up, like a pool of guilt, in his look." César Vallejo, *The Complete Poetry. A Bilingual Edition*, ed. and trans. Clayton Eshleman (Oakland: University of California Press, 2009), 22.

36. Bruno Bosteels, *Marx and Freud in Latin America* (Durham, NC: Duke University Press, 2013) ends his book with a tentative call to liberate us from ethics. However, it is

through a third instance, which, as Jacques Rancière argues, should be called aesthetic insofar as a redistribution of the sensible is at stake in it.[37]

The aesthetic problematization of reality does not create any new knowledge but it affects the economy of truth upon which the real relies for its own stability. The reinforcement of aesthetic neutrality dissimulates the lasting disagreement between literary thinking and philosophical thinking. Insofar as it sustains a claim on the real, literature resembles the tradition that Alain Badiou calls an anti-philosophy.[38] Evoking Pascal's line "Men are so necessarily mad that not to be mad would be another form of madness,"[39] Badiou characterizes anti-philosophy in terms of a clash between integrity and reason. Nietzsche, Pascal, and Wittgenstein are the quintessential anti-philosophers in Badiou's eyes—although he wonders if Heidegger shouldn't be thrown into that heap as well. Integrity, however, is another word for unreason. As Jacques Lacan, the anti-philosopher that Badiou is really after in his book, put it: "Madness is freedom's more faithful companion, following its every move like a shadow."[40] In Vallejo's poem the man turns "his maddened eyes" ("los ojos locos"). To some extent, the turn always happens against reason. One turns at the expense of one's sanity. Although perhaps one turns because one needs to regain one's sanity because there is no reason outside the sphere or possibility of the turn.

---

not clear if the ethical has not shifted places with the political in his argument. Bosteels notices, that there is no reason why "[Enrique] Dussel's book could not have been called *Política de la liberación*" (instead of *Etica de la liberación*) (305). While I believe that ethics does have a field of consistency, it also seems apparent that we are witnessing an instrumentalization of the ethical in some dominant lines of academic and social discourse today. This instrumentalization is rooted on the prevalence of what Alain Badiou calls "democratic materialism" as the hegemonic way of forming notions and ideas in the present. (Alain Badiou, "Democratic Materialism and the Materialistic Dialectic," *Radical Philosophy*, vol. 130 (2005): 20–4). Rescuing ethics from its permanent co-optation in a discourse of rights is one of the conceptual battles of our time.

37. The idea that a political revolution always demands an aesthetic correlation is characteristic of Jacques Rancière's work. See *Aisthesis. Scenes from the Aesthetic Regime of Art*, trans. Zakir Paul (London: Verso, 2013). Interestingly, the same economy among ethics, aesthetics, and politics is discussed by Didi-Huberman, although in a different historical context. In *The Eye of History*, he speaks of "an epistemological decision" which "passes very quickly from the *aesthetic* register to *ethical* questioning and to the *political* position of the problem." Georges Didi-Huberman, *The Eye of History. When Images Take Positions*, trans. Shane B. Lillis (Cambridge, MA: MIT Press, 2018), xviii.

38. Alain Badiou, *Lacan. Anti-Philosophy 3* (New York: Columbia University Press, 2018).

39. Blaise Pascal, *Pensees* (New York: Penguin, 1995), 414.

40. Jacques Lacan, "Presentation on Psychical Causality," in *Ecrits*, trans. Bruce Fink (New York: W. W. Norton, 2007), 144.

The turn does not merely question the shape of the real; it also unveils the process by which the unintegrated, non-hegemonic moments of the total present are made of disavowed pieces of the past. This consciousness about the value of time in the production of life constituted one of the most significant accomplishments of the artists of the turn. It provincialized hegemonic historical time by confronting it with its undead and undiluted remainders. Therein derives the tremendous appeal that the words of Nietzsche exerted upon Latin American intellectuals at the turn of the century. Nietzsche is the author that Mariátegui invokes not just once, but twice at the beginning of his *Seven Essays*, as an authority able to preside over the material elucidation of the Andean universe.[41] In a way that his Latin American readers could not but find enticing, Nietzsche declared that history happens through the suppression of other temporalities. But these temporalities do not vanish into thin air; they persist under the form of an exemplary obstinacy. That is the gist of the Nietzschean declension of the historical as the history of the will to power. In life, as in society, unity is merely the metaphor for the subordination of the multiple to the evolutionary vocation of what becomes actual. The unrealized alternatives do not disappear but survive in hiding, now and then finding their way into the consciousness of the time even if they are distorted as anomalies or as circumscribed forms of protest against the tyranny of a projective identity between the real and the rational.[42]

Questions of Archive

The reconceptualization of the political, the creation of new antagonisms, the re-temporalization of the historical—all the narrative, logical and cognitive operations I have described as proper of the nativist avant-garde—resemble the modalities of interrogation popularized in the 1990s by subaltern studies. Subalternism is what has always already happened to Latin American literature in the wake of the turn. However, the proper Latin American inscription of the question of subalternity was never established to full satisfaction, perhaps because its initial formulation (in the work of John Beverley, Alberto Moreiras, and Ileana Rodríguez) took testimonio as its starting point.[43] In doing so, they

41. Ofelia Schutte, "Nietzsche, Mariátegui, and Socialism. A Case of Nietzschean Marxism in Peru," *Social Theory and Practice*, vol. 14 (1988): 71–85.

42. Friedrich Nietzsche, *The Will to Power*, trans. Walter Kaufmann (New York: Viking Press, 1982).

43. The posterior production of some authors involved with Latin American subalternism attest to the insufficiency of the notion of voice (and derivative authenticity) in the original formulation of the paradigm. In *Latinamericanism after 9/11* (Durham, NC: Duke University Press, 2011). John Beverley moves in the direction of a "strategic" form of identity politics able to reinvigorate an increasingly weak political mediation

perpetuated a conceptual displacement introduced by Gayatri Spivak herself in "Can the Subaltern Speak?" At issue in Spivak's essay was the refutation of the liberal idea-force that speaking is a natural capacity of the *zoon logon*. There is nothing natural about speaking. There was a way in which arguing for the unnaturalness of speech confirmed the place of verbal expression as the foundational instance of every possible political subjectivation. Political action is associated with a declarative modality.

Some level of confusion was perhaps unavoidable. Although Spivak's formula was just an instrument of clarification, it was taken as a position to be confirmed or refuted. Some early signs of the problems encapsulated in conflating the question of subalternity with that of enunciation came from the objections raised in the field of Latin Americanism by people who contended that either "their" subalterns did speak, or that Spivak's position betrayed the estrangement of the third world cosmopolitan intellectual from the problems that he/she seeks to represent. There is a definitive sense in which, without being insubstantial, these objections missed the point. Subalternism, a theoretical construction, cannot be refuted empirically. And the argument that experience shows otherwise—a valuable idea when correctly grounded—can only be plausible if the empiricist argument clarifies the theoretical presupposition subtending its position. The fact that some subaltern people speak (the fact that the subaltern exists in a relationship of logical and historical continuity with the popular) does not discredit in the least the thesis of a subalternizing structuration of power and discourse, that is, the idea that as a form of the domination proper to the modern political realm (in which power is symbolically apportioned and distributed) representation cannot but be based on exclusions.

Instead of focusing on an impending, contained, or suppressed will to speak, in this book, I propose the figure of the archive as the objectified register and condition of possibility of a subaltern-popular expression.[44] The archive puts in play an element that the metaphysics of the voice always manages to miss: there is no self-foundation for a discourse. The voice that constitutes the present has a share in the dimension of the immemorial.[45] I borrow my archival impulse

---

from the standpoint of movements grounded on community and solidarity. Alberto Moreiras's notion of infrapolitics maintains a subalternist impulse in its rejection of representation (or incarnation) as a satisfactory rendering of antagonism or universality. Alberto Moreiras, *El no sujeto de lo político* (Santiago de Chile: Palinodia, 2008).

44. I am not suggesting that the archive avoids exclusion. In the first pages of *Archive Fever*, Derrida produces an elaborate etymology of the archival that would demolish any pretension of archival neutrality. However, archives are always open to associations and appropriations. They can be used as a foothold for those who have no social ground to stand on.

45. The symbolic is not a site of deliverance but a place of alienation. However, there is a material, recalcitrant—in the end, *real*—aspect of every symbolic; and this

from Horacio Castellanos Moya's 2004 novel *Senselessness* (*Insensatez*).[46] The novel tells the story of a foreign journalist who is hired by the Catholic church (an institution he abhors) to go over a 1,100 pages report that contains firsthand testimonies of 422 massacres perpetrated against indigenous communities in Guatemala by the army and right-wing paramilitary groups. Castellanos Moya's unnamed narrator filters the report in a notebook that he plans to keep to himself and smuggle outside the country and away from the church. In this way, the diary becomes the fantasmatic and projective figure of a popular archive. The scene that interests me is presented in the novel as a rumination of the compiler about a future fictional text that he plans to write based on his current work once he leaves Guatemala. The story concerns a civil registrar in a town called Totonicapán.

> An idiot whose foolish behavior led to them cutting off with a machete each and every one of his fingers ... as the soldiers kept him pinned to the ground after they had beaten him so hard they had broken who knows how many bones to teach him not to underestimate them and that dedication to one's work had a limit and that this limit was the authority of the lieutenant, who know brandished the machete, letting fall one decisive blow that split the head of the civil registrar of Totonicapán longitudinally, as if it had been a coconut and they were at the beach and not in the battered living room of the civil registrar's house, splattered with the blood and brains of the aforementioned, who had refused again and again the lieutenant's request to turn over the village's register of the dead, who knows why he behaved so foolishly, for the lieutenant urgently needed a list of the villagers who had died in the previous ten years so he could bring them back to life so they could vote for the party of General Rios Montt.[47]

The insignificant nature of the archive befits its historical role to the letter. The archive in question is the record of lineages and genealogies of the town, a list of names and dates whose obtuse and dumb status the narrator displaces onto the registrar by calling him an idiot with unfeigned admiration. What is the civil registrar of Totonicapán dying for? Despite the way the narrator enlightens us about the situation, the civil registrar is not the martyr of a "transparent democracy" against the perverse forces of "state terrorism." In a way that recalls

---

is the aspect that comes to light in the archive at the moment of its liberation from the institutional and hermeneutical forms which police it.

46. Horacio Castellanos Moya, *Senselessness*, trans. Katherine Silver (New York: New Directions, 2008), 60. Although the novel has no temporary markers, we know that it is framed by the brutal repression of Guatemala's civil war, which produced some 300,000 deaths between 1960 and 1996.

47. Moya, *Senselessness*, 60.

the Hegelian topic of recognition, he dies for something that would be able to survive his own biological death. The civil registrar dies for the archive not insofar as it contains "valuable information," but insofar as the archive does not contain in itself the clear precepts of the practices that it may authorize. Generations may pose to the archive the question about their being, with the constant reassurance that they will never receive a final answer able to annihilate the drift of their practical and political life.[48]

In a world in which literary creation is mediated by the figure of an author, all materials that enter a literary text do so, like Heidegger's animals, afflicted by a poverty of the world. However, one of the most important consequences of the early twentieth-century aesthetic revolution lies, precisely, in emphatically denying that the process of aesthetic incorporation of secondary materials renders their previous history inconsequential. The use of the word "material" to designate the building blocks of fiction is already revelatory since it is overwhelmingly critics, rather than writers, who use this expression. To the critic, the so-called materials seem inert and easily manipulated; to the writer, they represent nothing but bewitched reminders of alien presences. Augusto Roa Bastos never considered the building blocks of his fiction to be mere materials. Instead, entirely possessed by an archival logic, the Paraguayan author spoke of an absent language and an absent discourse.[49] Sometimes the archival resuscitation of the discourse of the past is literalized and performed in the texture of the present. The impossible line uttered by Pablo Neruda in "Alturas de Machu Picchu"—"Decidme: aquí fui castigado" ("Tell me: Here I was punished")—belongs to this operation of conjuring a necessarily absent intentionality.[50] Similarly, a fragment of speech that seems to come from another time inserted by Arguedas in one of his novels (such as the dialogue between Don Bruno and the *cholo* Cisneros, in which the former humiliates the latter by bringing to light the system of duties that undergirds the *gamonal*'s claim to political hegemony), or a mythical matrix superimposed on the

---

48. Like any "authentic" archive, popular archives easily acquire a heuristic function regardless of how fragmentary their composition may be. Stephan Palmié offers a compelling treatment of this possibility of popular archivization in his discussion and reconstruction of José Antonio Aponte's "libro de pinturas." A nineteenth-century Cuban free Black executed by the colonial authorities, Aponte composed a palimpsestic text with drawings and paper cuts representing the main events in history. He also wondered about the place of Black Cubans and himself in those events. Colonial authorities found Aponte's book senseless, maddening, inscrutable, and subversive. Stephan Palmié, *Wizards and Scientists: Explorations in Afro-Cuban Modernity and Tradition* (Durham, NC: Duke University Press, 2002).

49. See Augusto Roa Bastos, "El texto ausente," in *La obra posterior a Yo el Supremo*, Augusto Roa Bastos, 9–16 (Poitiers: Centre de Recherches Latino-Américaines, 1999).

50. Pablo Neruda, *Canto General* (México: Talleres Gráficos de la Nación, 1950), 62.

recognizable narrative devices of the literary profession (such as the ambiguity of the human/animal divide in the Indianized world of *Men of Maize*) are no longer literary materials or objects in any traditional senses. If they are not objects, then they are subjects. It is the subjective function of the material that gives a testimonial chromatics to the tradition of the turn as well as to the work of the nativist avant-garde.

Is all this obscure, even obscurantist? How can the mere material of creation *speak*? ("Who has spoken? Is it you or some other?" the surprised *gamonal* asks his *pongo*, who, as we know, speaks from the depth of an archive.)[51] Does not the merely present-at-hand nature of the literary material exude the type of instrumentality commonly associated with our dealings with what is remote, with what is past? And yet, how can a time that has reduced almost the entire constellation of existence to the dimension of language ever be surprised that things and stories talk back to it?

The great challenge faced by the nativist avant-garde was the decision to reckon with the obstacle and the attempt to translate this intuition into meaning. Literary criticism—and the social sciences on which the latter was often molded—caught up with this project only belatedly. And when they did, it was not without hesitations. Considering the totality of the social from the perspective of an emerging antagonism carries with it important questions. Hernán Vidal voices one of them in an introduction to a special issue of *Revista Iberoamericana* that examines literary and cultural developments in US-based Latin Americanism during the period 1978–2008.[52] By that time, the subaltern, which was once the most occult, has become in a certain sense the ideal of the visible subject itself. This move threatens, if it doesn't completely ruin not completely ruin the synchronization between antagonism and social reality that Vidal sees as a condition of possibility of a productive analysis, and derivatively of political action. According to Vidal—and his opinion is not entirely off the mark—today's intellectuals trust the subaltern hanging on a feeling that is no more than faith (although an alternate name could also be solidarity). Vidal believes that a particular poetics in subalternism comes too close to postulating a sort of inverted eugenic paradigm that makes the bare life of the people a eulogy of its transformative power. In Vidal's own words: "It is worth asking if humanism can sustain itself outside a notion of 'rights'" (49). My answer would be "no." But this does not mean that in accepting the notion of "rights" we should simultaneously accept a bourgeois ownership of this notion. The democratic event cannot be historically exhausted or socially particularized in

---

51. José María Arguedas, "El sueño del pongo," *Obras Completas*, vol. 1 (Lima: Horizonte, 1983), 253.

52. Hernán Vidal, "Introducción," in *Treinta años de estudios literarios/culturales latinoamericanistas en Estados Unidos: Memorias, testimonios, reflexiones críticas* (Pittsburgh: Instituto Internacional de Literatura Iberoamericana, 2008), 9–60.

terms of its appropriation by a contingent subjective formation. The closure of the liberal metaphysics of the subject conditions all our perceptions and theories about the social, cultural, and political present. It is the horizon of this closure that allows—or rather demands—that Vidal's pertinent question be inverted and, in the legacy of the writers of the turn, ask: can a notion of rights sustain itself outside a demand for which humanism will always be a misnomer, but a demand nonetheless which in its subaltern intonation has proven to be one of the engines for the constant reimagination of the sense and role of the political in the whole continent?

Chapter 2

MIGUEL ANGEL ASTURIAS: THE SCIENCE OF LITERATURE

> I am a committed writer, but my commitment is to a reality and a world.
>
> —Miguel Angel Asturias

In the introduction to his remarkable edition of *Hombres de maíz* (*Men of Maize*), Gerald Martin expresses his puzzlement at the poor critical reception enjoyed by the novel.[1] Asturias's predicament is not new to the Latin American writer. Critics in the 1940s remained ambiguous regarding Jorge Luis Borges's stories, and in the 1970s it took some time for the critical establishment to warm up to José María Arguedas' *The Fox from Up Above and the Fox from Down Below*. The cases of Borges and Arguedas teach us not just that real innovation is difficult to recognize, but also that for such recognition to happen, a context of reception must be somewhat in place. The rather immodest intention of these pages is to provide such a context for *Men of Maize*.

The word "context" does not refer to any historical or sociological reconstruction of the world when the novel was first published. The context of reception of a work of art is always internal to the field in which that work appears. We can use the Lacanian notation of the subject as what one signifier represents for another signifier (S1, S2) to render the situation more graphically: How should S2 be constituted such that S1 can achieve its proper meaning?

Martin Lienhard had this question in mind when he included *Men of Maize* in the current of ethno-fictions that the Swiss critic showed to be characteristic of Mesoamerica.[2] While *Men of Maize* exhibits many of the features proper of ethno-fictions, we are still left with the question of why a novel that keeps such close links to ethnography should include the rejection of ethnographic

---

1. For the many mishaps in the critical reception of the novel, see Gerald Martin's critical introduction, "Introducción del coordinador," in Miguel Angel Asturias, *Hombres de maíz*, ed. Gerald Martin, Colección Archivos (Madrid: ALLCA XX/Fondo de Cultura Económica, 1996), xxi–xxxiii.

2. Martin Lienhard, *La voz y su huella* (Lima: Horizonte, 1992).

authority as one of its fundamental gestures. Gerald Martin has surrounded *Men of Maize* with the most exhaustive, sophisticated, and learned academic apparatus ever enjoyed by a Latin American novel.[3] Martin scrupulously pursues figures and implicit references toward an original source, only to discover that most of the time the consistency of the path that leads from one mythical allusion in the novel to a book like the *Popol Vuh* dissolves in a vast ramification of meanings whose consistency comes more from their redoubling (from the exercise of their creative potentialities) than from their supposedly venerable origin. The archaeological gesture through which so many readers have tried to trace the novelistic meaning back to an ancestral origin is compromised when such a procedure ends, over and over again, in dis-appointment.

We must recognize in this disappointment the structural effect of the encounter between the discourse of witnessing and the expressive demands of the historical avant-gardes. This encounter makes possible the politicization of the aesthetic sphere. As John Kraniauskas suggests, "it is only with the relative privilege socially inscribed in literary autonomy that the real conditions of artistic responsibility are given."[4] Asturias's aesthetic responsibility confronts him to the recognizable paradox of all auto-ethnographic writing, namely: how to portray an intimate world without positioning the narrative voice in the space of an observer alienated from the reality he tries to depict. Asturias answers this challenge by making life itself—in an almost phenomenological sense—the ultimate referent of his literary endeavor. Any literary criticism of literature is necessarily antinomical—as Adam Shellhorse put it.[5] Any gesture through which literature opens itself to its other only exists in interior of that infinite dialogue to which literature testifies by its mere existence. In the case of Asturias, his wager for existential immediacy is compromised by the fact that in order to disclose the rawness of the Indianized world, Asturias takes a detour through the Maya Quiché archive as a site of authorization. In this way, what presents itself as present acquires a double valence. The world as presence (immediate existence) is made possible by the presencing of an interpretive framework—the indigenous archive as a schema for the interpretation of reality.

The dis-appointment was also a feature of the time, visible in the political crisis of the 1920s and in the doubts that assaulted the project of European civilizations; doubts that were bespoken by movements like Cubism in the sphere of art and phenomenology and psychoanalysis in the orders of philosophical

---

3. And yet, Gerald Martin does not offer a reading of *Hombres de maíz* in the customary sense of the word. The critical relationship here is closer to what in English is called "a companion" than to the exegetic tradition proper of literary criticism.

4. John Kraniauskas, *Capitalism and Its Discontent. Power and Accumulation in Latin-American Culture* (Cardiff: University of Wales Press, 2017), 104.

5. Adam Joseph Shellhorse, *Anti-Literature. The Politics and Limits of Representation in Modern Brazil and Argentina* (Pittsburgh: University of Pittsburgh Press, 2017), 125.

and scientific knowledge. It is not by chance that all these movements unveil reality as a construction. The European order, like every order, was grounded on a belief. The belief allows its subjects to extract a rule for their actions. They act as if their actions are in agreement with what works as a ground. The belief then is not so much a lie, as it is a reference to something subtending that, even when it cannot be fully articulated, works as the reference point for all the "as ifs" that conform the imaginary of a culture and a society. Guatemala (Latin America at large) was no less in crisis than its European counterpart. The imaginary that articulated the projection of the nation was already in tatters when Asturias left for Paris. He did not need to write *Men of Maize* to bring it down. Asturias's project was not to dismantle the fiction of the nation, but to refound it on a different basis. His procedure involved challenging not so much the hegemonic façade of the Guatemala he knew, but that subtending element in reference to which all reality takes its bearings. It is an operation that touches on the level of the archival fictions that guarantee the historical continuity of a people or a nation. These observations may clarify the meaning of "the science of literature" in my title. The expression involves a playful allusion to Hegel's *The Science of Logic*, in which the German philosopher developed the idea of an alignment between reality and thought. My claim is that Asturias—to be more precise the Asturias of *Men of Maize*, his most emblematic novel—has such an Adamic alignment as his goal. The procedure, as we know, took the form of a revitalization of the Maya Quiché mythological lore. This fact authorized some people to read the novel as an almost academic act of cultural rediscovery—or even as an escape into the past. However, the time of *Men of Maize* is the present. Everything that belongs to the past appears in the novel verbalized, vocalized, enunciated.

Mythological references are fundamental to the world of *Men of Maize*—there can be no doubt about it. I would even say that the novel involves an actualization of the Maya Quiché mythology. But under what form? My argument is that the myth becomes a tool for the exploration of what is *real* in reality, of what presences in the present. This simple function changes the status of the myth. The myth becomes an archive. The actualization of the myth puts the validity of the social link (of its imaginary hold upon the social) in question. The myth begins to behave antagonistically toward the dominant social formation. It begins to represent a new language for the constitution of the present. If Asturias's literary creation really has the stature I attribute to it in these pages, it is not because it brings its rescues and memorializes a glorious past. *Men of Maize* is an event of language that seeks to redraw the coordinates through which a culture established a link to its world. These links are mostly discursive and linguistics. What leads me to characterize Asturias's novel as an event of language?

A literary triumph—some may say. This could be true if it not were the case that literature is as much on trial as ethnography in the pages of the novel. It is from this trial of literature that *Men of Maize* acquires its traits of unintelligibility.

Nothing proves the point better than the pristine, eminently readable pages of the second part of the novel. Compared to them, the first part—the events that transpire among the creoles and indigenous people of Pisigüilito, before the narrative moves to San Miguel de Acatán—reads like a traversal of a jungle of words, half-muttered convictions, and inscrutable passions. However, without the second part, we would not know how to read the first. It is only by contrast with the second part that the first part appears as an excess of life and a carnival of cultures. Asturias distorts literature to make it answerable to a world that could only be approached through an ethnographic sensibility, but one which an ethnographic diction will inevitably deface. The science of literature carries the project of canceling what Mary Louise Pratt once called "the paradox of auto-ethnography,"—the paradox involved in looking at oneself with foreign eyes. At some point, Asturias felt that literature could give him the edge he needed, and which ethnography could not deliver. In the end, he realized that by becoming a science, literature too becomes the more or less mute witness to a world that is no longer its lot to constitute.

The Paris Years

Asturias arrived in Paris in 1924, the year André Breton published the surrealist manifesto. Political commotion in the interwar years had sent hundreds of artists and intellectuals flocking to the French capital. In the city's streets, university classrooms, and cafés the most variegated traditions came into contact: Cubism and Einstein's relativity; Hegel's panlogism and Marx's dialectic; Freudian psychoanalysis and Husserlian phenomenology; a passion for the primitive and a reverence for the technological—all seasoned with intense interest for the comparative study of civilizations. This mélange of discourses formed the primordial soup out of which structuralism and post-structuralism would emerge a few decades later. This convergence between artistic avant-garde and the sciences of man could not but appeal to Asturias, who went to Europe as the author of an infamous positivist treatise and returned to Guatemala as an avant-garde writer committed to the vindication of the Maya Quiché lore.[6]

James Clifford noticed that already in the 1920s surrealist procedures were clearly identifiable in the style and practices of the rising field of comparative ethnography. Ethnography and surrealism found a meeting point in the figure of the collage. On the collage, Clifford defers to the famous dictum of Isidore-Lucien Ducasse (Comte de Lautrémont), "A chance encounter on a dissecting

---

6. Asturias's relationship with ethnography is well documented. Shortly after arriving in Paris, he enrolled in a course on Maya culture taught by the eminent Americanist George Raynaud. A man of vast knowledge, Raynaud covered not only the Maya world, but Incan and Aztec civilizations as well.

table of a sewing machine and an umbrella."⁷ The technique is recognizable in *Men of Maize* where it takes the form of a conceptual enjambment that overlaps distinct temporal orders:

> La tierra de *Ilóm* olía a tronco de árbol recién cortado con hacha, a ceniza de árbol recién quemado por la roza.
> Conejos amarillos en el cielo, conejos amarillos en el agua, conejos amarillos en el monte.

In Gerald Martin's translation:

> The air of Ilóm was heavy with the smell of newly felled trees, the ashes of trees burned down to clear the ground.
> Yellow rabbits in the sky, yellow rabbits in the water, yellow rabbits in the forest.⁸

Given the prominence of film in the language of *Men of Maize*, we might also call this procedure a cutting or a montage.⁹ But the transition between the two shots is not temporally seamless. The time of capitalist accumulation announced in the *roza* that clears the forest space for sowing contrasts with the mythical temporality that announces the conspicuousness of the past in the narrative present. From this aspect alone, we can see that the surrealist procedure differs from Asturias's enjambment in a fundamental sense.¹⁰

For Clifford, both surrealism and modern ethnography are counter-discourses leveled against the standardization of experience characteristic of a rapidly modernizing European ethos. Since perception has already been assumed to be misperception, the literary artifact and the ethnographic

---

7. James Clifford, "On Ethnographic Surrealism," *The Predicament of Culture* (Cambridge, MA: Harvard University Press, 1988), 119.
8. Asturias, *Hombres de maíz*, 7. Miguel Angel Asturias, *Men of Maize*, trans. Gerald Martin (New York: Delacorte Press/Seymour Lawrence, 1975), 3.
9. In Chapter one, I pointed to Martin Lienhard's observation that Eisenstein's *¡Que Viva México!* was one of the formal models for Asturias for the composition of his book.
10. For a discussion of Asturias's relation to surrealism see Stephen Henighan, *Assuming the Light: The Parisian Literary Apprenticeship of Miguel Angel Asturias* (Oxford: Legenda, 1999), 137. Carlos Rincón offers an exhaustive and critical appraisal of this relation in "Nociones surrealistas, concepción del lenguaje y función ideológico-literaria del 'realismo mágico' en Miguel Angel Asturias," in *Hombres de maíz*, ed. Gerald Martin, 695–722. A recent exploration of this subject can be found in Adrian Taylor Kane, *Central American Avant-Garde Narrative: Literary Innovation and Cultural Change (1926–1936)* (Amherst, MA: Cambria Press, 2014).

intervention implement different strategies united under a common commitment to deautomatization. But by focusing on the level of the procedure, surrealism condemned its argument to raise the question of deautomatization in the restricted sphere of consciousness. This implicit individualism is precisely the objection that the intellectuals of the Collège de Sociologie leveled against the surrealists.[11] Meaning is a communal affair from the start. The decisive step undertaken by Asturias in *Men of Maize* lies precisely in socializing the surrealist approach and making of it the point of interaction of vast symbolic orders. In Asturias's hands the surrealist procedure became—as was also the case for Lacan, whose surrealist leanings are well documented—a tool for exploring the collective organization of experience and the limits of overlapping injunctions and forms of habitation of a common world. In *Men of Maize*, we witness the emergence of networks of meanings in which the characters come to be described and made patent.

Asturias, the Gran Lengua

The surrealist collage does not only shock the modalities of perception of the viewer; it also implies a severe questioning of the author function. The banal idea that *Men of Maize* was not a product taken to its desirable level of perfection reflects this fundamental trait of its composition. Undoubtedly, its incorporation of different levels of narration and verisimilitude, its construction of complex symbolic articulations, and its postulation of universes of meaning that depend on the generalization of principles quite alien to those of its readers, all conspire against the novel's possible narrative smoothness. Asturias was quite conscious of the palimpsestic nature of his work. In an interview given in Caracas in 1967, Asturias said, "Beyond any doubt, my writing is a continuation of the great Maya and Quiché narratives."[12] The word *continuation* may play tricks on the reader. As occurs often in his case, it is easier to determine what Asturias did *not* mean to say. He did not mean to suggest that he is (pace Raynaud) an indigenous author. He was not claiming any privileged relationship vis-à-vis an origin called Maya or Quiché. Asturias did not know any indigenous languages; he was never even interested in learning the rudiments of these

---

11. Michèle Richman, *Sacred Revolutions: Durkheim and the Collège De Sociologie* (Minneapolis: University of Minnesota Press, 2002).

12. Quoted in Guillermo Yepes Boscán, "Asturias, un pretexto del mito," in *Hombres de maíz*, Asturias (Madrid: ALLCA XX/Fondo de Cultura Económica, 1996), 680. Gerald Martin recalls a similar assertion made by Asturias in a conference held in Guatemala in 1968: "There is in *Hombres de maíz* a richness of language born from the people, not from me." Gerald Martin, "Génesis y trayectoria del texto," in *Hombres de maíz*, Asturias (Madrid: ALLCA XX/Fondo de Cultura Económica, 1996), 483.

languages. Nevertheless, he spoke of himself as the *Gran Lengua* (the Great Tongue), suggesting a direct line of interpretation between his literature and that of indigenous people.

So, the question arises: How close is Asturias, the writer, to the complex worldview that he insinuates rather than presents in his novel? His self-described role as *Gran Lengua* is not that of a translator; if anything, it is closer to Dr. Francia's secretary in Roa Bastos's *I the Supreme*. And like the Supreme's amanuenses, the *Gran Lengua* confuses everything, sometimes in order to remain loyal to the surrealist injunction to reveal the undertone of the dreams that permeate all reality. The results are pages and paragraphs of difficult intellection, in which different ways of constructing meaning overlap.[13] The novel unfolds in a multiplication of seemingly incompatible registers so that, despite the sober efforts of a critic like René Prieto, it is quite difficult to come up with a convincing structural model of the novel as a whole.[14]

Although Asturias's literary practice opposed any absorption of the singularity of existence into a conceptual language (even that of literature), there was a constructive side to his project that was difficult to reconcile with the pervasive negativity proper of the avant-garde. James Clifford describes the critical charge of the surrealist collage in terms of its ability to expose culture as a set of "artificial arrangements susceptible to detached analysis and comparison with other possible dispositions."[15] Asturias may have found such questioning of naturalized cultural hierarchies appealing, but he also may have found it insufficient. The work of aesthetic negativity washes away not only the recalcitrant elements of the dominant but also those subordinate forms of cultural existence that Asturias sought to vindicate. On the other hand, it would be reductionist to claim that modernism or the avant-garde were closed to any form of constructivism, since both include the reconstitution of experience as a fundamental goal.[16] This trend, visible in the Situationists of

13. Mario Vargas Llosa notices that "*Hombres de maíz* unfolds in unexpected comparisons and vertiginous litanies, *jitanjáforas* [jabberwocky] and puns, a verbal pyrotechnics at once musical and poetic in which the properly narrative element catches fire and goes up in smoke only to return, a few paragraphs later, incarnated in a writing of an almost documentary realism." Mario Vargas Llosa, "Una nueva lectura de *Hombres de maíz*," *Hombres de maíz*, Asturias, 649–53.

14. René Prieto proposes a structural model for the novel, grounded on the modeling effect of a mythical substratum. See *Miguel Angel Asturias's Archeology of Return* (Cambridge: Cambridge University Press, 1993).

15. Clifford, "On Ethnographic Surrealism," 119.

16. In *The Culture of Time and Space*, Stephen Kern underlines the universal reach of a revolution in the forms of perception in the early twentieth century. The renovation of space made famous by Cubism ended up questioning not just the nature of spatiality but that of materiality as well. Kern contrasts the legacy of Democritus, from which we inherited the view that the world should be constituted by "solid bits of matter," to

the 1960s, was already part of the Cubist revolution, whose multiplication of planes and reconfiguration of spatial logics lead to a "reinvention of the notion of experience itself."[17]

Curiously, it was Martin Heidegger, a philosopher without major connections to modernism, who penned one of the most lucid descriptions of the necessary multi-perspectivism that presided over the possibility of an authentic knowledge of the present. As in the case of Heidegger's *Being and Time*, Asturias's novel appears implicated in a formidable effort of uncovering the "primordial spatiality" of existence.[18] Like Heidegger, Asturias rejects consciousness as the embodiment of the human. Nahualism—the belief that every human has an animal counterpart—is a perfect incarnation of the anti-Cartesianism characteristic of Heidegger's *Being and Time*, even if the German thinker doesn't pay much attention to animals in his book. Before the body could even be thematized, the world in which such body "happens" needs to be brought into phenomenological perspective. The situated nature of Dasein—like the situated nature of Asturias's characters—is fundamentally environmental: a being "bound up with beings."[19] These beings with which Dasein is entangled are not restricted to those present. One of the ways in which Heidegger establishes the importance of the non-present is through the notion of de-distancing (or de-severing). De-distancing makes the most distant star and the closest blade of grass to stand at the same existential distance from Dasein—but not without costs. "When one is primarily and even exclusively oriented towards remoteness as measured distances ... the primordial spatiality of Being-in is concealed."[20] The interplay between the most distant (the Maya Quiché past) and the closest (the world as it is revealed in the present) constitutes the fundamental structure through which *Men of Maize* renders its unparalleled view of the historical process.

But how do we know that we have the right access to what functions as ground? Reflecting on this problem, Heidegger advances a series of concerns that Asturias could have made his own: "When tradition thus becomes master,

---

J. J. Thomson's corpuscular physics. By 1914, a book about atoms explained that matter had a "spongy" consistency and was "prodigiously lacunary" (133). Kern argues that one of the consequences of this movement was the regrouping of the conditions for existence around the notion of simultaneity (another name for the collage).

17. Georges Didi-Huberman, *Devant le temps. Histoire de l'art et anachronisme des images* (Paris: Les Editions de Minuit, 2001), 287.

18. Martin Heidegger, *Being and Time*, trans. John Macquarrie and Edward Robinson (Oxford: Basil Blackwell, 1978), 141.

19. Martin Heidegger, *Discourse on Thinking*, trans. M. Anderson and H. Freund (New York: Harper & Row Publisher, 1969), 48.

20. Martin Heidegger, *Kant and the Problem of Metaphysics*, trans. Richard Taft (Bloomington: Indiana University Press, 1997), 141.

it does so in such a way that what it 'transmits' … become inaccessible … it blocks our access to those primordial 'sources' in such a way that Dasein has no ground of its own to stand on."[21] The problem is that modernity's vertiginous process of archivization (which Asturias fully experienced in Paris) creates new possibilities in the order of de-distancing while it also generates new distortions in the dimension of the symbolic. Archivization and increasing modernization made the problem that Heidegger calls "the ground" ever more urgent for Asturias. What we have to ponder now is why is it that Heidegger succeeds at the same task that Asturias cannot but fail.

The unity of experience that Heidegger searches for in *Being and Time* already constitutes a premise of his study. Heidegger relies on a hermeneutics whose circularity (as he has already warned us in the introduction) does not vitiate the investigation, since it testifies to "a remarkable relatedness" without which an ontical investigation cannot even start.[22] By contrast, *Men of Maize* begins with the staging of two irreconcilable propositions upon a single action, that of planting maize, "Sown to be eaten it is the sacred sustenance of the men who were made of maize. Sown to make money it means famine for the men who were made of maize."[23]

If *Being and Time* can be said to have solved the question of rootedness of Dasein, it is so insofar as Heidegger managed to disengage the issue of rootedness from any form of empiricism, consigning it to the encircling force of language.[24] What the phenomenological intuition discloses is, fundamentally, of the order of signification. The only reason why Heidegger could bend upon the world-as-language is because a whole tradition already has paved the road to an immanent relationship between the world as language and the language of philosophy. Heidegger was the heir of a linguistic purification, of a political purge that extricated from philosophical discourse the ghosts and debts that could tie the present of philosophy to the history of its "as-having-been."[25]

In the case of Asturias, this schematism that allows the "I am" to stand in continuity with the "as-having-been" is simply not there. It is, surely, the occasion and excuse of the literary work itself, and we can say that the novel

21. Ibid., 43.
22. Heidegger, *Being and Time*, 28.
23. Asturias, *Men of Maize*, 5–6.
24. Theodore Kiesel, *The Genesis of Heidegger's Being and Time* (Berkeley: University of California Press, 1993), 33–5.
25. The creation of a philosophical language by authors like Baumgarten, Leibniz, Kant, and Hegel proceeded through a double strategy of vindication of the vernacular German and a reflective evaluation and purging of the past. In this process, some ties were severed—with the Arab and Judaic world, but also with colonialism and the exploitation of the Black body—while others were reinforced or created anew—mainly with the classical Greek past.

comes to the place of the absent schema. But it can become so—a schema—only as an event of language. Asturias's novel appears as the other side of Rancière's repeated claim of an essential solidarity between the noun *politics* and the noun *literature*, which together produce "a specific sphere of experience in which certain objects are posited as shared and certain subjects regarded as capable of designating these objects and of arguing about them."[26] Any reader who has lost himself/herself in the pages of Asturias' novel knows that this is not the case in *Men of Maize*. Meaning is not available to be taken as an object in the world. Instead, it has to be wrestled from a universe in which everything communicates but not necessarily to the figure of a preformed reader. The readers of *Men of Maize* (and sometimes its characters as well!) are constantly reminded of a crisis of designation, a dispersion of the referential function of language born precisely from the fact that the symbolic apprehension of the world happens in such a way that the gap separating the "I-am" from the "as-having-been" becomes an obstacle for some (the *ladinos*) or an unachievable utopia for others (the indigenized people). How could it be otherwise if between those two spaces, stand not only two times, but also (at least) two languages and two rationalities as well?

Mythical Repetition

The *Gran Lengua* articulates the validity of the myth as a point of orientation for the present. But the temporality of citation involves considerable perils. The interplay of archive and experience always risks losing sight of either the power of the origin or the originality of the present. The fundamental operation of the novel seems to be one by which its different "geological" layers (the image belongs to Gerald Martin) is worked out in such a way that it travels forward rather than backward, so much so that a plunge into an assumed past results in a resurfacing in an intractable present. This trajectory in itself excludes the simplistic idea that the mythical dimension represents a fundamental bedrock whose meaning and consequences are repeated either consciously or unconsciously in the becoming of time. The idea of a mythical repetition is a proposition mostly alien to the formative principle of Asturias's novel. As far as myth is concerned, we could adopt here an observation that Stephen Henighany made about *Leyendas de Guatemala*: In everything that pertains to the materials, "the pattern of Maya images ... is governed by Asturias's artistic and narrative requirements rather than by the Maya tradition."[27] But what are these "requirements?" In their essence, as Arturo Arias notices, they are not

---

26. Jacques Rancière, *The Politics of Literature,* trans. Julie Rose (London: Polity Press, 2011), 3.

27. Henighany, *Assuming the Light*, 138.

indigenous in nature.[28] It is the *indigenista* attitude in Asturias (René Prieto resolutely includes *Men of Maize* in the *neoindigenista* camp) that bespeaks his fatal assignation to the sphere of the present world rather than to a mythical past. The myth and the constellation of meanings attached to it are charged with the task of producing another perspective upon the world. Myths—ethnographers tend to agree on this point—are cosmogonies, tales about the justice under which the world came to consist. It is fitting that once they are redeployed in what is at all lights an unhinged reality, they should acquire a double edge. As memories, they mark the history and the drift of the subjectivity that constitutes itself through their mediation; as incarnated ideas, they bring a power of commotion to bear upon the hegemonic organization of the present.[29]

In the horizon of *Men of Maize*, the myth is an archive: the objectified memory of what was once alive and which now endures under different registers of inscription and forgetting. The myth is the point of origination of a convoluted process of inheritance by which the past is made into a condition of an aesthetic, ethical, and political apprehension of the present. This is why Asturias never needed to learn an indigenous language to become the Great Tongue. The function of the author is not to prove the continuity of a Maya Quiché heritage in his blood, but rather to show the binding character that the past holds for the present, even when the chain and the links that connect the "as-having-being" to the "I-am" lie shattered under the unredeemable shadow of a colonial history.

This does not mean that the rich tradition toward which Asturias turns has no purchase in his novel. Nahualism—that is, the belief that human beings can transform into animals—plays a significant role in *Men of Maize*. And the same can be said of other mythical elements in the work. Among those, I single out one that, in my opinion, has the most far-reaching structuring effects. There is an existential earnestness in Asturias's novel that makes the characters true to their world. Chalo Godoy behaves exactly as we expect him to behave; the Tecúns do not doubt for a second that a *daño* has been perpetrated against their *nana* and that only the severed heads of the Zacatón family hanging before her can restore the old woman's health; Goyo Yic is as honest a blind beggar as Chigüichón Culebro is the most reliably brutal of all *curanderos*. One would be hard-pressed to elicit in these cases the sharp differentiation that Mikhail Bakhtin establishes between epic and novelistic characters.[30] There is something epic in

---

28. Arturo Arias, "Algunos aspectos de ideología y lenguaje," in *Hombres de maíz*, Asturias (Madrid: ALLCA XX/ Fondo de Cultura Económica, 1996), 562.

29. As Gerald Martin notices, *Men of Maize* "is the only work by Asturias about the indigenous people of Guatemala that examines the indigenous cosmovision in its contemporary dimension." Gerald Martin, "Genesis y trayectoria del texto," in *Hombres de maíz*, ed. Gerald Martin, 472.

30. That is, while epic characters speak and behave in agreement with their ethical environment and are therefore predictable characters, the novel form introduces a

the miserable, disenfranchised bodies that crisscross the geography of *Men of Maize*. While at the semantic level the novel at times betrays a certain excessive Spanish barroquism (even a churrigueresque tendency), I do not think that this epic dimension comes to the novel by way of its peninsular antecedents. Instead, this epic ethos results from Asturias's attempt to instantiate a set of characters and emotions that stand in obvious dialogue with classic Maya Quiché lore in a narrative that is primordially novelistic—and therefore far more concerned with the question of experiencing the world than with enacting a structural quest into that world's origins.

This tension sets the stage for the fundamental antagonism of the novel. This antagonism emerges first and foremost through the pluralization of the symbolic function of culture.

The Multiple Symbolics

When Saussure defends the arbitrary character of the sign, he reasons that if linguistic signs were motivated people would quarrel endlessly about why to call a tree a tree instead of something else. At a structural level, language bans deliberation. So, language is not just a model for the law; it is the initial law of any human community whatsoever; the law of nomination by which all the objects of the world insofar as they are named are also ordered, classified, asserted, or suspected. The role of language as the wellspring of any possible contractualism comes to the fore in words like friend, daughter, husband, lover, or enemy. They are nouns that contain, if not promises, at least expectations, but whatever value they may have, it is one redeemable only before an immaterial tribunal to which we commit ourselves by the mere fact of speaking. The alien nature of language—Lacan refers to it as simply the Other—accounts for the fact that in human communication misunderstanding is often more common than true understanding. All misunderstanding is grounded in the simple fact that the subject is not the origin of meaning. More often than not, he struggles to make himself understood by himself.

Although the law hits the subject from the outside, its nature is not of the order of the unhuman. The law secures its binding nature by giving us something in exchange for the sacrifice of our Adamic freedom. What language offers is recognition. Without this tacit recognition that inhabits almost every word, human life itself would be impossible. (The recognition in question has nothing to do with the liberal notion of recognition in which the subject preexists the honor bestowed on him.) When I couch Asturias's relationship to

---

dimension of accident proper to modern subjectivity. See Mikhail Bakhtin, "Epic and Novel," in *The Dialogical Imagination*, ed. Michael Holquist (Austin: University of Texas Press, 1982), 3–40.

his materials in terms of language and archive, I am trying to underscore the symbolic charge of those materials, how, in them, the fundamental structure of binding and recognition comes to the fore.

"Begin by thinking that you don't understand," Lacan tells a perplexed audience of analysts around 1953.[31] How good is this advice? When Asturias says that maize is sacred, the didactic content of the phrase is inescapable for the reader. We understand. We even know that corn is not sacred for us, so the writer may be putting in play the values of some "other." We even understand Calistro when he says that in killing the deer he also killed the wizard who commanded the assassination of the Zacatons, because wizard and deer were "énticos" (identical). The word *éntico* itself—a reality effect in Barthes's sense—solicits and obtains our acquiescence. But does this understanding mean that we recognize the symbolic network that subtends Calistro's reasoning? I don't think so. Our contract here is with literature, not with the intuition of which literature is a distant echo. What we understand in this story depends on our own approach to the primitive under the form of an ethnographic gaze—surrealist or not. The symbolic mobilized in such an understanding is not the other's symbolic but our own, one on the bases of which we take our bearings and declare those others to be primitive. From this example we can already intimate why Lacan is so keen to preempt understanding. For the French psychoanalyst, understanding introduces in its very essence a principle of regulation, a homeostasis of meaning. In literature, full, complete understanding would eventually derail the goal of presenting the alternative symbolic, and this, once again, is the reason why the commitment of witnessing should pass through a separation from its sources.

In contrast to the easy capture of language in the networks of the digestible and understandable, we find a passage like the following:

> The warrior who smells of peccary disguises his trial and adorns himself with orrisrot. Heliotrope water hides the odor of the deer and is used by the warrior who gives off little deer-drops of sweat. Still more penetrating is the spikenard, most suitable for those who are protected in war by night birds, frozen and perspiring. Likewise the essence of the gardenia is for those who are shielded by snakes, those who have scarcely any odor, those who do not perspire in combat. (10)

At the end of this description, a timely note by Gerald Martin informs the reader that this difficult passage represents a list of *nahuales* and as such bespeaks the ethnographic acumen of the *Gran Lengua*. What is unique about the enumeration—and sets it apart from similar ones that we find in

---

31. Jacques Lacan, *The Seminar of Jacques Lacan. Book I. Freud Papers on Technique. 1953-1954* (New York: W. W. Norton, 1995), 71.

costumbrista or *indianista* works—is the way in which its enunciative value is not exhausted in its referential quality but brings with it a whole constellation of expectations.[32] The list of nahuales (which is not presented as such in the novel; we only know it to be a list of nahuales thanks to Gerald Martin) is a performance of committed speech enacted in terms of a collusion between an ethical interruption and an aesthetic insinuation of an alternative ordering of the world. I say "interruption" because when considered in relation to its context in the page, the list of nahuales comes from nowhere, cutting through an entire scene centered on the figure of Colonel Godoy and his actions. The fragment's sudden appearance simulates the return of the repressed, as if history itself had suffered a slip of the tongue. But this is not all. What does the *Gran Lengua* facilitate in this enumeration of nahuales? Surely not meaning in its reduced ideality. The passage is meant to be effective regardless of an intervention such as Martin's—whether or not Asturias foresaw such a philological intervention. Understanding or not understanding does not concern merely, and only the semantic matter of thought. In this passage, the only thing to understand is that there is a law of understanding from which we are excluded by and large. If *Men of Maize* can be said to say something, what is most insistently said in its pages is: there are multiple symbolics. The different symbolics rub elbows. They touch each other. People and landscapes, beasts and events are harnessed to them. Everything begins and ends with the horizon of meaning, the contracts, and the confusions that these symbolics made possible.

After helping Colonel Chalo Godoy exterminate Gaspar *Ilóm*'s rebellion by poisoning the Indian chief, la Vaca Manuela Machojón gives a farewell to Machojón's son, who is going to a nearby town to marry his fiancée.

> Vaca Manuela ... blessed him with the sign of the cross, and advised him that if he was to marry he should be a good husband, which in a word means a man who is neither sour nor syrupy, neither a madcap nor a milksop. (23)

The advice is given in standard, recognizable Spanish and in vernacular Spanish. The *Gran Lengua* translates from one to the other but without letting the reader know what came first on the plane of enunciation. While everything in the scene conveys a sense of foreboding (the marriage is conditional, the blessings apotropaic), language both alludes to and instantiates its relationship to the law, but more interestingly to its plurality. A list of injunctions is conveyed

---

32. In discussing Asturias's novel, Arturo Arias has talked about the discovery of the signifier as well as—in an earlier text on a slightly different register—"the discovery of the word." Arturo Arias, *La identidad de la palabra: Narrativa guatemalteca a la luz del siglo XX* (Guatemala: Artemis-Editer, 1998), 107. In a similar vein, René Prieto notices that a critical aspect of *Hombres de maíz* lies in "sign association" (*Miguel Angel Asturias's Archaeology of Return*, 101).

through specific idiomatic forms. They would be nothing outside these idioms. Neither the concept of heterogeneity nor that of transculturation, anchored as they are in an ideality of meaning, can properly capture the subtlety of this linguistic operation. What Asturias executes here is the givenness of the archive approached from the ethical perspective of someone who sees himself existing in the destining of that process of archivization.[33] In this sense, it is interesting to ponder here the function of the middle voice, the voice of the middleman, the one that says, "which in a word means." Its function seems quite similar to the glossaries that accompanied *pre-indigenista* literature until the first decades of the twentieth century. (And certainly, *Men of Maize* contains a much-needed glossary in the Archivos edition.) These glossaries were not only helpful for clarifying a textual meaning obscured by the use of local or ethnically marked locutions; their function was to underline a sort of ontological distance, marking the limit of a world that is no longer ours. Insofar as their function was to indicate the remoteness that separated the reader (and perhaps the author) from the narrated material, they are the opposite of the fundamental phenomenological condition of all literature, which depends on the merging or overlapping of consciousness rather than on their differentiation.[34] If the glossary does not play the same role here, it is because the indigenous world and its popular voices are not quoted but instead vocalized as Martin Lienhard aptly put it.[35] The reader of the novel soon finds out that the glossary is of limited utility, and this is so because the function of the ethnographically marked nouns and expressions is not so much semantic as performative.

Now, even in the restricted space of the Machojón household, this is not the only symbolic that intersects the farewell scene. Machojón's father, Don Tomás, is prostrate, speechless under the weight of a curse. After the gendarmes killed Gaspar *Ilóm* and all his followers, the sorcerers foretold that the killers would die by fire and leave no descendants. Don Tomás takes the omen seriously; after all, he himself was part of Gaspar's tribe before his ladinization through marriage with Vaca Manuela.

The young Machojón never solicits his lover's hand; he disappears, enshrouded in a rain of fireflies that resembles a hailstorm of winged gold. Soon, the lost rider, whose body is never found, reappears among the flames

---

33. As Mario Vargas Llosa noticed, "The primary indigenous materials that Asturias retrieves come from historical erudition rather than from an immediate knowledge of the folkloric features of the Guatemalan culture of his time." Llosa, "Una nueva lectura," 652.

34. George Poulet, "Phenomenology of Reading," *New Literary History*, vol. 1, no. 1 (1969): 53–68.

35. René Prieto notices that language in the novel is not used for description: "Rather than indoctrinate his readers [Asturias] decided to demonstrate the originality of a Maya Quiché civilization" (*Miguel Angel Asturias's Archeology of Return*, 127).

of the *roza*, the fire used by the corn planters for sowing. The story serves the maiceros well. Feverish to see his lost son one more time, the old Machojón releases more land to be burned; until the whole story backfires. (No one is master of the symbolic.) Frustrated that he cannot see his son among the screams of "right there," "I just saw him," Machojón dresses like his son, mounts his best horse, and lets himself be consumed by the fire. Except that he is no longer burning forest, but the crop with which the maiceros had hoped to end the misery of their lives once and for all. The story marks the defeat of the supernatural—there has never been a Machojón among the flames—but also fulfills the promise of the *brujos*: because his father took part in the murder of Gaspar Ilóm, he dies by fire and without offspring.[36]

The same fire reappears, threatening Colonel Chalo Godoy as he descends toward the Corral de los Tránsitos with the rest of his patrol. In hindsight, we know that Godoy and his men ride to their death. They are certainly nervous, since despite representing the forces of rationalization, they are assaulted by the strangeness that is linked to a landscape for which they lack the nouns, the enchaining of stories, and in the end all the consolatory functions that come from having duplicated a reality on the scale of language. This extreme uncertainty about the anchoring of the world in the density of the word is parallel to the revitalization of the supernatural viewpoint as the chapter unfolds. It is at the end of this chapter that Vaca Manuela will evoke the omen, when the fire started by her husband reaches the maiceros and the troops of Musús, Godoy's second lieutenant, who have just arrived in the valley. Wondering about the fire that threatens to set the whole valley ablaze, Musús, who obviously knows the old Machojón has been tricked into burning as much *monte* as possible, wonders "who was playing with fire?" Vaca Manuela, who may sense in his words an interpellation to her husband, retorts in a way that displaces the agency of the impending catastrophe as much as it resignifies it.

> Colonel Godoy, your leader, was the one who played with fire, when he made me and my man poison Gaspar Ilóm, *the fearless male who had succeeded in throwing the noose of his word round the fire running wild through the mountains*. (47)

36. *Men of Maize* is an extraordinarily polysemic novel. The episode of Machojón's death condenses a reference to the *maiceros's* avid search for riches in the constant repetition of gold used as an adjective to describe the color of the lost son and his horse, but this color comes from the fact that he was killed by the fireflies that represent the sorcerers, which as they fall onto Machojón are said to resemble a hailstorm of winged gold.

The italics are mine and are used to emphasize the fact that although syntactically these words stand in apposition to "Gaspar *Ilóm*," it is not Manuela Machojón who proffers them. A piece of epic talk—even of Homeric interposition, in the style that Auerbach taught us to recognize—bestows a note of grandeur on a piece of miserable life that is touched, as it were, by the dignity of legends. More prosaically, the words of Vaca Manuela show how the intersection of competing symbolics is the permanent driving narrative force in the novel. They also show in what sense they are symbolics and not just stories or remembrances: they constitute the building blocks of the law of understanding by which subjects take their bearings in the world. The invincibility of a repressed symbolic may well be the fundamental lesson that the novel tried to teach to its initial readers.

Men of Maize is without doubt the product of an enlightened mind, and yet the magical always touches on the level of causality. It is true that the magical explanation never goes uncontested, but the same can be said of non-magical causality in the work. In following this strategy, Asturias renounces any attempt to validate one worldview over the other; and in this sense his ethical commitment to the world is also instantiated by his relationship qua author to the characters of his novels qua characters. We see Goyo Yic or Vaca Manuela Machojón through a scrupulous objectivism, and at no point does Asturias try to break into the consciousness of his creations through a trick of omniscience. What is singular in the procedure is the position taken by the narrative voice. And this position is such that it restores its secret to the other by never belying its interpretation of the world.

It would seem that Asturias is doing no more than saving appearances: under certain conditions, the indigenous worldview is validated. All Asturias does in presenting and upholding a popular view on the temporality of events is restore to the other's symbolic its field of application. What is essential is that the narrator does not treat popular, vernacular consciousness as unable to map the space in which it exists and, second, that he conceives the political effects of the novel as discursive rather than as merely indexical. It is in this sense that I take Gerald Martin's assertion that Asturias's novel presents a "deeply political notion of writing."[37] Asturias is not saying that Guatemala is populated by magic. He is saying, in a language inflicted by otherness, that Guatemala is a country populated by antagonistic forms of consciousness and by equally antagonistic discursive formations, and that these are not superstructural features added to the world but an essential part (perhaps the most essential part) of reality itself. This is, after all, what the word antagonism means: more real than reality.

---

37. Martin, "Introducción del coordinador," xxiii.

Spatiality, Environment, Umwelt

René Prieto has observed that: "Asturias ... always maintained that the one and only function of a Latin American author was to unveil the political reality of his country. And yet ... *Men of Maize* ... remain[s] misunderstood to this day."[38] Certainly, our notion of the political has undergone significant changes since Prieto wrote these lines; however, his question remains legitimate. How was the political presented in Asturias in such a way that it went misrecognized and unread "to this day?" I've already anticipated my own answer: The political element in Asturias went misapprehended because critics looked for it in the reified forms of politics (police, in Rancièrean terms) rather than in the particular strategies that are proper to what, with Gerald Martin, we can call a "deeply political notion of writing."[39] I take Gerald Martin's description to mean that Asturias's engagement is with the conditions of possibility of engagement. Through his writing, Asturias intervenes on the discursive forms that take charge of stabilizing a reality. This is why, nowhere is the fundamental position of the political in Asturias more obvious than in the treatment to which he subjects the notion of spatiality in his novel.

If mapping represents the fundamental political operation of literature in modernity, how are we going to understand the profound crisis of spatial logics in *Men of Maize*? Many critics have noticed the disorientation that seizes the reader in those pages in which a Baroque style merges with a general absence of geographical markers and points of reference. However, popular characters move quite comfortably in this world that is so disorienting for the reader. At some level, there is a positive side of disorientation insofar as the latter results from the affirmation of an originary *world-as-lived* which the phenomenologists take to be the ground of any experience whatsoever.

In *Men of Maize*, the popular world is understood primarily as environment: the world around insofar as it is more than a backdrop; the world insofar as it nurtures. *Umwelt*—the key notion coined by biologist Jakob von Uexküll, whose investigations, as Giorgio Agamben reminds us, "are contemporary with both quantum physics and the artistic avant-gardes,"[40] deeply reshaped our contemporary notion of reality. Agamben continues: "Where classical science saw a single world that comprised within it all living species hierarchically ordered ... Uexküll supposes an infinite variety

---

38. Prieto, *Miguel Angel Asturias's Archeology of Return*, 1.
39. Martin, "Introducción del coordinador," xxiii.
40. Giorgio Agamben, *The Open: Man and Animal*, trans. Kevin Attel (Stanford: Stanford University Press, 2005), 39. The fundamental references here are to Jakob von Uexküll's *Theoretical Biology* (New York: Harcourt, Brace, 1926) and his *Mondes animaux et monde humain, suivi de Théorie de la signification* (original German publication 1956), trans. Phillipe Müller (Paris: Pocket Collection, 1965).

of perceptual worlds that, though they are communicating and reciprocally exclusive, are all equally perfect and linked together as in a gigantic musical score."[41] The idea of *Umwelt* stands in solidarity with the nahualism of the first part of the novel. However, as a historical form, the novel is antithetical to any *Umwelt*. Where the *Umwelt* was, literature makes emerge an environment. That the mythological substratum cannot be repeated in the present simply means that the popular *Umwelt* must be subjected to the conditions of spatiality. The environment can be considered pre-political, in the sense that it implies reality as primordially given. On the other hand, nothing can be more political than questioning the modalization of the real on whose basis the subject relates to the totality of appearances. Asturias intimated that much when he wrote: "I am a committed writer, but my commitment is to a reality and a world."[42] Why does Asturias need two objects of engagement—a reality and a world—instead of just one? Moreover, in what sense could a reality be different from a world?

Reality and world had been subject to two diverging destinies in the hermeneutics of the modern. While "reality" evokes an entity that is the object of heavy policing, "the world" has rested for most of our history as a reservoir of experience. This fundamental distinction between world and reality increasingly came under assault throughout modernity and is today on the verge of disappearing. Already in 1755, Jean Jacques Rousseau noticed that the more Europeans traveled around the globe, the greater their ignorance of the world.[43] By the beginning of the twentieth century, the paradox of increasing information leading to increasing anaesthetization became one of the most pervasive questions in the sphere of art and culture in general.

The dimension of a fundamental popular *Umwelt* is simultaneously enacted and abandoned in the movement of the novel. This enactment and this abandonment—with a timid return toward the end that really doesn't settle the matter—constitutes the proper action of the novel. The importance of spatial logics in *Men of Maize* is well represented by the fact that everything the reader gets to know about the world is disclosed primordially through the characters' *movement*. While Asturias's novel presents us with different groups bound together in terms of the localized languages they speak and the beliefs to which these languages testify, the most noteworthy trait of the novel is that whatever is disclosed to us about their reality is ultimately related to the comings and goings of its characters. Some of the modalities of that movement are flight (María Tecún), search (Goyo Yic), mission (Coyote Aquino), punishment (Colonel Chalo Godoy), promise (Machojón), traversal (Hilario Sacayón), visiting (the comadres), and business (Revolorio and Goyo Yic). Movement in the novel is

---

41. Ibid., 40.
42. Quoted by Martin, *Hombres de maíz*, 477.
43. Jean-Jacques Rousseau, *Discourse on the Origin of Inequality*, trans. Donald A. Cress (Indianapolis, IN: Hackett, 1992).

not presented under a Euclidian geography of departing from or arriving at. Space itself is engendered by traversal, and this disclosing of space through traveling novelizes the narrative. It makes literary characters out of the epical stubbornness of the popular types. And yet, insofar as people travel, insofar as travel is one of the dominant modalities in the novel, there has to be an arriving at and a departing from. The departure is always from a protective enclosure that these characters must abandon in order to become fully visible to a literary process that exposes them to a sociability grounded on spatial modalities that are the exact opposite of those they have abandoned. It is not until we arrive at Chapter XIII, situated in San Miguel de Acatán, that nomic spatiality asserts its grasp on the narrative. It is only then that geography and abstraction precede the journey.

Among all the characters, Goyo Yic plays a significant role, since it is his traversal of space that will eventually bring the novel to a close. However, no chapter is named after him. He appears toward the middle of the novel, in a chapter entitled "María Tecún." The honor is well deserved because left to himself, Goyo Yic would be an utterly stationary character. It is the flight of María Tecún from her husband—the old man who rescued her as a baby from the massacre of the Zacatón family—that jump-starts the narrative process around a story that possesses a structuring function for the entire novel. María Tecún's flight sends Goyo Yic to the coast, where he will find the first thing resembling a state (in the form of a prison). But in order to find María Tecún, Goyo Yic needs to first acquiesce to her line of flight. The blind man needs to see. For that, he submits to a brutal eye surgery at the hands of the curandero Chigüichón Culebro. The homemade surgery restores Goyo Yic's eyesight, allowing him to travel the precarious roads, encounter religious festivities, and visit unknown towns in search of his escaped wife. At first, it looks like Goyo Yic's new status as a seeing person results in little more than a cheap commentary on the proverbial blindness of love: although he can now look for her, his former blindness means he has never set eyes on her. He cannot even describe her to other people. However, sight does not result in his transformation into a contemplative person. The criticism of abstraction takes in Asturias's hand a turn that is absent in Heidegger. Goyo Yic's deep immersion in his quest and surroundings is attested by his almost becoming one with his pet animal, Tatacuatzín, which significantly becomes Goyo Yic's nickname on the road. This aspect of the novel, a reference to the subtending nahualismo, cannot be in any way reconciled with Heidegger's intransigent separation between the animal and the human.[44] The fact that the agent of disclosure in Asturias can indistinctively be human or animal is not to be read

---

44. On this point see Peter Sloterdijk, "Rules for the Human Zoo: A Response to the *Letter on Humanism*," *Environment and Planning D: Society and Space*, vol. 27, no. 1 (2009): 12–28.

in naturalistic terms. Nahualism reintroduces the heuristic value of myth in the entire constellation of the novel. Whenever Asturias refers to the world, it is not merely the world offered up as a passive entity for interpretation. It is a world traversed by the gaze that Asturias bears testimony to when he places himself in an indigenous line of interpretation.

The world created by this radical interpretation of reality is not easy to navigate. The reader is continuously faced with a lavish landscape of mountains, rivers, trees, and plants described, moreover, in an exhilarating, almost delirious language. The cognitive limit created by this style of representing space reminds us of how much our sense of the real depends on operations of concealment that we strive to criticize even though it is from them that the objects of the world receive the law of their intelligibility.

The Economy Lesson

His sympathy for the experiential adventures of his popular characters does not blind Asturias to the dominant forces shaping the life of rural people in Guatemala. Slowly but relentlessly, capitalism encroaches on the life of the periphery. All in all, it is not the logic of the gift but instead the logic of capitalist profit that forces the characters into a form of action that can be properly novelistic.

Joseph Vogl notices that the rise of capitalism is inextricable from the emergence of a new form of realism in the field of social interactions.[45] In *Men of Maize* the expansion of capitalist rationality is uneven, and its domination only "formal," as attested by a series of episodes that remark how difficult it is to combine the calculative requirements of capitalist accumulation with the primacy of a disintegrating *Umwelt* at the level of the spatial distribution of bodies. Asturias seeks to present his readers a world that is not yet fully mapped through economic rationalization. There are also networks of meaning, correspondence, circulation, and forms of iteration that are only feebly articulated to the economic power of money. Entire sociabilities and even towns are constructed around this way of life. It is in one of these towns that Goyo Yic meets Domingo Revolorio, who offers him a business proposal that will lift them both out of poverty. Goyo and Domingo will use all their savings to buy a stock of *aguardiente* in a nearby town, and they later march to Santa Cruz where the alcohol will be sold by the glass.

Domingo Revolorio alerts Goyo Yic that the success of the enterprise depends on a specific conversion not unlike the one that, according to Max Weber gave birth to capitalism in the North Atlantic Protestant world. "I once

---

45. Joseph Vogl, *The Specter of Capital*, trans. Joachim Redner and Robert Savage (Stanford: Stanford University Press, 2015), 17–23.

had a cantina, but I drank it all up; the second one my friends drank up; I had two cantinas and was left with just experience."[46] It is tempting to read the whole episode of Goyo Yic and Revolorio as a parody of *The Protestant Ethic and the Spirit of Capitalism*. Asturias's first stop in Europe was London, the capital of that ethics, where he was supposed to study economics, a subject he soon changed to ethnography and literature.

There is a disciplinary function of experience and objectivity that Revolorio exhibits in his admonition to Goyo Yic. The warning seems even more urgent given the miraculous nature of capitalist accumulation even at such a small scale. The two men manage to collect eighty pesos between them, enough to buy a *garrafón* (carboy) of aguardiente for which they expect revenues in the order of 1,200 pesos.[47]

After paying for the aguardiente and receiving a *guía*—which, more than a receipt, is a safe-conduct to be presented to the authorities in order to justify their possession of the merchandise—they start out for Santa Cruz in the early hours of the morning. Fatigued and cold, Goyo Yic daydreams of taking just one sip of the aguardiente, but Revolorio snaps:

> It might do your belly good, compadre; but we can't afford it … We didn't make our agreement for the fun of it, we gave our word we wouldn't give anyone, not even ourselves, a drink out of this flagon without due payment.[48]

But when Goyo starts exhibiting all types of bodily afflictions, Revolorio offers him six pesos, left over from the purchase, for him to buy just one drink and thereby regain enough strength to reach the city, to which Goyo agrees. As soon as he is in possession of the sum, he offers it to Revolorio, so he, too, can buy a drink. The six pesos change hand dozens of times until a patrol finds the two entrepreneurs irremediably drunk on the side of the road. There is a tragic dimension in this economy lesson that should not be missed. The commodity through which the two characters have sought to cancel their misery is precisely the one they need the most in order to forget how gripping that misery is in the first place. Questioned by the patrol, they can neither explain what happened to the aguardiente in the *garrafón*, nor produce the *guía* that would prove the alcohol was purchased and not stolen. A calculation is needed to understand the Dionysian nature of the economy lesson. If Goyo and Revolorio expected to earn 1,200 pesos at 6 pesos per glass, that means that they consumed 200

---

46. Asturias, *Hombres de Maíz*, 127. My translation.

47. This section contains another story which functions as the negative of calculative capitalism and expresses the liberating effects of intoxication. Revolorio tells the story of a group of white miners and their slaves. After a long work day, when they were all drunk, "the whites served the blacks and they all called each other brothers" (134).

48. Asturias, *Men of Maize*, 146.

glasses of aguardiente in just one morning—hardly a Protestant ethic by any measure. Such an ethic fails in the case of Goyo and Revolorio, insofar as what they precisely cannot do is postpone their desires. The aguardiente is a commodity only from the perspective of the value it may generate once it starts to circulate in the economic process. Goyo Yic and Revolorio have difficulties conceiving the aguardiente as a commodity, to the point where its use value ends up triumphing over and nullifying its exchange value. The money they circulate is not capital, but merely cash put at the service of buying an object of consumption and use. What the economy lesson teaches is the anthropo-technological nature of capitalism, or, as Weber would have it, capitalism's intrinsic relationship to the abnegation of self and enjoyment.[49]

The end of their capitalist adventure sharply divides Goyo Yic and Revolorio. They both suspect the other of cheating, and even after sobering up they cannot come up with a satisfactory explanation for how they ended up in financial ruin even after paying for every one of their drinks.

In the end, since they cannot prove to the authorities that they were in legal position of the alcohol, Goyo Yic and Revolorio are sent to prison—a place that, in ways not unique to Guatemala, is also a school and an education of sorts. Being sent to this prison fulfills Goyo's desire, because there he finds one of his lost sons, who is revealed to him, not through the vision that he reacquired to search for María Tecún, but through hearing and language: by the fact that the lost son bears Goyo Yic's name.[50]

The economy lesson takes place in the María Tecún chapter, and it is her figure that Asturias uses to counterbalance the non-calculative style that Goyo Yic wants for his own life. Once María Tecún is reunited with Goyo Yic, she explains that it was not a lack of love that estranged her from her husband, but instead, her certainty that the feeble old man would be unable to support the many children he had been fathering. In her flight, she accomplishes the abstraction and calculation that Goyo Yic cannot abide. Some modicum of Protestant ethics—of curtailment of enjoyment—is, after all, necessary if life is not to be consumed in the abyss of its own productivity. The conquest of time as futurity will lead to the restitution of mythical time: Goyo Yic and María

---

49. The capitalist genealogy drafted by Max Weber, 1905, *The Protestant Ethic and the Spirit of Capitalism* (London: Routledge, 1997), has been disputed in recent years by a number of authors. For some of them, racism and colonialism are at the origin capitalist accumulation (Eric Williams, *Capitalism and Slavery* (Chapel Hill: University of North Carolina Press, 1944)) while others have argued that it is not saving but instead expenditure that grounds capitalist expansion. Colin Campbell, *The Romantic Ethic and the Spirit of Modern Consumerism* (London: Blackwell, 1987).

50. While in prison, the now sober Revolorio and Goyo Yic reproduce the economic experiment of paying several drinks with a few pesos only to arrive at the same puzzling result.

Tecún will return to the lands desolated by Chalo Godoy, the maiceros, and the old Machojón in order to tend the milpa; but this restitution only takes place though the experience of a spatiality that exceeds the limits of these characters' original emplacements. Finally, let's notice that the mythical return of Goyo Yic and María Tecún to the land of Ilom is an integral part of the economy lesson. Through such a return, the myth actualizes itself as a limit to the boundless nature of capitalist enjoyment that the economy lesson both unveils and derides.

Naming the Cause

This novel that so prodigiously proliferates a dense network of names to sustain the reality of its local *Umwelts* (to a point where a glossary is needed, which is still insufficient) seems simultaneously hesitant when it comes to declaring the stakes of its own position in more mainstream, recognizable terms. Asturias leaves no doubt that capitalism itself is to be blamed for the social tensions that lie at the root of the military intervention in Pisigüilito. The reader can legitimately extrapolate that the same capitalist drive is the one that is contested and resisted by the different forms of lived experience the narrator finds so admirable. However, the fact that Asturias blocks the emergence of any level of explanation that lies above the consciousness of his characters (not only a recognizable subalternist narrative ploy but also the constitutive fiction of an auto-ethnography) complicates if not completely nullifies the novel's pedagogical potential. Many progressive critics remained nonplused about the rather fleeting nature of the indictment of capitalism in its pages. Carlos Rincón chastised Asturias for his lack of knowledge of historical materialism, openly suggesting that if Asturias had a better grasp of Marxism, his novel could have thrown a better light on the nature of social and economic exclusion in Guatemala.[51] Gerald Martin, on the other hand, lists historical materialism as one of the driving discourses of the novel.[52] There is a portion of truth in both positions. Certainly, *Men of Maize* manifests, as Martin argues, a desire to transcend the capitalist determination insofar as it is untrue and nihilating. Nevertheless, Rincón is also right when he suggests that Asturias describes the standoff between tradition and innovation, but he seems unable or unwilling to map their line of flight, the wheretofore of their dilemma—and it is clear that for Rincón myth does not provide such a road map.[53] What rings untrue for Rincón (and it is difficult to fault him on this point) is that a phrase such as "the corn is sacred" could act as the battle cry for an anticapitalistic discourse. For

---

51. Rincón, "Nociones surrealistas," 707.
52. The other two discursive threads he identifies are psychoanalysis and popular magic (Martin, "Introducción del coordinador," xxiii).
53. Rincón, "Nociones surrealistas," 706.

Rincón, the novel ends up trapped in a circular movement, one in which the contradictions of history seem to be sublated into the space of a mythical hope that may well be one reason why the representatives of the popular are losing the historical battle in the first place. In Rincón's view, Asturias's socialist leanings and protestations are condemned to remain at the level of good intentions insofar as he cannot imagine (or does not know how to codify) a more strictly socialist solution to the problem of capitalist alienation and exploitation. It is here that Asturias's engagement with the world and with forms of lived *Umwelt* becomes relevant. While Rincón's socialism is developmentalist out of programmatic necessity, Asturias's protest against capitalist reification takes a form we can call, a bit anachronistically, "conservationist." Rincón cannot conceive of a discourse that would be anticapitalistic and antidevelopmentlist at the same time, and this is precisely what Asturias is willing to think. Moreover, it is what has become thinkable for us in our own present, as the future of life itself on the planet hinges on the potentiality of an all-annihilating environmental catastrophe. Certainly, around 1949 (the year of the novel's publication), a conservationist socialism sounded like a contradiction in terms, and Asturias lacked the concepts or the vocabulary to force his way out of that contradiction. (The problem of development itself, as a theoretical topic in Latin American social sciences, emerged at the moment Asturias was putting the final touches on his novel.)[54] What Asturias did have was a language able to turn upon itself and to open, in this very movement, a set of ethico-political possibilities that were almost unthinkable in the developmentally inflected discourses of the social and political rationality of the postwar era. This was the language of literature, but even that language remained suspect to his eyes.

Twice-Told Tales

Men of Maize seems neatly divided into two parts. The first one, extending from Chapters I to XII, is mostly concerned with the events that transpire in Pisigüilito with Colonel Godoy's military intervention. The events of the second part, centered on the provincial town of San Miguel de Acatán, seem to take place years, if not decades, after the events of the first part; however, the last chapters of the book are also traversed by a mythical temporality that make the chronological differences relative. My analysis so far has concerned only the first part of the novel—the one that I deem most significant.

---

54. Maristella Svampa offers an insightful reconstruction of developmentalism and its relationship to dependency theory in Latin America in her recent book, *Debates latinoamericanos: Indianismo, desarrollo, dependencia y populismo* (Buenos Aires: Edhasa, 2016).

The action that takes place between chapters XIII and XVIII is like a strange body inside *Men of Maize*. For Gerald Martin, these sections "represent a sort of retrospective vision that contrasts the ladino Europeanized world with that other indigenous world partially witnessed by Asturias between 1904 and 1908 and re-discovered ... between 1924 and 1933."[55] In fact, Asturias developed this second part as a separate story, initially written around 1948 that he conjoined to the larger narrative when he was completing the book. An array of romantic characters populate its pages: don Deféric, a Bavarian composer stranded in the highlands of Guatemala who periodically sends his musical scores to Germany for publication and recognition; Neil, an American sewing machine salesman forever in love with Miguelita de Acatán (who rejects him); Hilario Sacayón, a poet muleteer who doesn't know who dictates to him the lines of the poems and songs he recites in the cantinas; Father Valentín, a priest writing a diary that is also and simultaneously a piece of ethnographic literature; and—most prominently—Nicho Aquino, who is said to transform himself into a postal coyote ("Correo-Coyote") in order to deliver the mail from San Miguel to the capital in the blink of an eye.

This final sequence of chapters represents the novel's only sustained narrative track told from an urban perspective—from the depths of a symbolic utterly occupied by colonial values. Even when previous chapters present the reader with the perspective of Colonel Godoy or of the landowner Machojón, the ethical worldview of that perspective remains popular in nature. It is only when we reach Chapter XIII that events are discussed, overwhelmingly, from the point of view of the upper echelons of a provincial society. The characters of San Miguel de Acatán only relate to the popular through the distancing lenses of an evaluative judgment rooted in a normative understanding of time. As soon as a glimpse of a popular discursivity emerges, it is immediately consigned to the sphere of the obsolete and the outmoded. Everything that was world forming before—the traversing of space that endowed experience with meaning—is now subordinated to stories that everyone knows and on whose meaning everyone seems to agree. Unanimity presides over this world; and if Antonio Gramsci could once describe hegemony as persuasion protected by the armor of force, we could call the persuasive last story of *Men of Maize* a coup de force protected by the armor of historicized time.

The highly esteemed but poorly paid mailman Nicho Aquino does not know that while he was on one of his routine trips from San Miguel de Acatán to the capital his wife abandoned him. As if to leave no doubt that we are already in the trace of a repetition, the fugitive woman loses her name. She is to don Nicho Aquino and the rest of the townspeople *una tecuna*. After discovering the woman's absence, Aquino files a missing person report at the municipal

---

55. For Martin what Asturias experienced in Guatemala, he rediscovered in France. Martin, "Genesis y trayectoria del texto," 490.

office, where an employee retells him the story, now become myth, of Goyo Tic and María Tecún:

> Remember what they say happened to that blind fellow who fell down a ravine on account of him running after that María Tecún. He heard her speaking; and just as he caught up with her, he recovered his sight, only to see her turned into stone. He forgot he was on the edge of the precipice; and for your knowledge and governance, they're still looking for him.[56]

While the story as remembered in the town represents a beautiful rendering of the intertwinement of popular memory and literature, spiced up with some pedagogical elements, the legend of María Tecún is presented in a unidimensional fashion that strips it from any trace of perspectivism. Everything that was lively, world forming, and *Umwelt*-like in the previous episodes is subjected, in the case of "Correo-Coyote," to a law of recursivity by which events and discourses are weighted up rather than experienced. It is only in the second part of the novel that the reader can literally hear the murmurs of the characters' thoughts and where, even for the characters, consciousness becomes a matter of self-inspection. These are pages that should be read not only as an indictment of a ladino appropriation of popular cultural lore, but also as pages casting a heavy doubt on the possibility of literature representing a successful transcultural operation. No doubt it was literature itself that opened for us the problem of the *Umwelt* in the first part of the novel; what is at stake in the second part is the antithesis of that gesture, one that for Asturias takes the unmistakable form of the degradation of voice into its written form. As soon as the word *cartas* appears in the narrative, Asturias is compelled to write "letters full of lies … how many lies in San Miguel de Acatán." Is it not extraordinary that the word *lie* plays no role in the first part of the novel and is used to characterize the second part as a whole? This coincidental assertion of the structural unworthiness of the written word in the most openly literary chapter of the book suggests an indictment of the literary process itself. Asturias reacts against fiction as the fundamental limitation of the writer's responsibility.[57]

The history of María Tecún has degenerated at this point to the level of a legend. "Legend" comes from the Latin *legere*: things to be read—like the letters full of lies that Aquino duly distributes between San Miguel and the capital. But surely Asturias is doing something other than deploying a simple-minded schism between the written and the oral. At the opening of this chapter, I ciphered Asturias's operation with the archive in terms of a voice: Asturias

---

56. Asturias, *Men of Maize*, 150. Translation modified.

57. On the paradox of responsibility, see Jacques Derrida, "This Strange Institution Called Literature: An Interview with Jacques Derrida," in *Acts of Literature*, ed. Derek Attridge (New York: Routledge, 1992), 33–75.

speaks to us about something that has spoken to him. But I do not use the figure of the voice and its attendant metaphors (to listen to, to reverberate, to vocalize, to write in the earshot of) to merely suggest the intimate relation of the writer to his material. I use them to underline the uniqueness of a process of inheritance and hosting. As a matter of fact, the stories told in the first part of the novel are neither oral nor written but instead are in between these two ideals—this is so, in part, due to the heuristic role of myth in the mapping of the world. By contrast, the second part introduces a thorough reconstitution of reality as a cohesive totality in which each discourse and each language are allocated its right place. All characters can quickly reflect on the nature of discourses which no longer constitute them in any significant way. Fiction is a second time whose very repetition betrays a fallen relationship to experience—a failure of deseverance. In certain ways, legends preserve the underlying heterogeneity upon which they rest (a heterogeneity that in the immediately successive chapters will open for Nicho Aquino and for him alone); but legends are not preserved as different valuations of the world. They are not preserved as symbolics rubbing elbows, but instead as narratives that, stripped of their poietic power, are also stripped of their most intractable antagonistic features.

To the transposition of existence into a rationale and perhaps even an alibi corresponds the register of knowledge, incarnated in the novel by the quasi-ethnographic passion of Father Valentín. The indictment of amateur ethnography in the hands of a well-meant Father resembles Asturias's own trajectory too closely to be dismissed. The priest keeps a personal diary where he reenacts the proverbial anthropological stance of the first great intuitive ethnographers of the Americas (Motolinía, Bernardino de Sahagún, J. F. Lafitau).[58] These European men and their indigenous counterparts were the first ones to grapple with the tragic dimension of loss inherent to the colonial conquest. Father Valentín is puzzled by the flight of Aquino's wife. Since the constant flight of women from households is a recurrent fact in society, what could be the origin of this behavior? The answer he arrives at is that these women have been administered a poison that provokes their actions. And with this simple answer—which is itself part of the legend that the priest is trying to analyze—Father Valentín restores an element of causality, a teleology of sorts, that has been mostly absent in the novel thus far. From a strictly narrative perspective, the important thing is that Father Valentín's inquiry works through the reduction of all symbolics to the dominant gaze of the onto-theological reason he incarnates.

The recognition of an antagonism often demands a turn from the writer. This turn results in a shift in perspective. Perspective is one of these ambiguous words that name two opposite operations. The unassailable singularity of my

---

58. The point is also made by Gerald Martín in an extensive note in *Hombres de maíz*, 366.

perception of the world is a matter of perspective. But perspective names also the overcoming of any singular position. Since the architectonical writings of Brunelleschi about Renaissance's perspectivism, the notion stands for the absolute mathematical rationalization of space. Such rationalization implied a simultaneous triumph of reason and fate, since the vanishing point of perspectivism was no other than God.[59] Merleau-Ponty spoke of such perspective as the eagle's gaze or even as God's gaze—and it is not by chance that it is a priest who tries to bring the end of perspectivism into the novel by recasting the entire complex of nahualism within a closed sphere of Christian interpretation.[60]

Once Coyote Aquino takes to the road as a new victim of *tecunismo*, the citizens of San Miguel de Acatán fear he could end up repeating the (falsified) story of Goyo Yic and disappear into a mist of legends along with all their messages, parcels, and valuables. A muleteer is sent to look for him, but he cannot be found, since he has already half entered the land of legends.

Don Nicho Aquino has descended into a cave where he will find his nahual, his animal protector, his other self. In the cave, one of the "firefly wizards" is waiting for Aquino to initiate him in the mysteries of a form of memorization which is not of this world. ("No one who is not an animal and a man can understand me.")[61] And yet, the narrator insists: "Life beyond the peaks that come together is as real as any other life. Not many men, however, have succeeded in going beyond the underground darkness."[62] And shortly after, "Those who resolve, come what may, to penetrate a few leagues beneath the earth," return (if they return) with new eyes, eyes able to perceive "the secret path down which they strode accompanied by hundreds of other animals, the shadow of grand-father animals."[63]

How to interpret this sudden withdrawal from the world into a sort of surrealist beyond from which Aquino, we know, is not coming back? ("those who return"/"if they return.") The similarities with the depiction of the

---

59. Brian Rotman notices that the visual mathesis of the world involved an unmistakable reference to Christian spirituality. For Rotman, this step was first accomplished by Nicholas de Cusa who tied the question of perspective to the presupposition of an omnivoyant God already by 1543. Brian Rotman, *Signifying Nothing: The Semiotics of Zero* (Stanford: Stanford University Press, 1987), 21.

60. Father Valentin writes: "But what cannot be explained, without the help of the devil is how the Indian can change himself into the animal that protects him, the animal he uses as his nagual ... They say this Nichón turns into a coyote as he leaves the town ... and for that reason, when he delivers the mail, the letters seem to fly." Asturias, *Men of Maize*, 176. Translation modified.

61. Ibid., 305.
62. Ibid., 297.
63. Ibid., 299.

Freudian unconscious produced by European artists are striking. It is plausible also to read in these images an invocation to the Mayan schema of the tree of life. This symbol, familiar to most Mesoamerican cultures, organizes existence according to an axis mundis that tie together the realms of heavens, earth, and the underworld. Is this, then, a rite of initiation? However, the Aquino that emerges from under the mountain and goes to meet Goyo Yic in the last pages of the novel is a diminished being, an outlaw that in their rage because of the lost parcels, the authorities of San Miguel de Acatán charged even with the death of his wife. The fate of Aquino remains puzzling since it marks a limit beyond which the true knowledge of the community cannot be reintegrated into its historical drift.

Stylistically speaking, Aquino's descent into the cave belongs neither to the first nor to the second part of the novel. It does not belong to the first part, because it lacks the modalities of sociability and reciprocity that characterize all the exchanges in the horizon of the popular *Umwelt*. We are not dealing with a symbolic, strictly speaking, but instead with an experience that is presented as intensely individual—that is, as already idealized and subtracted from the actual world of causes and effects. It does not belong to the cognitive modalities of the second part of the novel, because it is a story that violently shuns any possibility of simply translating it into the beautiful forms of literary *leyendas*. The descent into the cave is another scene, and it does not require a commitment to a psychoanalytic viewpoint to see that the moral of this scene should be read to the letter: the cave represents the going under of a popular modality of witnessing and inheriting. This going under, the whole novel seems to claim, figures that repression from which literature itself is born. Literature's desire to be reintegrated into the world only makes sense in light of its inescapable and structural distance from that reality. This separation from the existence to which it wants to testify constitutes a sort of original sin for literature, a sin from which Asturias is not ready yet to absolve his beloved instrument.[64]

---

64. There are several reasons to suspect that the second part of the novel disseminates—as if in a dream—the figure of the writer's ego in a variety of subject positions: not only can Hilario Sacayón be considered an alter ego of Asturias, but there is also the curious encryption of the name Miguel in a variety of positions: San Miguel de Acatán and Miguelita are the most salient.

Chapter 3

SEEING WOMEN PHOTOGRAPHED IN REVOLUTIONARY MEXICO

There is a photo, credited to Mauricio Yañez and numbered 8756, in the archive of the Fototeca Nacional at Mexico's National Institute of Anthropology and History (INAH) that shows General Ramón Iturbe posing with four heavily armed women. Although the presence of women in the officialdom of the revolutionary armies is a well-known and documented fact, such women rarely performed their femininity for the camera. The four señoritas surrounding Iturbe are presented manifestly as *women*. The photograph, which circulated widely in Mexico at the time, gave rise to the myth of General Iturbe's "female military staff" (*estado mayor femenino*). As Iturbe later explained, there was no such thing as a female staff in his army.

The women in question had been introduced to the general by the American consul in Durango in 1911. As Iturbe and his troops entered Topia, the four daughters of Durango society thought their honor would be best safeguarded at the home of the American consul. Once Iturbe's army occupied the city, they became intrigued by what everyone described as the general's courteous manners. They asked the consul to invite Iturbe for dinner and then persuaded him to pose with them for a photo.[1]

John Mraz, who reproduces the photo in *Photographing the Mexican Revolution*, notices that this type of photo constituted an extended trope in revolutionary Mexico, one that historian Gabriela Cano considers simultaneous with the emergence of the Maderista revolution.[2] In this type of photo, middle-class women (often daughters of wealthy ranchers) posed with rifles and crossed cartridge belts in an intended mimicry of revolutionary armies and in

---

1. There is scant historical evidence regarding this episode. Several conflicting sources agree, however, on the essential traits of the story which became a popular fable in revolutionary Mexico. The amount of conjectures and storytelling to which the photo gave rise is not without relevance for my reading of this photograph in terms of interpretive anxiety.

2. John Mraz, *Photographing the Mexican Revolution: Commitments, Testimonies, Icons* (Austin: University of Texas Press, 2012), 68.

a perhaps unintended reference to the popular soldaderas. The trope results, then, in a complication of roles of gender and class, since these women posed as what they were not—and yet this not-being-something is what constituted the truth of their representation.

General Photographic Theory and the Photography of the Mexican Revolution

It is one of the ironies of photography that there should be no direct path to its study. In the opening pages of *Camera Lucida*, Roland Barthes makes an uncharacteristic admission: it is "very difficult to focus on Photography."[3] As Jacques Lacan says, images are notorious for their traps.[4] Hence the need to proceed with some caution by approaching our subject through deviations and concentric circles of interpretation. At stake is finding our way in the dimension of the evident, where things are distinct, and mirages abound. Optics has a name for this phenomenon: distortion—sometimes even aberration. It is from the heart of an experience of distortion that Carlos Monsiváis launched his well-known indictment against nineteenth-century photography in Mexico:

> No one should be surprised by the absence of a Mexican nineteenth-century equivalent of the work of Atget in France, Julia Margaret Cameron in England or Matthew Brady and Jacob Riis in the United States … It is a question of priorities and patronage: the nineteenth-century middle class relied on pictures only to eternalize the majesty … of their exterior, physical appearance.[5]

The revolution put photography on a completely new ground. The naturalness with which the photo of General Iturbe and his four señoritas was exhibited, distributed, and discussed speaks of a time in which the vitality of the medium could not be contested. That vitality does not make things any easier for the commentator. In writing on the photographic archive of the revolution, I have found myself in a peculiar position. Many of the critics and texts of photographic theory that seemed essential to me as I read them "to become informed" seemed only partially correct when I was confronted

---

3. Roland Barthes, *Camera Lucida: Reflections on Photography*, trans. Richard Howard (New York: Hill and Wang, 2000), 6.

4. "The picture is … a trap for the gaze." Jacques Lacan, *The Seminar of Jacques Lacan Book 11: The Four Fundamental Concepts of Psychoanalysis*, ed. Jacques Alain-Miller, trans. Alan Sheridan (New York: W. W. Norton, 1998), 89.

5. Quoted from Olivier Debroise, *Mexican Suite: A History of Photography in Mexico*, trans. Stella de Sá Rego (Austin: University of Texas Press, 2001), 26.

the photographic corpus that interested me. I am not talking about questions of style but of essence. Questions such as: what is photography, how is it constructed and read, and what expectations can we legitimately pose upon it as both an art and a social practice? These are the types of questions that Barthes ciphered in terms of "an eidetic science of the photograph."[6] Perhaps the critics I am referring to (Susan Sontag, Sigfried Kracauer, Andre Bazin, Vilém Flusser, to name just a few) would have come up with a different account of photography had their archive been comprised of photos similar to those in the Casasola archive: images of state ceremonies and civil parades, and something resembling street photography taken at the height of the revolution by able professionals who had to invent a canon for their practice amid the roar of social upheavals and military campaigns.[7] Like these photographers, we too have to invent our canon if we want to do any justice to their practice. Which opens some interesting perspectives: Why not conceive of the Mexican photography that emerges simultaneously with the revolution not as a derivation of the photographic practices of the metropolis but instead as a photographic practice of intrinsic novelty and originality? What happens if we think the conditions of photography in general from the set of dispositions implied in the peculiar situation—the most peculiar and yet common situation in human history—of a revolution?

Such an exercise in critical freedom would certainly not disavow the geopolitical conditions under which photography evolved. It was only in the most advanced nations in the world—and around the 1830s, this means England and France—that the pace of technological innovation and the existence of an extensive market created the conditions for the feverish and yet slow progress of what, starting in 1839, was called photography.[8] These were bourgeois societies in a way that Latin American societies would only become half a century later and never so thoroughly.[9] Moreover, the daguerreotype

---

6. Barthes, *Camera Lucida*, 20.

7. I discussed the photography of the Mexican Revolution in the final chapter of my book *Culture and Revolution: Violence, Memory, and the Making of Modern Mexico* (Austin: University of Texas Press, 2017). The present essay continues and expands some arguments made in that book.

8. "The word 'photography' was coined by John Herschel in 1839 and won out slowly over competing terms that were more egotistical (daguerreotype, talbotype) or less descriptive of the unique properties of the medium (calotype, photogenic drawing, heliotype)." Anne McCauley, "The Trouble with Photography," in *Photography Theory*, ed. James Elkins (London: Routledge, 2007), 411.

9. By 1860, London boasted over two hundred photo studios. Even according to the most optimistic calculations, this figure is several times larger than the number of photo studios across Latin America at the time. Finally, while both in England and France photography was readily and productively grafted into the inner structure of the state (both Louis Jacques Daguerre and William Henry Fox Talbot obtained important state

and the collotype emerged against the background of cultures already familiarized with the mediating force of the image. That familiarity helped soften the most culturally shocking aspects of the photographic innovation.[10] So when I say that we have to look for our own canon, it is not a matter of imagining a centrality that Latin American photography never enjoyed and could not have structurally enjoyed.[11] It is, instead, a matter of thinking what certain significant images from Latin American photography—and in this case Mexican photography—reveal about the experience of photography as such, and, specifically, how a particular historical context such as a revolution impacted the very theory on which any photographer depended in the instant of pressing the shutter.

Mexico did not have a Brady, a Cameron, a Riis. At first sight, it may seem that Monsiváis naturalizes the history of photography that we have been told—that of Beaumont Newhall, the curator of The Museum of Modern Art (MOMA's) department of photography, and his successor John Szarkowski.[12] However, what Monsiváis bemoans is not the absence of aesthetically minded people in the world of photographic imagining. The first photographers who populated Mexico's principal cities since the middle of the nineteenth century (Olivier Debroise dates the opening of the first studio at around 1858) did not lack in technical dexterity or artistic training—in fact, many of them had a direct affiliation with the prestigious art school of San Carlos.[13] What Monsiváis laments is that nineteenth-century photographers in Mexico did not take advantage of the fundamental ambiguity of the medium to venture toward an encounter with the thickness of a lived world.

support to promote their inventions), in Latin America, photography was precariously harnessed to equally precarious states—with the sole relative exception of Brazil, where Emperor Pedro II himself became a photographer and a champion of the medium. On the latter see Natalia Brizuela, *Fotografía e Império: paisagens para um Brasil moderno*, trans. Marcos Bagno (Sao Paulo: Companhia Das Letras, 2011).

10. Pierre Sorlin, *Le fils de Nadar: le "siècle" de l'image analogique* (Paris: Nathan, 1997), 17.

11. Given the fluidity of its relationship with Europe—in part due to its amicable colonial severance from the metropolis—Brazil received the largest number of early European photographers and developed a field of artistic photography almost simultaneously with France, England, and the United States. Photographs (daguerreotypes) were shown in the Imperial Academy of Fine Arts in Rio de Janeiro as early as 1842, making it perhaps the earliest admission of photography into an artistic salon. John Hannavy, ed., *Encyclopedia of Nineteenth Century Photography* (New York: Routledge, 2013), 206.

12. Beaumont Newhall, *A History of Photography: From 1839 to the Present* (New York: Museum of Modern Art, 1982), 133.

13. Debroise, *Mexican Suite*, 58.

If we consider the short list of photographers against whom Monsiváis measures the insufficiency of Mexican photography, what first jumps to attention is that Julia Margaret Cameron, Jacob Riis, and Matthew Brady represent wildly different photographic practices.[14] Cameron was mostly a portraitist, an upper-middle-class Victorian woman born in India whose images were famous (and derided) for their soft focus. Matthew Brady, one of the great photographers of the American Civil War, stands at the opposite pole of Cameron's dreamy photographs of reenacted historical events. Some of the photos attributed to Brady are dry and informative; those that shocked American audiences for their graphic presentation of death were taken, we assume, by his employees Alexander Gardner, James Gibson, and even others, anonymous ones. Finally, the Danish-born New Yorker Jacob Riis was a crime reporter with an intense investment in social reform. He photographed the dark and concealed corners of American life where poverty met crime at night and at a moment when flash photography was in its infancy.

Monsiváis criticizes early Mexican photography for being concerned only with the outward forms of social recognition. That recognition entailed a misrecognition of existential proportions.[15] Photographers failed to make photography relevant by submitting too quickly to their sitters' request for banality. Mexican photographers seem to have been invested in the ceremonial reproduction of the dominant, paying little or no attention to what constantly pierces the fictitious cohesiveness of the real.

The photos that go to compose an archive share a certain tonality—a monotonous quality. In the case of revolutionary Mexico, this discourse was slowly distilled from the standing photographic archives of the revolution—which we identify overwhelmingly with the *archivo Casasola*. A compacted and protean version of this archive was published by Agustín Casasola in 1921 under the title *Historia gráfica de la revolución mexicana*. The photos in the *Historia gráfica* were intended as indexical evidence of the object they portray. These objects, in turn, appear implicitly grouped under two domains: everydayness and the historical. Neither the everyday nor the historical were easily definable terms in this context, since the revolution has uprooted them from the principles of periodicity and reproducibility under which they are normally thought.

---

14. Monsiváis constructs his personal canon on a conceptual ambiguity between documentary photography and artistic photography. This ambiguity characterizes the photographic phenomenon as a whole. Abigail Solomon-Godeau notices that in photography images are moved in and out of the column of the aesthetic with an ease not encountered in other artistic forms. See *Photography at the Dock. Essays on Photographic History, Institutions and Practices* (Minneapolis: University of Minnesota Press, 1991), 4.

15. One of the subtitles of the essay condenses Monsiváis's scorn for the class pose: "Soy porque me parezco" (I am because I look like myself).

Agustin Victor Casasola, Pete Hamill writes, "was one of the giants of twentieth-century photography, and yet his name is barely known beyond the frontiers of his native Mexico." Nobody could be surprised that the name Casasola is absent from the first photographic exhibition mounted in 1932 by the Museum of Modern Art in New York on the bases of which Newhall wrote his influential *The History of Photography*. One of the main argumentative lines in Newhall's book concerns the struggle of photography to assert itself as an artistic form. In the nineteenth century, this struggle opened the road to an exaggerated stylization whose pinnacle lies in pictorialism. Pictorialists staged their photos as paintings, and often the taking of a picture was preceded by a careful sketch of the elements and characters to be admitted into the frame.[16] It is very difficult for us today to appreciate pictorialism because it was defeated in the history of photography by "straight photography," a movement defined by the aim to exploit the camera's technical capabilities to produce images sharp in focus and rich in detail.[17] The use of sharp focus and rich detail to define photography opened the question of what distinguishes then artistic photography from other uses of photography that are equally fated to exploit the internal capabilities of the camera. The traditional answer points to composition and modernist sensibility. In compositional terms, modernist photography emphasizes the discovery of the formal qualities of reality itself. The photographer sees the same world that we see. He/she just discovers a hidden geometry in the real. Unlike as in pictorialism, there is no arrangement of the world to facilitate an artistic message. Instead, the photographer relies on a series of limited technical decisions: the angle from which the picture is taken, a frame which no longer defers to the primacy of the sitter, the subtraction of objects from its worldly entanglements, and their redeployment in a renewed field of visibility. The final product is a shift from the testimonial function of the camera to the instance of photographic production. Photography becomes a discourse about photography.

The promotion of the aesthetic as the fundamental and exclusive criteria from which to judge photographs radically changed the notion of what matters in a photo and consequently determined which photos matter. The history of photography is told in reverse with the sensibility of modernist photography

---

16. Henry Peach Robinson, perhaps the best-known representative of commercial pictorialism, divested photography of any documental value. His polemic photograph "Fading Away," a technical breakthrough on many accounts, depicted a staged scene where all actors were photographed posing independently and then assembled into a melodramatic photograph.

17. As can be expected, movements similar to straight photography erupted simultaneously in different parts of the globe. The German "new vision" (Neues Sehen) movement and the closely connected "new objectivity" emerged in the middle 1920s in the framework of a widespread challenge of German artists to romantic expressionism.

acting as a teleological disposition inherent in photographic practices across time. It is clear that some examples of the photojournalism that blossomed around the revolution constitute such an instance of exploitation of the camera capabilities. Many of the emblematic photos taken in Mexico between 1910 and 1920 partake of the qualities of street photography although they are routinely excluded from any canonic history of photography. Interestingly, this exclusion has less to do purely formalistic criteria as with a sociological definition of art. The rise of formalism resulted in a criticism of indexicality in which it is not always easy to separate claims grounded on epistemology from claims grounded on taste. The discrediting of photography's evidentiary claim is inextricable from the crisis of realism at the hands of high modernism—which means that judgments about indexicality are passed in the shadow of an interpretation of photography as art, and of art as radical disinterest. As a result, even photographic expressions produced and situated outside the domain of the artistic became epistemologically suspect.[18] André Bazin

18. In 1976, a debate took place in the pages of *Cahiers du cinéma* between film critics Alain Bergala and Pascal Bonitzer about the merits and reliability of historical photography. For Bergala, the development of photographic rhetoric has fatally compromised the medium's capacity for witnessing. Even snapshots are ideologically saturated and cannot be said to give us any access to the materiality of existence—or, to the reality of human suffering. This is so because, through manipulation, the photographer preempts the viewer's interpretation by coding his/her reaction in the texture of the message itself. Here the photo acts (like every studium, as Barthes seems to me to suggest) as an apotropaic device, giving us a diluted version of reality. By saying too much, photography ends up showing too little, even while the entirety of its promise was made of supplanting the verbosity of saying with the plainness of indicating. (For a similar argument, see Pierre Bourdieu, *Photography: A Middle Brown Art*, trans. Shaun Whiteside (Stanford: Stanford University Press, 1990)). Bergala's criticism begs the questions of an unparergonic form of representation (On the parergon see Jacques Derrida, *The Truth in Painting,* trans. Geoffrey Bennington and Ian McLeod (Chicago: University of Chicago Press, 1987)). The weakness in Bergala's argument comes by way of what, with Barthes, I will call Bergala as a Spectator. Bergala's judgment on photography can be "phenomenologically" described as Kantian and elitist. It is Kantian in its rejection of pathos as a form of interest that compromises the aesthetic value of the photo—which shows, indeed, that the aestheticism Bergala attacks remains a horizon of expectation for him, that a "bad" form of representation is pitted against a good, originary un-parergonic one. It is aristocratic because what judgment resents in historical photography is the emergence of a popular form of showing itself whose conventionality is not enough to dismiss it as inauthentic. This polemic foreshadows the subsequent, most famous one that erupted in 2001 when Georges Didi-Huberman included in an exposition four photos taken by prisoners of a Nazi concentration camp and smuggled to Poland around 1944. Gérard Wajcman wrote a vehement

notices that photography exacerbates an impasse proper of representation that is constitutive of Western art at least since the renaissance: the irresolvable "conflict between style and likeness."[19]

The formalist reorganization of the history of photography did not go uncontested. Richard Bolton objected that the formalist canon implied a regrettable reduction of the photographic field grounded on a complete disregard for "the social function of photography and the social role of the photographic artist."[20] The criticism of aesthetic formalism appealed to a number of Latin American critics. In *Mexican Suite*, Oliver Debroise approvingly quotes Douglas Crimp's attack on the reading of images in terms of increasing formalization, in detriment to their historical or pragmatic value.[21] I share this criticism, although on different grounds. It seems that endorsing the distinction between aesthetic and non-aesthetic photography in its traditional intonation deprives us of any language to talk about "non aesthetic photos" other than the language of historicist reconstruction. This is an absurd situation, since as even the most mundane experience would confirm, there is no such thing as a non-aesthetic photograph. The overwhelming factor that guides the taking of a picture is memorialization, and the condition for memorialization regarding images is fundamentally aesthetic—also in the case of images that can be considered ugly, disgusting, or abject. Even the most informative of photos always include an aesthetic claim, even if such a claim is the saturation of the principle of likeness proper of realism.[22] Likewise, the reason why we look at photos (rather than overlook them) are almost never intrinsically sociological.

It is instead in the dimension of freedom that the artistic and the nonartistic seem to part ways. It would appear that Edward Weston took in Mexico the photos he wanted to take, while the Mexican photojournalists took the photos

---

retort to Didi-Huberman's exhibition under the title "De la croyance photographique" in the pages of *Les Temp Modernes*. Didi-Huberman's measured response, along with Wacjman's piece, the photos, and other material, was later turned into Didi-Huberman's book, *Images in Spite of All: Four Photographs from Auschwitz*, trans. Shane B. Lillis (Chicago: University of Chicago Press, 2008).

19. André Bazin, "The Ontology of the Photographic Image," in *What Is Cinema?* trans. Hugh Gray (Berkeley: University of California Press, 2005), 13.

20. Richard Bolton, "Introduction. The Contest of Meaning: Critical Histories of Photography," in *The Contest of Meaning: Critical Histories of Photography*, ed. Richard Bolton (Boston: MIT Press, 1992), ix.

21. Debroise, *Mexican Suite*, 4.

22. As Anne McCauley writes, "The features that make photographs interesting or captivating to many people are not necessarily accidental effects of automatic recording. They are more often the results of conscious (or at times intuitive) manipulations of posing, focus, or exposure by the photographers (or others in the production process)." McCauley, "The Trouble with Photography," 419.

they had to take. There is a series of incidental clues that support this position, starting with the fact that there is a whole range of themes (the dramatic close-up, the nude, the isolated piece of nature) that remain the province of artistic photography. It is telling that when the Casasola archive was composed, Casasola and his heirs systematically cropped several images so as to endow them with the artistic charge and prestige recognizable in the modernist close-up.[23] That the photojournalists did not practice the close-up portrait (at least in a significant way) does not mean that they were not concerned with aesthetic questions. As I said before, disregard for the aesthetic is profoundly alien to photography in general. However, there was something in the revolution that barred this most apparent path of photographic inquiry. As if revolutionary photography had to choose between the face and the world, but in doing so—and this is the whole point that needs to be debated—it was not choosing between art and testimony but transforming the meaning of both.

The Image as Art and as Testimony

A reading of Newhall's *The History of Photography*, able to pay attention to the ethical choices of the photographic gaze will encounter a photographic corpus centered on concerns and places characteristic of the European and North American modernity. Some of its dominant themes are: monumentality, the portrait of the illustrious man, the ruin, progress signaled by the slow twilight of a rural world, the stylization of the human figure along with conventions inherited from fine arts (as in the case of the nude), the overtly staged pastoral scene (a favorite of pictorialism) and the colonial gaze—in either its ethnological or monumental version: a shack in Ecuador, the almost sublime proportions of monumental ruins in Egypt. These contexts represent the ethical fantasy that subtends the West as gaze. As with any fantasy, its role lies in taming what may appear in excess of the play of intentions in the photographic act. What remains unseen in any dogmatic reading of photographs is the world as an object of attunement.

---

23. A photo titled "Revolutionary Fighter with a Winchester in a Train," reproduced by Pablo Ortiz Monasterio in his compilation on Mexican photography of the revolution is a cropped version of a photo published in "Revista de Revistas" on December 12, 1915. The uncropped photo is credited to Manuel Ramos, and it is printed in sepia, while the version attributed to Casasola is printed in high contrasting black and white. For the cropped Casasola reproduction see by Pablo Ortiz Monasterio, *Mexico. The Revolution and Beyond* (New York: Aperture, 2003), 50; the uncropped version attributed to Manuel Ramos is reproduced in Miguel Angel Berumén and Claudia Canales, *México. Fotografía y revolución* (México: INAH-Conaculta, 2009), 118.

Let's imagine that, paying attention to this attunement, we read the two archives (Newhall's and Casasola) side by side. A man sits in his studio against a heavy backcloth, a group of soldaderas climb a train; an explorer is dwarfed by a Mesoamerican monument half eaten by a growing vegetation, a dog crosses the street; the wife of a merchant rests her hand on a velvet sofa in Bourdeaux, demonstrators spontaneously fill the frame; an Italian village clings to bygone centuries by an almost invisible thread, a young girl with her mom wait amid a sea of soldiers and horses; I did not invent these examples. These are how things stand in two very different traditions. What is that the Mexican side of these series uncovers? Or to put it in terms of the gaze-like nature of the visible: what draws the camera-eye? What calls it with unstoppable passion? I would say that it is above all the obtrusiveness of the body—the lack of connaturalness of body and world. The welcoming of the unexpected that Monsiváis found lacking in nineteenth-century photography takes the form of an attempt to couple existence and materiality. It is with the recognition of such materiality that Claudia Canales ciphered in terms of "the overwhelming force of … (a) singularity," that the photography of the Mexican revolution begins.[24] But what exactly begins? A change in the modalities of the photographic act itself. The center of attention of photographic analysis has always been the activity of the photographer. (The notion of photography as art is inextricable from the notion of style.) The photography of the revolution tips the balance of photographic power to the context and to the demands that this context poses for its revelation.

The photography of the revolution can never be simply documentary or historical. Historical photography is possible because reality itself ("the historical") is a highly codified production. A historical photo takes as its subjects recognizable historical figures or events. It is, so to speak, the image of an image. Things are different when photography takes as its object the figures of an unscripted social event. In this case, the relationship between photography and the presence to be memorialized becomes less certain. The photojournalist that took the pictures of Madero's entering the city of Mexico in 1911 or the decena trágica in 1913, or even more pertinently, the soldaderas at the train stations in 1914–15, did not know (they were even far from suspecting) that their images will be one day called "DNA of the nation."[25] The revolution as historical event and the photographic now did not produce an exact match. The present was not something that this photography could simply show. Instead, it became one of its essential problems. This misadjustment between

---

24. Claudia Canales, "La densa materia de la historia," in *México: Fotografía y revolución*, ed. Miguel Angel Berumen (México City: Conaculta, 2010), 51–118, 56.

25. The expression "DNA of the nation" is taken from Carlos Monsiváis's "Soy porque me parezco." Different authors believe that the distribution of dead bodies in several photos of the "decena tragica" had been arranged post-factum.

the *now* of the instant and the *now* of history left an important mark in the rules of photographic composition. Since the revolution could not be "shown," photography needed to take recourse to all sorts of artifice to accomplish its testimonial goal. In consequence, the questions that this photography elicits are less of the order of verisimilitude than that of signification. This explains why although many of the most important photographs of the revolution are obviously staged—Villa in the presidential chair comes readily to mind—that staging does not compromise the historical and documentary value of these images.

Like his Mexican counterparts, Alexander Rodchenko sought to photograph the everydayness of a city struck by a revolution. Rodchenko found that the photographic gaze of his time conformed too easily to prevalent historicist and ethical demands. The Russian artist sought to revolutionize perception in order to release the potential for revolutionary change implicit in the world itself. Hence, the recourse to the unsuspected angle, the play of mirrors, the vertical revelation of layers of awareness. Rodchenko catches his subjects in the process of coming to terms with modernity as a metaphysical corset weaved all around the body's potential for expressivity. One can claim that Mexican photography confronts the opposite problem. A reality that is already insurrectional assaults the frame. Two daughters and the wife of a wealthy rancher decorate their bosom with cartridges and saber in hand look defiantly to the camera. An officer to be executed embraces his accomplice seconds before the fatal hour. The dust from a wall ascends to the sky following the discharge, while four or five bodies fall slowly to the ground. The aesthetic force of these images is increased rather than tempered by the use of medium shots or eventually of long shots that aim to bring all the determinations of the world into the photographic drama.

Eugene Atget had secured a place in the history of photography well before Berenice Abbot sold to the MOMA her collection of prints by the French master in 1968. Among Atget's merits, critics often emphasized his knack for the transient and his ability to expose types and characters that were doomed to disappear in a rapidly modernizing world of turn of the century Paris. What the camera often finds in Mexico are arrangements that are also transient, but not organized around the axis of socialized time (past, present, future) but under the modality of irruption. Atget shows us window shops. Mexican photographers show us women out of place, actually, women ruining the notion of place itself by a permanent misuse of the disciplinary features inherent in socialized spatiality. In another place, I offered a sustained reading of "Women on top of a train" by Hugo Brehme, in which a group of peasant women take over the top of a train and organize a makeshift house among the rattle of troops and the coming and going of trains and armies.[26] Brehme was

---

26. Horacio Legrás, *Culture and Revolution: Violence, Memory, and the Making of Modern Mexico* (Austin: University of Texas Press, 2017), 150.

not a photojournalist; however, there was something in the real that threw him into the arms of straight photography.

For most of his "heroic heads" pictures, Edward Weston instructed his sitters to close their eyes. It is possible to see in this demand the radicalization of the formalist requirement that all worldly conditions are removed for the occasion of the photographic act. Insofar as they are the point of origination of an alternate valuation of the world, it is better if the eyes of the sitters stay shut tight. In the opening paragraph of *La Chambre claire*, recalling a photo he once saw of Jeromé (Napoleon's brother) Roland Barthes exclaims, "I am looking at the eyes that look at the emperor." He is right. He sees the eyes that are not looking at him.[27] The photography of the revolution abounds in images in which what we see are not the eyes that saw Emiliano Zapata or any other figure, but rather the eyes that look. This is particularly perceptible in the case of children and women—whose looks are often described as defiant. This note of defiance is not so much an intentional posture before the camera as it is an index of the irruption of new themes and positions in the field of visibility. (Didi-Huberman's distinction between pose and position may be pertinent at this point.)[28] A photo attributed to Agustín Casasola (and taken probably at the Buenavista train station) shows an assortment of different social types. The photo, reproduced by Berumen and Canales in *México. Fotografía y revolución* (page 115) and beautifully analyzed by Leonard Folgarait in *Seeing Mexico Photographed* includes a number of children in different postures.[29] There is in this image—and in other similar ones like the one titled "Soldiers and Wives Leaving Sonora" (caption in English written on the negative, reproduced in Berumen's and Canales's book) peripheral but poignant depiction of childhood that indicates a correspondence (or attunement) between the self-display of life and the ability of the camera to capture it.[30] Despite the fact that the title only mentions soldiers and wives, the conceptual punctum of the photo is the little girl holding her mother's hand at the bottom of the picture. Her figure is not just an image taken from the real—but a historical accomplishment in its own right.

The implicit dialogue that I have been constructing between the canon of modern photography and the development of the documentary photography

---

27. Roland Barthes, *Camera Lucida*, 3. Since the semantic comprised by "seen" and "looking at" is meaningful in this context, I add here the original French, which reads: "Je vois les yeux qui ont vu l'Empereur." Roland Barthes, *Chambre claire. Note sur la photographie. Ouvres Completes*. III (Paris: Du Seuil, 1980), 1111.

28. Georges Didi-Huberman, *The Eye of History. When Images Take Positions*, trans. Shane B. Lillis (Cambridge: MIT Press, 2018), xix.

29. Leonard Folgarait, *Seeing Mexico Photographed. The Work of Horne, Casasola, Modotti y Alvarez Bravo* (New Haven, CT: Yale University Press, 2008), 19.

30. Berumen and Canales, *México. Fotografía y revolución*, 87.

of the revolution does not seek an aesthetic vindication of the work of the photojournalists. There are images produced in Mexico between 1910 and 1930, which would merit a place in the photographic canon on aesthetic grounds alone. Cartier-Bresson picked a photo attributed to Casasola as his favorite picture of the twentieth century.[31] The incorporation of new names into the canon of photography is not the goal of these pages. The benefits of such a move seem limited. Fundamentally, it will obscure a far more genuine problem that I can now phrase in terms of the possibility of uncovering the historical conditions of the beautiful and the aesthetic premises of the historical. This path should take us beyond the opposition between the formalist aestheticism of the museum operator and the strong sociologism of the champions of photography as document. At stake, then, is the creation of a framework of reference for a photographic practice that could not have been viable without partaking simultaneously of the aloofness of art and the commitment to the testimonial since it is tied to both in virtue of its material organization.[32] This framework of reference will not establish the world as existing beyond the camera—as one would say beyond the text. In the end, it is to the texture of the revolutionary experience as an event of perception that we need to reintegrate at least part of the photographic archive of the Mexican revolution. Nothing offers a better possibility of producing such reintegration than the photographs of women.

Women in the Field of the Visible

Let us start by noticing a fact already mentioned in this essay: some of the most recognizable and reprinted photos of the Mexican Revolution are of women. The image of two apprehensive waitresses serving breakfast to the Zapatista revolutionary troops at Sanborns in 1914 is as emblematic of the peasant armies' occupation of the capital as the iconic photograph "Villa and Zapata at the Presidential Chair." Hugo Brehme's "Soldaderas on Top of a Train" (his original German title reads simply, "Zapatista Camp on Top Of a Train") and the candid figure of an Adelita hanging from the rails of a train coach rival the iconic value of Pancho Villa's gallop in front of the camera or Zapata's grave

---

31. The photo in question is titled "Fortino Sámano Smokes a Cigarette before Being Shot, 1917." For a reproduction and discussion of the photo, see Andrea Noble, *Photography and Memory in Mexico: Icons of Revolution* (Manchester: Manchester University Press, 2010), 78–9.

32. Borrowing words from Didi-Huberman, the task is tracing a path equally removed from "an aestheticism that often fails to recognize history in its concrete singularities," and a "historicism that often fails to recognize the image in its formal specificities." Didi-Huberman, *Images in Spite of all*, 26.

gesture while posing with a presidential sash crossing his chest, a rifle on his right arm, and his left hand gripping his saber.

In *Photography and Memory in Mexico*, Andrea Noble expresses a certain skepticism about this recognition of women in the photographic archive. For Noble, this recognition produces a discourse which by suggesting the idea that women were *also* engaged in the revolution and that they *too* were historical participants betrays a subalternizing logic. The presence of women in the photojournalist record and the careful reconstruction of the context for their appearance "Does not necessarily solve the problem of inserting women as agents into that narrative."[33] Too often indeed, Noble continues, visibility is constructed in terms of invisibility.[34] Noble does not specify the meaning of this assertion beyond the intuitive level at which it solicits (and obtains) our agreement.

Insofar as women are concerned, what value should we place on the quantitative increase in representation when the latter is measured against the background of a qualitative inertia in which the effacement of women may take on a new and yet repeated form? Let us begin by discarding the untenable, namely the idea that throughout the revolution women (and of course there are already too many inside this signifier) were kept in a subaltern, silenced position in an affair that was, after all, marked by the macho bravado of the revolution. Such an assumption cannot withstand even the most modest historical scrutiny. The mobilization of women is one of the most salient traits of the transformations brought about by the Mexican Revolution in the sphere of the social. The revolution—Mary Kay Vaughan notices—not only "assaulted Victorian morality and rules of sexual repression" but also "brought women into public space in unprecedented ways."[35] The revolutionary destruction that took place primarily in the countryside uprooted provincial life, sending thousands of women from their homes into urban centers, where they encountered a modernization that was transforming the landscape of the feminine in its own way.[36] The photographic record testifies to this movement, and yet the force

---

33. Noble, *Photography and Memory in Mexico*, 102.

34. Hubert Damisch, "Cinq notes pour une phénomenologie de l'image photographique," *L'Arc*, vol. 21 (1963): 34–7.

35. Mary Kay Vaughan, "Pancho Villa, the Daughters of Mary, and the Modern Woman: Gender in the Long Mexican Revolution," in *Sex in Revolution: Gender, Politics, and Power in Modern Mexico*, ed. Mary Kay Vaughan, Gabriela Cano, and Jocelyn H. Olcott (Durham, NC: Duke University Press, 2007), 26.

36. The encounter between rural uprooting and an urban revolution that took gender as its index gave way to novel articulations of subjectivity like the one incarnated by Benita Galeana, the communist leader of peasant origin whose life Carlos Monsiváis uses as evidence for his claim that the Mexican Revolution was also and perhaps fundamentally an erotic revolution. See Carlos Monsiváis, "La aparición del subsuelo: Sobre la cultura de la Revolucion Mexicana," *Historias*, vols. 8–9 (1985): 150–66.

of the testimony remains suspect, since, as Noble points out, visibility can be constructed in terms of invisibility.[37] For Noble, mere indexical evidence already poses unique "interpretive challenges."[38] With indexicality, Noble refers to a sort of natural attitude vis-à-vis the photograph, by which the image appears as an impartial record of a standing reality.[39] Certainly, photos allow inferences and deductions, but very rarely can they constitute the ultimate proof of the hypothesis mounted in their always uncanny evidence. The fact that the archive presents us with a variety of women in several historical functions does not authorize us to decide on the nature and value of the social change that, apropos the revolution, takes women as both its agent and object.

Women is here apprehended as a signifier in the set of the popular. This has not always been the case. So, what does this (relatively) new positionality mean? In the social, where a pose and a position are already constituted, the task of signifying the revolution falls upon the common men and women in their average everydayness. In part, this is so because everydayness itself, especially of the popular type, had been proscribed and dissimulated in the previous, Porfirian, distribution of the sensible. The poetic unveiling of reality is undertaken without straying beyond an informative and realist style. Carlos Monsiváis is surprised by this trait of the photographic archive, and he charges Agustín Casasola with imposing it on Mexican photography. For Monsiváis, Casasola is responsible for the fact that the archive has been combed and explored only partially, favoring certain types of images over others. Monsiváis notices the conspicuous absence of "fotos de denuncia" (social indictment photos), and he ventures, as an explanation that Casasola's own historicist style

37. Noble, *Photography and Memory*, 101. On the visualization and yet invisibilization of women see Andrea Noble, "Zapatistas en Sanborns (1914): Women at the Bar," *History of Photography* 22, no. 4 (1998): 366–70.

38. Noble, *Photography and Memory*, 111. Mraz criticizes what he considers the psychological reading of photographs in several of his books and essays. See for instance, *Photographing the Mexican Revolution*, 23.

39. Margaret Iversen is one of the authors claiming that the use of indexicality as a synonym for likeness is fundamentally misleading. She defends the validity of a realist photographic inference on the grounds of the actual indexical nature of photographs, stressing that a photo is materially connected to its origin. Physical objects "impregnate" a film through a combination of the physics of light and a set of chemical reactions. See Margaret Iversen, "Indexicality: A Trauma of Signification," in *Photography, Trace, and Trauma* (Chicago: University of Chicago Press, 2016), 17–30. I am not sure how relevant this approach is to the question of realism—even if the chemical process that leads to the reconstitution of the image is conceived in terms of residual trauma of the once-real, the question of realism cannot be settled through a reference to the relationship between reality and representation, because that relationship—causal as it is—is as much the ground for realism as for irrealism.

molded the way photographers related to reality. Simply put, the photographers of the revolution thought they were witnessing history in the making and they recorded the present as if it were history. Although in normal times this may mean merely photographing state representatives, eminent scientists, or successful social figures, the photographers of the revolution had to calculate the historical relevance of their photos against the background of a very mobile political process.[40] Photographers were looking at the present with the eyes of the future—as if it were already the past. In this twilight, human subjects may be falsified in the very act of their presentation: for instance, women's visibility may be constructed in terms of invisibility.

Four Señoritas and a General

In *Understanding a Photograph,* John Berger speaks of the widespread assumption that if one is interested in the visual, one's interest must be limited to a technique of somehow "*treating* the visual ... And what is forgotten—like all essential questions in a positivist culture—is the meaning and enigma of visibility itself" (41). We can borrow Heidegger's expression "the worldhood" of the world to approach "the enigma of visibility," that emerges in the photography of the revolution. This photography bears witness to a world which is almost the opposite of what Heidegger understood as a world: a set of intelligible references whose mutual interconnection unveils a fundamental design. In a revolutionary world, every attempt at representation backfires, since reality itself is shown in all its inconsistency. In the most representative pictures of the revolution, the system of assignments is broken and inoperative. Women appear out of place, and their representation elicits all types of questions. It is a pity that we do not have a photograph of those wonderful descriptions that have come down to us via written testimonies—such as the one portraying revolutionary times as those in which "a dispute over a stolen piano was equitably resolved by dividing it in half with an ax."[41]

If we do not have most of these images, it is not so much because the opportunity did not arise, but because one of the fundamental functions of the photography of the revolution was to appease a wild reality. Olivier Debroise has observed that unlike the two other major wars of the time—World War I and the Russian Revolution—the unpredictability and dynamism that

---

40. Of interest here is the work of Sabino Osuna, a photographer who initially specialized in portraits and architectural studies, but whose work shifted to a careful record of the impact of the revolution on official Mexico in the period 1910-14. An important collection of these photos is held at the University of California-Riverside's Special Collections section.

41. Manuel Gómez Morín, *1915 y otros ensayos* (Mexico City: Cultura, 1927), 23.

characterized the photography of the Mexican Revolution made it the point of origin of a lasting mythology.[42] However, there is also a way in which the unscripted nature of the revolt conditioned the Mexican photographers to take a step in the direction of the idealization (and disavowal) of revolutionary chaos. Think, for instance, of those photos showing revolutionary groups more or less neatly formed, their rifles cocked and pointing at an imaginary enemy. These traditional photographs—war postcards—seem to reassure the viewer that the horrific stories told about the revolution cannot be all true; that the force that irrupted all over Mexico, shaking centuries of traditional allegiances and instituted forms of domination, can be mastered after all. The photos seem to say: see here, these unruly people can be gathered, formed, made to stand still, and finally captured in the grip of a reassuring representation.

But what happens when the same type of war postcard photography shows women and not men? What happens when these women are not revolutionary soldiers or soldaderas marching behind their men, but middle-class women who will under no circumstance leave their homes, take up weapons or charge into battle? What exactly is appeased in this case? Well, what is appeased is unmistakably women. Beyond the important point of who receives the entitlement of representing *all* women, I think that the following point stands on its own. In the context of the Mexican Revolution, the political status of women cannot be conceived under an attributive model—that is, as a compounded image in which the signifier *woman* is supplemented by another signifier that politicizes it (working women, peasant women etc.). Rather, the figure of woman by itself politicizes the entire photographic register. And that figure does so, primordially, because in the context of the revolution, the signifier women became the most versatile sign of political desire and social incompleteness.[43] Women bring to this photography—and this remains true of all representations of women in the revolutionary archive—not a sense of urgency but of insurgency, and insurgency is the undisputed meaning of all photography of the revolution. It is because insurgency is the meaning of this photography that appeasement is one of its functions.[44]

42. Debroise, *Mexican Suite*, 218. The absence of state censorship—when not of the state itself—greatly facilitated the task of photographers. As John Mraz comments, unlike the First World War, where European commanders restricted the access of photographers to the front, in the Mexican case "all the caudillos understood the importance of projecting themselves and their movements visually." Mraz, *Photographing the Mexican Revolution*, 13.

43. As Joanne Hershfield noticed "modernity in Mexico was marked by debate and anxiety concerning the rapidly changing role of women," *Imagining la Chica Moderna. Women, Nation, and Visual Culture in Mexico 1917-1932* (Durham, NC: Duke University Press, 2008), 12.

44. This does not mean that women can appear in all possible subject positions (nobody can). I have not encountered photos of women being executed: the privilege of

What needs to be appeased are women, and along with women—or, rather, apropos women—desire. All we know about this photo of General Iturbe and the four women confirms that women's desire is what is at stake in it, even more than the dreaded desire of the revolutionary troops. Already at the level of the anecdote, everything starts with four women imagining or fantasizing a male desire and then going to some lengths to incite and domesticate it. To judge by the photo, they even "(cross)dressed" General Iturbe in an exacerbated display of revolutionary masculinity. The fact that Iturbe is invited to perform his masculinity in the photo is for me a clear indication that what is at stake in this image is gender itself.[45]

When Judith Butler says that gender is performed, she is also saying that gender belongs to the sphere of projection—in the sense that it is a project rather than a given.[46] Any representation of gender is provisional because, in the end, gender remains beyond representation. Or more accurately, it is a representation that appears in place of another representation that fails to consist—it is not a thing, but a sign. This form of semiotic relativism does not account however, for the efficacy and the politics of the images of women. To the realm of the former belongs the traumatic, to that of the latter the consolatory operations of the patriarchal gaze. The gist of Laura Mulvey's famous essay "Visual Pleasure and Narrative Cinema" is even more justified if we are to speak about photography.[47] For Mulvey, the dominant forms of image production are perpetually engaged in a fetishization of the feminine because its figure is a constant reminder of the centrality of castration in the order of human existence.

The overlapping of the enigmatic desire of women and the enigma of revolutionary desire created the coordinates in which the interpretations of this photo have unfolded. It is not merely because there were so few women photographers in revolutionary Mexico—although there were undoubtedly

appearing before the absolute master seems reserved for men. One can read the "Nacha Ceniceros" episode in Nellie Campobello's novel *Cartucho* as a pronouncement on revolutionary death as privilege. Nellie Campobello, *Cartucho, and My Mother's Hands*, trans. Doris Meyer and Irene Matthews (Austin: University of Texas Press, 1988).

45. The poster photograph for Paul Leduc's film *John Reed Insurgent Mexico*, a thoughtful meditation on the revolutionary image, presents us with a patriarchal order that struggles to reassert itself in the medium of the revolutionary turmoil. The fact that maleness also needs to be performed tells us to what extent this attribute has lost its "naturalness." The poster image can be viewed at "Reed, México insurgente," IMDb.com, http://www.imdb.com/title/tt0069168/.

46. Judith Butler, *Gender Trouble: Feminism and the Subversion of Identity* (New York: Routledge, 1990).

47. Laura Mulvey, "Visual Pleasure and Narrative Cinema," *Screen*, vol. 16, no. 3 (1975): 6–18.

more than what has been reported—that I can assume that the person who took this particular photo was male. If a photo represents the photographer's intuition, is his desire at stake here? The question is worth bearing but is unable to immobilize the analysis, for the simple reason that it is in the nature of desire to be transindividual. The enigmatic character of desire comes from the fact that it is not connatural with its object. The desire expressed in the photo does not easily fit into the picture Monsiváis envisioned of the revolution as preeminently erotic, as an unveiling of a long-repressed sensuousness.[48] Questions of honor and the history of revolutionary sexual violence against women had their share in the (mythical) origin of the photo. However, they don't have much purchase on how the scene is organized. Four women surround Iturbe: but nothing in their posture suggests a primacy of a patriarchal organization of meaning. The phallic is certainly present—but is it masculine? Instead, female desire is stated at a level of absolute generality: what this desire was for is something that the photo cannot tell. So, in the end, what is it that these four women want? (The fact that there are four of them contributes to the image's allegorical charge.) Even while knowing close to nothing about them, I can venture that no concept accommodates the desire expressed in the scene—unless there is in the world something that is not of this world; and what is not of this world is, as Alexandre Kojève used to say, desire that knows itself to be without object, desire that desires desire.[49]

In Kojève, desire that desires desire is the formula of the universal. What is extraordinary in this photo is that the position of the universal is identified with the figure of women: the ones who desire nothing in particular and, therefore, may desire it all. This constitutes the symbolic weight of this image. That the weight of the image is symbolic means, in this case, that the figures of the four señoritas become placeholders for the projection of all kind of social fantasies—rather than a political statement in its own right. There is here, as Noble feared, an erasure of women, partially because its figure exceeds any conceivable positive adscription—any possible territorialization of its desire. Since the desire in question is not of this world, it belongs to the sitters only partially. They are—or consist—under its shadow. Or, to say the same thing historically, when the photo was taken, the concept "woman" had already been overrun by its reality. This overrunning of the concept by its incarnation constitutes the distinctive feature of a true political subjectivation. Hence, the proverbial function of appeasement proper to the photographic register. What is appeased in this photo? Not the general, who is supposed to look threatening. Not the revolution in its masculine manifestation, which is already domesticated and

---

48. Monsiváis, introducción to Salvador Novo, *La estatua de sal* (Mexico: Fondo de Cultura Económica, 2008).

49. Kojève popularized the expression "all desire is desire of the other (desire)" in the context of his commentary on Hegel's *Phenomenology of Spirit*.

out of sight. I would say that what is appeased is the meaning of *women* once this signifier is intersected by the signifier *revolution*. Is it not extraordinary that gossip circulated about a revolutionary general whose entire military staff was constituted by women? Is not the urgency to attribute a role to these women a form of appeasement? The image seems not to be enough. A leftover is still to be conjured or exorcised, and it is to this leftover that the fable of the "female military staff" is directed. What are these señoritas doing side by side with a revolutionary general? Whence this carnivalesque overlapping of appetites and virtues? Someone came up with a story. Ah, yes: these women are Iturbe's female staff! It all makes sense now; everything is solved through an indexical trick. However, look at the photo again, and you will see—right between the imaginary space that connects the sitters and the photographer—that something does not add up. The lack of psychological connection among the sitters lends an eerie effect to the scene. In the end, there is something deeply apotropaic in this image: a masquerade of women is mounted in order to show women.[50] What is it that the apotropaic conjures? One thing, for sure, is sex. Abigail Solomon-Godeau suggests that every time that gender is at stake in a photo, the logic of disavowal proper of fetishism can hardly be overlooked.[51] This logic tells us that Iturbe can only be a figure that reassures us that we are indeed in the presence of women since, after all, he is undoubtedly a man. This apotropaic nature of the image is an index of its deep historicity. Patriarchy, Monsiváis writes, "is nothing if not an endless strategy of concealment."[52] The end of concealment doesn't necessarily mark the beginning of revelation. This is so because against any style of positivism—even the phenomenological one—a subject acquires the dignity of the historical by no longer being equal to its concept. Where have we learned the most enduring lessons on this point if not in revolutionary Mexico?

50. Roland Barthes notices that myth attaches decisively to photography to reconcile "the Photograph with society." Immediately he adds, "Is this necessary?—Yes, indeed: the Photograph is *dangerous*." Barthes, *Camera Lucida*, 28, emphasis in original.

51. "Recalling Freud's definition of the fetish ('To put it plainly: the fetish is a substitute for the woman's [mother's] phallus which the little boy once believed in and does not wish to forego') we should not be surprised to find it cropping up, so to speak, in the place of the feminine." Abigail Solomon-Godeau, *Photography at the Dock*, 248. Sigmund Freud's quote belongs to his essay "Fetishism," in *Sexuality and the Psychology of Love*, ed. Phillip Rieff (New York: Collier Books, 1963), 215. Jacques Lacan's interpretation of fetishism differs from Freud. The fetish is not a substitute of a lost imaginary organ, but the veil of its absence.

52. Carlos Monsiváis, "When Gender Can't Be Seen amid the Symbols: Women and the Mexican Revolution," in *Sex in Revolution. Gender, Politics and Power in Modern Mexico*, ed. Jocelyn Olcott, Mary Kay Vaughan, and Gabriela Cano (Durham, NC: Duke University Press, 2010), 5.

A Split between the Eye and the Gaze

Appeasement is by definition, an ambivalent trope. It cannot itself appear without conjuring the object it abhors. In *Specters of Marx,* Jacques Derrida conceives of this conjuring by which a peasant is a peasant, a general is a general, and a woman is a woman, as an ontologizing gesture whose function is to ward off the anxieties that always arise when the consistency of reality wobbles. Yet, the work of ontologization always fails. An ontology that equates being with presence soon finds out that the distinctive traits of the real are not given in the perceived reality itself.[53]

The question of a subject of history in its own right acquires a new significance in light of these discussions. Such a subject can only appear in the folds of a dialectic between conjuring and appeasing. Undoubtedly, we should be able to deconstruct the fictions of historicism without any recourse to photography. If photography is nonetheless a privileged site for such a deconstruction, it is on account of the role that evidence—and, derivatively certainty, and so on—plays in the history of the photographic art. The indexical trap has always been a bourgeoisie trap. Its inconsistencies are the inconsistencies of liberalism at large. At this point, the problem of avoiding a merely indexical reading of images overlaps with the question of a subjectivity able to ground itself beyond the liberal *récit*. In a revolution, more than in other instances, the categorical apparatus of liberalism can no longer sustain the system of fictions that had the autonomy and self-sufficiency of the subject as both its goal and its presupposition. In this context, the old rhetoric of individualism, of the subject as the owner of his/her fate, comes increasingly under fire, to the point where even sociologists find it fashionable today to call for a "no intentional" analysis of revolutions.[54] To be a historical subject means to belong to the moment in which one lives in all its transitory indetermination. It is a form of actuality, both in the sense of living in the present and being present. What can be simpler than that, especially for photography? What can be simpler than just taking the shot of the subject that is present in my presence? If the solution is not that simple, it is because we cannot blindly equate the present with the actual. The immobile nature of any present is a peculiar positivist credo. In reality, things do not stay put. In film, a trick is played upon the brain by a rapid succession of images that simulates movement. What is the equivalent yet inversed illusion implied in the stillness of a 1/60 shot? The assumed objectivity of all photography, which is at the center of every realist aesthetic of the photographic act, needs to be relaunched upon bases that are no longer positivist, that are no longer liberal.

---

53. Jacques Derrida, *Specters of Marx. The State of the Debt, the Work of Mourning & the New International*, trans. Peggy Kamuf (London: Routledge, 2006).

54. Theda Skocpol, *States and Social Revolutions: A Comparative Analysis of France, Russia, and China* (Cambridge: Cambridge University Press, 1979).

The photos portraying women in the revolution do not do them justice. Nor do they do them an injustice, either. The women of the photos that concern me here—the Maderista trope of the rancher's daughter dressed in full war attire—use their poses and their dresses to signal the belonging of their figures to the meaning of the times, much like Villa seated in the presidential chair signaled the belonging of his actions to the realm of the political. But in the end, the symbolic weight of this image exceeded the intention of its sitters. The photo shows simultaneously the obvious and the impossible. It constitutes a sort of symbol of revolutionary expectations that allows the viewer to glimpse a strange moment at which an event had already happened and is still to come. We can understand this act of prescience in a psychoanalytic style of inquiry by asserting, for instance, that what defines a subject is not what he/she is, but what he/she lacks. Although images are said to be worthier than a thousand words, they are—like subjects—always lacking. Indexical readings are so popular precisely because they are the appeasement of this lack. The history of photography has been marked by an anxiety peculiar to the unanchored nature of the image. It is only apposite that this anxiety should be redoubled in the case of photographs of women. Insofar as it is a constant reminder of the possibility of castration (of what has always already happened) the figuration of women sends rips of anxiety through the social body. Anxiety has a special relationship to truth. Lacan called it the only affect that never lies.[55] Freud, who tarried with the notion of anxiety for decades, in the end reduced it to a signal of an unfathomable danger to come. In the wake of Freud, Lacan locates anxiety beyond language in the terrain of the real itself. Why should the subject feel anxiety vis-à-vis the real? Precisely because this real is the subject's counterpart. It was born from the same operation that begot the subject itself: a partition in the fabric of the indifferent performed by the force of the symbolic. The operation produces a leftover (the famous object petite *a* of the Lacanian algebra), and it is this object petite *a*—the sheer materiality of what is in total indifference—that is related to anxiety. It is the whole that reminds us that we are not one with the world, because we have been separated from it by language. Human beings only relate to this partition through myth, and above all through the myth of Oedipus in which the original partition is repeated at a more human scale. In his discussion of the castration complex, Freud recalls the myth of original hermaphroditism in Plato's *Symposium*, where Aristophanes explains Eros as the search for the lost unity of a humanity that once sufficed to itself. Aristophanes's ontology of the human views each person as a *symbolon* (token or part) looking for its supplement and its recognition in the larger fabric of the

---

55. Jacques Lacan, *The Seminar of Jacques Lacan Book 11: The Four Fundamental Concepts of Psychoanalysis*, ed. Jacques-Alain Miller, trans. Alan Sheridan (New York: W. W. Norton, 1981), 41.

world. Myth (or symbolic integration) works full speed in this photo: how do the different parts of the photo hang together?

Although the photograph of the four women and General Iturbe does not belong to the patriarchal morality whose yoke breaks under the pressure of revolutionary upheaval, nor are we in a state of the world in which the existence of women into the open has been sifted in the social imagination and stabilized around a series of conceptual markers. Neither are we at that moment where the female figure is transformed from the patriarchal rule of concealment to the biopolitical and hygienic kingdom of revolutionary reproduction. This photo belongs instead to a moment of indecision, to an arrest of historical time, to a bracketing of norms that makes room for a claim of recognition. This is the photo of a significant impasse, although it is no less historical or transcendental on that account—on the contrary.[56]

In the photo of the four women and General Iturbe, women are shown but also conjured. All conjuring is always the conjuring of the in-apparent: of what does not appear, even in a photograph. In stressing the debt of the real to the unreal for its realization, we are not inviting a retreat from an interpretation of the visible. The question of representation cannot be circumvented entirely. But if indexicality is a trap, it is so because reality is always structured around a void. Photography, painting, and even looking-at are ways in which we work our way through the debris of the visible. That a woman is a woman and a rifle is a rifle is the predictable statement of liberalism's entrenched belief in the autonomy and self-presence of every subject, as well as of positivism's credo on the objective nature of the world we inhabit. However, as Bolívar Echeverría writes in an adventurous moment of his essay on and translation of Karl Marx's *Theses on Feuerbach,* there is no true objectivity inside the capitalist determination. Having in mind a process that cannot be any other than that of the Mexican Revolution, the Mexican philosopher continues: "To think a revolutionary process means to revolutionize thinking."[57] This statement seems to suggest that a revolutionary photography can only be seen with revolutionized eyes. Are periods of ideological conformism therefore condemned to a sort of analytical blindness? We know from experience that this is not the case. Since the reality

---

56. Woman is not the only visual signifier that suffers a transformation at this moment: the pressure looks formidable in the case of the patriarchal figure whose archetypical modalities of presentation are almost wiped out by the revolutionary winds—and reconstituted later on different grounds. The disintegration of both notions come together in the Maderista trope of white middle-class women dressed in combat attire. In these photos, women dressed in war attires appear alongside their fathers. The masculine figure works as a *point de capiton* of a representation that seems to border on the *desmadre*.

57. Bolívar Echeverría, *El materialismo de Marx* (Mexico City: Editorial Itaca, 2010), 20.

of domination is a constant of capitalism, the movement of its resistance fatally emerges everywhere as a counterbalance from which we can glimpse another world, just as the desire of the four señoritas surrounding Iturbe invites us to glimpse another possible structuration of gender relations in Mexico. In Echeverría's bold argument, what Marx meant by objectivity in the theses is a full immersion in the materiality of perception. This materiality is fully overdetermined. This means that the act of interpretation itself—of which any accurate perception partakes—is a form of praxis. We interpret, Echeverría writes, either in domination (inside an interiorized regime of police) or in rebellion: that is, we make of interpretation a transformative practice.[58]

Anxiety relates to something that is outside the picture, although simultaneously, it is without doubt inside the text. Where does this plus of signification come from? And how could it emerge in a photo, which is concerned primarily, fundamentally, with the tautological reassertion of the world? The photographic image is appearance, John Berger says, playing on the ambiguity between what seems to be and what resolutely is. The result of this tension is that "appearances in themselves are oracular."[59] The trap of indexicality is the trap of a naive belief in the intrinsic intelligibility of the world. So, Berger concludes: "The positivist view of photography has remained dominant, despite its inadequacies, because no other view is possible unless one comes to terms with the revelational nature of appearances."[60] But since an appearance appears, indexicality—and for that matter, a minimum of ideological liberalism—can never be completely wiped out from our interpretive horizon. Very likely all the subjects involved in the photo that occupy us—General Iturbe, the four women, and the photographer—were ethically (if not politically) liberal subjects and their whereabouts in the world were guided by a positivism of sorts. But the combination of these two ideas, the autonomy of the subject to determine its context and the tautological reduction of the existent to what is "actually there, before our eyes" can never produce the image that we have before us. Neither can the meaning of this photo be obtained by adding a revolutionary general to four upper-class señoritas and adorning them with the predicates of the revolutionary. Something else is needed. This something else does not pertain to the photo itself, and it is only in terms of what is not given in the photo that the photo makes sense at all.

From these observations, some general conclusions become possible. The world or objectivity (although they are clearly not the same) are never mere objects present at hand. A battle for the constitution of reality—or for the meaning of that reality—is always the fundamental political battle of a given

---

58. Ibid., 18.

59. John Berger, *Understanding a Photograph*, ed. Geoff Dyer (London: Penguin, 2013), 74.

60. Ibid., 76.

time. The consequences of this axiomatic decision are always exacerbated in Latin America, since historically, its reality can never be said to be a reality out there, to be simply grasped or even interpreted. Our praises and our objections are never directed to representations—to entities merely at hand, naturalized in the very act of our contemplation. To see, we need "to become involved and agree to enter, to face … without wavering, without concluding."[61] As Bolivar Echeverría writes, for a true objectivity—that is, for a form of apprehension that interprets in rebellion rather than in submission—there is no opposition between looking at the world and transforming the world. Interpretation as a form of praxis (rather than as a reading of a master code) seems to require, out of necessity, an always-renewed criticism of the imaginary structuration of the world. This renewal of the critical question inaugurates a movement that is circular only in appearance.

At some point in history, women emerged in Mexico as if in a new light, so to speak, and we wonder if photography could or could not be a faithful register of that irruption.

---

61. Didi-Huberman, *The Eye of History*, 3.

Chapter 4

DIALECTIC OF DIASPORIC CONSCIOUSNESS: THE AFRO-CUBAN VOICE AND THE HYPOSTASIS OF MEANING

The scant five pages that constitute Lydia Cabrera's foreword to *El Monte* are among the most daring methodological discussions ever produced by a Latin American author faced with the familiar task of giving an account of a subordinate group. In these pages, Cabrera informs her readers that her masterfully woven text about Afro-Cuban popular religiosity is not a study but a series of notes; that she, who composed the book, is not after all its author, and consequently that ideas of writing and cultural transmission themselves cannot survive untouched the adventure to which *El Monte* bears testimony. Cabrera also explains that this learned book dismisses all learning, that dictionaries are vicious instruments when it comes to cultural understanding, and that the path to a certain knowledge of the other lies in the radical abandonment of all paths that, until then, have been thought to constitute the proper access to the cultural recalcitrance of the excluded.[1]

These five pages are the only ones that Cabrera claims as her own in the book. But even in them, authorship is in question. The section bears no title and only its readers would call it a *foreword* or *preface*. Its difference from the rest of the book is marked typographically: it is all in italics, simulating the change in the register of a voice. The technique is not accessory, since *El Monte* itself seems a text composed of voices, each bringing forward its own universe, its own convictions. Among all these voices, Cabrera's own is distinguished by its marked humbleness. Authority is always deferred to her informants. How

---

1. Cabrera's emphasis on the abandonment of ethnographic mediation in favor of an immediate presentation of the informers has an antecedent in Rómulo Lachatañeré's 1942 *Manual de santería*. Lachatañeré vows to let the voice of Afro-Cubans structure and dictate the pace of the book. For Jorge Castellanos, the *Manual de santeria* does not achieve the same effect as Cabrera's *El Monte,* since Lachatañeré's corpus of testimonies is too small for the author to accomplish his intended design. Jorge Castellanos, *Pioneros de la etnografía Afrocubana: Fernando Ortiz, Rómulo Lachatañeré, Lydia Cabrera* (Miami: Ediciones Universal, 2003).

could it be otherwise? If the book is an inroad into the knowledge of an-other, it follows that authority rests with those who are the proprietors and origin of that knowledge. The history of the book's reception confirms this disposition. *El Monte* speaks to a mixed audience, the audience that it finally received, since the book circulated widely among experts and the general public but also became an object of consultation for religious practitioners themselves, in no small measure because of its impressive catalog of 555 herbs classified following multiple criteria that pay attention to their scientific names, the afflictions they can treat, the orishas they represent, and their magical uses.[2]

Afro-Cubanists Jorge Castellanos and Isabel Castellanos acknowledge that the effacement of the figure of the ethnographer represents a formidable conceptual breakthrough, but they also point to the many academic contributions Cabrera introduces to the study of Black popular religiosity: the rigorous distinction between Regla de Ochá and Regla Mayombe (or Palo Monte), which previously had been somewhat confused under the heading of *santería*; the pioneering discussion of the Abakuá secret society; an encyclopedic presentation of medicinal herbs; a daring photographic appendix in which a *nganga* is photographed for the first time; and finally, a courageous stance against the criminalization of these rites and their followers.[3]

These positive contributions remain somewhat hidden behind Cabrera's stylistic demeanor. An informative style, an objective or scientific description are all taboo in *El Monte*. Cabrera observes: "I publish [these notes] without a trace of scientific pretension—this much should be obvious. The method I have followed (if method could be indeed a word appropriate to describe this book!) has been imposed by my informants, with their explications and digressions

---

2. Castellanos, *Pioneros de la etnografía Afrocubana*, 187–234. Cabrera's herbolary also follows the idioms of her informants. Edna Rodríguez-Mangual comments on one specific entry that contains "seven and a half pages of explanations and anecdotes (many mutually contradictory)" and where "mostly quotations and dialogues are offered in place of the narrator's voice." See *Lydia Cabrera and the Construction of an Afro-Cuban Cultural Identity* (Chapel Hill: University of North Carolina Press, 2004), 69.

3. Given Cabrera's abhorrence of metalinguistic designations, her differentiation between *regla de ocha* and *Palo Monte* is not as straightforward as Castellanos and Castellanos suggest. Stephan Palmié notices that practitioners may participate in both reglas and most of them actually do so. Differences between the reglas are, however, notorious. While *regla de ocha* seems to emphasize a moral economy of persuasion and negotiation, *Palo Monte* is more commonly associated with a confrontational, crass, and antagonistic style of relationship between practitioners and the elements of the cult. See Stephan Palmié, *Wizards and Scientists: Explorations in Afro-Cuban Modernity and Tradition* (Durham, NC: Duke University Press, 2002), 163–75; and Jorge Castellanos and Isabel Castellanos, *Cultura afrocubana*, vol. 3, *Las religiones y las lenguas* (Miami: Ediciones Universal, 1983), 129–55.

that come invariably tied together in their discourses."[4] If the book follows no method, it is because what lies at its origin is an unscripted hearing. The whole book is the result of "a few years of patient application." The information that comes to light is not just owed to the other but discoverable in the other's terms: "We will use here the same terms [términos] used by those we have consulted to designate certain phenomena and practices" (9). The decision to avoid metalinguistic designations forces Cabrera and the reader to rely on the order of discourse to take their bearings in this strange world. With regard to that discourse, the reader is simply in the same position that Cabrera was in when she first encountered her informants during the years of patient application in which her function was restricted to listening and drafting hurried observations in her notebooks.[5]

The abandonment of traditional forms of authorship and authority is required not only by the nature of the subject matter but also by a complex political history overloaded with racial tensions. This much is clear when Cabrera explains the book's relationship to the world of learned Afro-Cubanism to which she was tied by links as much professional as personal and familiar: "It has been my intention to offer to the specialists, with all modesty and the utmost fidelity, a material that has not passed through the dangerous filter of interpretation, and to confront them [enfrentarlos] with the living documents that I have had the good fortune to find" (8). A book that is also for experts, but not an academic book; a book that, while providing its readers with a wealth of information about stories, *patakíes*, and rituals, also demands an involvement, a turn, an anatomo-scholarship capable of putting the disavowing experts eye to eye with those others who should not be perceived through the grid of religion or folklore since in the singularity of their existence they are both monument and actuality—or, as the text says, "living documents." Even if Cabrera's claim to immediacy is certainly disputable, the metaphor of the face-to-face confrontation ("enfrentar") leaves little doubt that here, too, the quality of the ethical encounter exerts a formative power over the dimension of presentation. From this tension emerges the momentous declaration of the preface: "The only value of this book lies in the role that the black informants have taken in its composition. They are the true authors" (10). The relinquishing of ethnographic authorship is congruent with the assumption (sustained

---

4. Lydia Cabrera, *El Monte, Igbo. Finda. Ewe Orisha. Vititi Nfinda (Notas sobre las religiones, la magia, las supersticiones y el folklore de los negros criollos y el pueblo de Cuba)* (Miami: Ediciones Universal, 1995), 7. All citations of Cabrera and other Spanish sources in this chapter are mine unless otherwise indicated. Page numbers for *El Monte* are hereafter cited parenthetically in the text.

5. Emily Maguire notices "Cabrera's text allows the reader to witness this ritual setting almost as if she or he were the participant," *Racial Experiments in Cuban Literature and Ethnography* (Gainsville: University of Press Florida, 2011), 57.

throughout the whole book) that this act of presentation is fundamentally an act of self-presentation.

It is difficult not to grant Cabrera her point. Rituals, anecdotes, the vivacity of life come and go through the pages with the distinctive stamp of the immediately given and lived. So much artifice may lead the reader to forget that *El Monte* is a text composed with the tightest, most rigorous handling of the tools of language. Every word, every turn of phrase is deployed with the utmost care and precision, starting with the title itself: *El Monte. Igbo. Finda. Ewe Orisha. Vititi Nfinda (Notas sobre las religiones, la magia, las supersticiones y el folklore de los negros criollos y el pueblo de Cuba)*.

The initial expression, *El Monte*, codes the entire book. As Cabrera explains, the word refers not just to "the forest" (or mountainous area) but to any uncultivated, overlooked place able to constitute a ritualized space, the hallway into a spiritual kingdom. Therefore, it is simultaneously space and a threshold. The reader crosses the threshold as soon as he/she steps into six words that Cabrera leaves untranslated and that, as the reading of the book will confirm, are perhaps untranslatable: *Igbo, Finda, Ewe, Orisha, Vititi,* and *Nfinda*. Eventually, the patient reader will find out that *Ewe*—of which Cabrera also offers other spellings, like *Eggue*—means "herb" in Lucumí. *Vititi* is the word for herb in Congo, but in the title it is linked to *Nfinda* as the residence of the spirits, which is the *Monte* but may entail also a further reference to the cemetery as a place full of spirits.[6] In the book, Cabrera offers not only different spellings of a word, but also different meanings altogether. Meanings are unstable, partly because even when they point to some common African roots (like Ki-kongo), they are used by different Creole groups who established their religions in Cuba over the long span of some three hundred years of slave trafficking.[7]

The title closes with a parenthesis in which everything immediate in the preceding words is now viewed through a distancing lens: *(Notas sobre las religiones, la magia, las supersticiones y el folklore de los negros criollos y el pueblo de Cuba.)* (Notes on the religions, magic, superstitions, and folklore of Cuba's Black creoles and of the Cuban people.) The last section of the title diagrammatically evokes a historicist narrative of progressive enlightenment and disenchantment. The word "notes" is the receding thread of a close ethnographic activity, whose perspective we now abandon, since increasingly the words used in the parentheses represent a white, dominant valuation: religion (*regla*, the practitioner would say), magic (a self-ascribed term but one that already interiorizes specific values of the dominant culture),

---

6. On this point see Castellanos, *Pioneros de la etnografía Afrocubana*, 195; see also John Szwed, *Crossovers: Essays on Race, Music, and American Culture* (Philadelphia: University of Pennsylvania Press, 2005), 77–9.

7. For an overview of the establishment of different African groups in Cuba, see Castellanos and Castellanos, *Cultura afrocubana*, vol. 3.

and finally, "superstition" and "folklore," which complete the shift in the point of view of the enunciation. These words seem to move away from living testimony and get closer and closer to objectification. However, any meta-narrativization of Afro-Cuban religiosity will fatally disavow the experience to which Cabrera became a witness in *El Monte*. It follows then that this progressive affirmation of a "professional" ethnographic gaze cannot be her stance in composing the book. Why, then, does Cabrera feel the need to state this point of view?

This conceptual instability at the level of the title is an index of an unresolved question that traverses the entire architecture of the book. In the first chapter, I argued that a cognitive turn similar is invariably a product of a social mobilization. *El Monte* seems to represent an anomaly in this configuration, insofar as politics plays no role in its construction. It is not just Cabrera who seems to avoid politics actively, conscientiously, but the experiences she tries to capture seems to shun the notion itself of political mediation. Cabrera (or her author-informants) feels no need to index the political as one of the active forces in the shaping of an Afro-Cuban worldview. It is clear that Cabrera believed that the political world was not one in which her informants could achieve a self-presentation—in other words, they could not be the book's authors. The recalcitrant nature of Black popular religiosity lies precisely in this simple fact that Cabrera acknowledges: the form of disclosure of that religiosity is incompatible with the forms of disclosure that are normative in societies organized around a liberal notion of rights. Igba and religion, Ewe and superstition are not words that can be uttered from the same subjective position. In the title, Cabrera pretends that all these differences can be collapsed into a final designation: "de los negros criollos y el pueblo de Cuba" (of Cuba's Black creoles—those born in Cuba rather than in Africa—and of the Cuban people). However, the doubling in the designation creates some hermeneutical unease. The question emerges as to how Black creoles stand to the Cuban people. Do they overlap or differ? If Cabrera had written "on white creoles and the Cuban people," her expression would have carried a certain redundancy. Insofar as it is historically correlative to the creation of the state, the expression "Cuban people" can only have a political meaning. However, by favoring popular religiosity as a key to understanding Black culture, Cabrera introduces a determination that is not only alien to political interpellation but also inimical to the founding and operating categories of the political itself. In this way, the political solicitation so scrupulously avoided in the body of the text reemerges carefully annotated in its title. This political inscription will remain weak, uncertain, and revocable all along the text. If any ground is offered to the recalcitrant difference of the Afro-Cuban to inscribe its voice in the great mantle of the word Cuba, this is undoubtedly the space of the book itself, from which Cabrera cunningly subtracts her learned authorship.

Interestingly, the dichotomy between a political and a religious form of presentation is indexed by the duplicity in naming that affects all those involved in the *santería* rites. Cabrera writes, "All the asentados, that is, all those who have been initiated in the trials that make them *omo orisha*, children, the saint's chosen, or *iyawós* (wives) of the santo … have two names: the Christian, Spanish one … and the African one that is given to them by the *orisha*."[8] There is an internal differentiation of these subjects, a differentiation that operates in terms that are symbolic as much as they are linguistic. From here on, the question will be if language can suture what the symbolic rents apart.[9]

Perhaps tired of these conundrums, at times Cabrera simply writes "nuestros negros" (our Blacks).[10] But the chiasmatic question is made even more patent. The phrase is shot through with historical and sociological aftertastes. "Our Blacks" seems to perpetuate the oligarchic patronage of the poor that surfaces everywhere among those who are nostalgic for the premodern forms of domination that characterized the first century of independent life in Latin America. The personalization of relations of subordination constitutes a pervasive feudal rhetoric of affect that only began to dissipate around the 1920s when new forms of identity replaced the old patrimonial ones. Cabrera cannot claim she is an outsider to this history. Her ethnographic interest in the Black population was if not sparked at least significantly consolidated by the time she spent in Paris.[11] Although she embarked on extensive ethnographic trips through Cuba, the information that facilitated the composition of *El Monte* was collected on the doorsteps of the hacienda San José, a property she purchased and shared with her lifelong companion María Teresa Rojas. Some of her *informantes*—especially the oft-quoted Teresa M. Omí Tomí—were longtime

---

8. Cabrera, *El Monte*, 25–6. While this doubled naming can be understood as an instance of syncretism, it is worthwhile to recall that the naming of the individual is a technology of social manipulation directly tied to the consolidation of modern state forms, as documented by James C. Scott's discussion of the relationship between the regularization of last names and taxation in *Seeing Like a State: How Certain Schemes to Improve the Human Condition Have Failed* (New Haven, CT: Yale University Press, 1999).

9. Achille Mbembe notices the uncertainties of nomination when confronted to "the one who is not where they say he is, and even less where they are looking for him." *Critique of Black Reason*, trans. Laurent Dubois (Durham, NC: Duke University Press, 2017), 28.

10. In her foreword (page 10), Cabrera muses on the properness of calling her informants "Black" against a more politically correct form of address such as "Afro-Cuban."

11. Cabrera lived in Paris between 1927 and 1938, training in drawing and the study of religions. Miguel Angel Asturias was in Paris between 1922 and 1933. Although both authors' stay in the French capital overlapped, I did not find evidence of substantial collaboration between them. Alejo Carpentier, who once claimed to have introduced Cabrera to her first *bajada de santo*, was in Paris between 1928 and 1939. See Any Nauss Millay, *Voices from The Fuente Viva: The Effect of Orality In Twentieth-Century Spanish American Narrative* (Lewisburg, PA: Bucknell University Press, 2005), 28.

employees in her parent's home. Cabrera was conscious of how this history of privilege conditioned the radicalism of her textual gesture. The Cuban slave-owning class had always held its knowledge of its Black servants in high regard, and it is perhaps for this reason that it seems so urgent to Cabrera to build her relationship to the Afro-Cubans in terms of trust rather than in terms of knowledge. In *El Monte*, she carefully depicts the scene of the acquisition of knowledge as the act of donation of a secret by Blacks to her. It is not uncommon for her informants to tell her things upon which she did not inquire. To mark her own position more forcefully, Cabrera describes herself as a "confidente" (confidant). She is first a confidant to Blacks and only then, derivatively, a friend to them. Because, we should point out, friend and confidant are two different forms of relationship. As Cabrera knew quite well—given her Francophile education, her long stay in Paris, her proximity to the founders of the negritude movement and her abiding interest in Afro-Caribbean culture—the word "friend" is a charged one when it comes to describing the legacy of slavery. The most prominent abolitionist group in France on the brink of the Haitian revolution was the *Société des amis des Noirs*, which played a pivotal role in persuading the national revolutionary assembly to support freedom for slaves in colonial Haiti. The friendship advocated by the *Société* depended on the universalization of the political agenda of the French revolution itself, and in that sense, it was as well intended as it was blind to the limits that Europe's colonial position will impose on any project of trans-Atlantic political sympathy. The word *confidente* points to a completely different set of relationships. In Spanish, the word invokes friendship as a possible yet not indispensable condition for the transmission of a secret. A confidant or *confidente* (etymologically, they are the same) is entrusted with a secret. The secret has its own force and creates the context of its reception. This heterogeneity is essential in order to separate confidence from its fallen existence in confession. To be entrusted with a secret is, first of all, to be asked to suspend the axiological value of the law, which is first and foremost a law of reception and understanding. This is why a relation of confidence cannot suffer the synchronization implied by any historically incarnated form of universality. This is why "our Blacks" cannot be simultaneously Blacks and ours even when speaking by themselves.

Testimonio

In 1966, Miguel Barnet published *Biography of a Runaway Slave*, a book heralded as an inaugural instance of Latin American *testimonio*. However, in its essential lines, the move to a testimonial expression had already been accomplished by Cabrera twelve years earlier.[12] Unlike Cabrera, Barnet does not claim that his

---

12. Barnet's book exists under two different titles in Spanish. The Galerna edition

material "has not passed through the dangerous filter of interpretation." This is so, in part, because Barnet could not escape the historical weight of the circumstances that surrounded the composition of his book. To say that much had changed between 1954 and 1966 would be an understatement. If one of the pervasive anxieties of intellectuals concerned with the Black population was the recognition of Afro-Cuban culture, the 1959 Cuban revolution changed the very context into which Blacks and their histories were to be integrated. In 1966, the prolonged exclusion of Black people from full membership in the Cuban nation was a fact that the revolution vowed to cancel. Undoubtedly, Barnet participated in the historical optimism that saw the Cuban revolution as crowning the different struggles for emancipation that had marked Cuba's history from the beginning. This conviction translates in his book into a more or less uncritical adoption of the timeline of the nation as the regulative framework of all historical occurrences whatsoever.

Barnet learned about the future subject of his book, Manuel Montejo, through newspaper interviews with some centenarians at a retiring home. Two of those interviewed caught Barnet's eye: a woman, a former slave who was a *santera* and *espiritista*; and a man who had fought in the wars of independence and had lived for an extended period in the *Monte* as a *cimarrón*, a runaway slave (9). Although Barnet is interested primordially in "general aspects of the religious practices of African origin" in Cuba, he does not conclude, like Cabrera, that knowledge about Blacks is the key to knowledge about the Cuban, but rather the other way around. Lured by the power of nationalist references, Barnet and his collaborators immediately "forgot about the woman and rushed to see … Esteban Montejo" (9). Barnet interviewed Montejo for several weeks. For the publication of the book, Barnet reorganized the material chronologically, thus making socialized time the appropriate schema to render the story of unscripted life. The gesture was made more forceful by the decision to write (or transcribe) the entire text in the first person. It does not occur to Barnet that the fugitive slave could be the subject of an alternate history, along the lines of Dipesh Chakrabarti's distinction between "History 1" and "History 2."[13] For Barnet, there is no such thing as a History 2. Politics, like history, exists

of 1968 bears the same title as the Cuban edition published two years earlier *Biografía de un cimarrón* (Havana: Instituto de Etnologia y Folklore, 1966). The testimony was published in Spain under the title *Cimarrón: Historia de un esclavo* (Madrid: Siruela, 2000). Miguel Barnet's book was translated into English as *Biography of a Runaway Slave*, trans. W. Nick Hill (New York: Pantheon Books, 1968); revised edition published by Curbstone Press, 2004; new revised edition published by Northwestern University Press, 2016.

13. Dipesh Chakrabarty develops the notion of History 2 as "a category charged with the function of constantly interrupting the totalizing thrust of History 1" in *Provincializing Europe: Postcolonial Thought and Historical Difference* (Princeton: Princeton University Press), 66. Chakrabarty's position remains somewhat problematic for one simple

since the beginning, and any antagonism indicates the a priori cotemporality of the slave and the historical situation. The slave is *in* history as he/she is in the world. As the Cuban ethnographer himself puts it, Montejo is "an authentic actor of the Cuban historical process."[14] So, unlike Cabrera, who does not quote a single passage in which Afro-Cuban ritual can act as a form of sociohistorical reparation, Barnet does include in his (or Montejo's) account scenes in which popular religiosity plays the role of political resistance.[15]

The perspective taken by Barnet in the reconstruction of Montejo's history has immediate consequences for the type of subjectivity that emerges from the pages of the biography. Whereas the trope that dominates Cabrera's account of the Black religious experience is *separation* (the loss of consciousness, the abandonment of decorum, the obliteration of normative cultural contexts in favor of a regression to a primordial form of interaction between gods and humans), Barnet organizes Montejo's remembrances around motives of *binding*. Politics, the most elusive form of relationship in *El Monte*, is foregrounded by Barnet from the very beginning of the book. *Cimarronaje* ("fugitivism") itself

---

reason: describing History 2 as a category leads unavoidably to posing it as a dialectical other of History 1. History 1 forces History 2 (itself a multiple) into a schemata. In Chakrabarty's account, it is History 1 that provides the unity of History 2, thus reducing the deep effects of multiple heterogeneous layers of non-History 1 and their field of action.

14. Barnet, *Biografía de un cimarrón*, 5. Some thirty years after the book's original publication, Miguel Barnet wrote a second introduction in which the fusion between Montejo's life and Cuban history is taken several steps further. See Miguel Barnet, "Quién es el cimarrón?" in *Cimarrón: Historia de un esclavo* (Siruela: Madrid, 2005), 9–13.

15. For instance: "When the master punished a slave, the other slaves [prepared a potion] and the master would fall ill or something bad would happen in his family" (31). Montejo's descriptions often underline surprising cultural continuities between the life of Blacks under slavery and life after emancipation. On the one hand, these continuities show that the temporality of lived life cannot be reduced to the social temporality of history and state. On the other hand, it is necessary to question certain positivistic reduction—partially advanced by Montejo himself—that belittles the effects of the end of slavery. Most of the traits Montejo perceives as a continuation of Black attitudes can be reconceptualized as memorialized forms of resistance to labor in general. Interestingly, the thesis that there is a fundamental continuity between slavery and post-emancipation life was a position popular among white planters. In *Insurgent Cuba*, Ada Ferrer quotes the testimony of Manuel Arbelo, a white sugarcane farmer who ten years after the official end of slavery is given command of a mostly Black infantry division. To Arbelo, these soldiers were "de facto slaves, though by right they were so-called free people, very few of them African, the majority of them children of Africans, rustic, and some semi savage." Ada Ferrer, *Insurgent Cuba: Race, Nation, and Revolution, 1868–1898* (Chapel Hill: University of North Carolina Press, 1999), 158.

is already a political notion of sorts since it is made the forerunner of many contemporary forms of political resistance and engagement. When reporting on the lives of other slaves or commenting on the cultural idiosyncrasies of the slave trade era, Montejos's perspective remains deeply rooted in History 1, the history of the liberal *récit* of hard-won rights and freedom with which the Black tradition itself is invited to identify. Deviations from that norm, which constitute the bread and butter of Cabrera's ethnographic effort in *El Monte*, are treated as just that: as deviations that, while interesting as cultural oddities, bear the unmistakable mark of a consciousness alienated from its own historical process. In most cases, when he talks about slaves or runaways, Montejo distances himself from them under the grammatical figure of the third person. As González Echeverría notices: "One of Montejo's most remarkable traits is that he assumes an ethnographer's perspective vis-à-vis the ethnic groups that surround him ... including his own."[16] One is tempted to invert Cabrera's declaration about the Blacks being the true author of "her" book, and say that insofar as authorship is concerned in *Memorias de un cimarrón*, Miguel Barnet is the true author.

Abolition and National Epic

Far from being a caprice of the author (be it Barnet or Montejo), this anchoring of the slave experience in History 1 honors the peculiar path to emancipation that characterized the Black experience in Cuba, where the history of manumission does indeed overlap with the history of a white Creole nationalist awakening. This history, too, has been overwhelmingly told from a History 1 perspective, facilitating, in the end, the subordinate position of the Black masses in the very horizon that supposedly welcomes them into the fold of a national community.[17]

Historian Ada Ferrer describes the multiracial coalition that achieved independence as a revolution within a revolution.[18] In its outward form, a Cuban army obtained independence from Spain, but in its inward dynamic the massive and paramount role played by Black soldiers and Black generals—some of them recently freed from slavery—marked the war as a unique attempt at revolutionizing race relationships in a completely unique fashion.[19] The revolution within the revolution was not only forgotten but was subjected to

16. Roberto González Echeverría, *Myth and Archive: A Theory of Latin American Narrative* (Durham, NC: Duke University Press, 1998), 168.
17. For a similar criticism on Barnet and a comprehensive treatment of his work see Jossiana Arroyo, *Travestismos culturales: literatura y etnografía en Cuba y Brasil* (Pittsburgh, PA: Instituto Internacional de Literatura Iberoamerica, 2003), 203–15.
18. Ferrer, *Insurgent Cuba*, 11–18.
19. Ada Ferrer notices "In an age of ascendant racism, as scientists weighed skulls and as white mobs in the U.S. South lynched blacks, Cuba's rebel leaders denied the

a brutal counterrevolution, even a restoration of sorts, in a process in which the occupying American forces after the Spanish-American war played a role.[20]

However, the wars of independence were the point of origin of a democratic promise that could not be reversed without invalidating the entire republican order that had been built upon it. Nothing is more significant here than the 1901 extension of universal suffrage to the Black male population, a measure fiercely resisted by the occupying American administration.[21] Universal male enfranchisement forced all parties to take notice of the Black vote, but simultaneously fragmented the political force of the Black population into a myriad of positions. Meanwhile, the race struggle continued unabated. The first decades of the twentieth century were years of massive economic disenfranchisement for Black communities, especially in rural areas, where Black land ownership suffered disproportionately at the hands of international corporations.[22] In the social sciences, the 1910s mark a high point of eugenics theory, of which Fernando Ortiz was—to his later dismay—a Cuban pioneer.[23]

existence of race, and a powerful multiracial army waged anti-colonial war." Ferrer, *Insurgent Cuba*, 1.

20. Once the conflict ended, the American intervention favored the landowning classes that had sided with Spain during the war of independence and rapidly restored a relentless racist outlook that identified the Afro-Cuban as a form of life unfit for modern democratic societies. See Alejandro de la Fuente, *A Nation for All: Race, Inequality, and Politics in Twentieth-Century Cuba* (Chapel Hill: University of North Carolina Press, 2001), 23–34.

21. De la Fuente, *Nation for All*, 12.

22. Ibid., 16.

23. It is possible to date Fernando Ortiz's turn on November 28, 1939, the day he delivered his lecture, "Los factores humanos de la cubanidad" (The Human Factors of Cubanness). It is in this piece that Ortiz first proposes his celebrated image of Cuban culture as an *ajiaco* (a stew). Ortiz finds that Blacks have contributed powerfully to the mix that he evokes in his culinary metaphor. Their work created the bases of modern Cuba; their rebelliousness (*cimarronería*) is the first warning of the fight for independence to come; and finally, and more important, Cuban sensibility itself (*emotividad*) is marked by the passion of Blacks for music, art, and syncretic religiosity. Ortiz's lecture was first published in 1940 (*Revista Bimestre Cubana*, vol. 14, no. 2 (1940): 161–86). For an English translation, see Fernando Ortiz, "The Human Factors of Cubanidad," *Hau: Journal of Ethnographic Theory*, vol. 4, no. 3 (2014): 445–80, trans. João Felipe Gonçalves and Gregory Duff Morton. The notion of the *ajiaco* has been mostly understood as a conceptual rendering of miscegenation and, as such, one that dissolves the ethnoracial and cultural characteristics of the groups at stake. Stephan Palmié convincingly argues that this interpretation—or simplification—completely misses the point and subtlety of Ortiz's thinking. See Stephan Palmié, *The Cooking of History: How Not to Study Afro-Cuban Religion* (Chicago: University of Chicago Press, 2014), 98–100.

Notices of Black inferiority and unfitness for modern life were telescoped in Cuban magazines that cited this or that American "authority" as their sources.[24] Segregation in the school system was unofficial but common. Racism boiled over into savagery in 1912, when four thousand Blacks—mostly poor, illiterate, and unarmed—were killed following the suppression of the Partido Independiente de Color.[25] Unsurprisingly, Black culture was often targeted in terms of one of its most idiosyncratic cultural features: its religiosity. Public opinion was constantly bombarded with the idea that the human bones used in some religious ceremonies were those of white children assassinated by Blacks expressly for this purpose. In 1922, the hysteria around *santería* allowed the administration of Alfredo Zayas to prohibit Afro-Cuban gatherings and costumes during carnival and even drumming in private houses.

However, starting in the 1920s, these variegated forms of racism began to coexist side by side with what Robin Moore calls "the first qualified valorization of Afrocuban arts by the intellectual elite." Increasingly songs, rhythms, and artistic expressions associated with the Black population became culturally acceptable, inaugurating a state of "uneasy pluralism" in the first republic (1902–33).[26] This opening to Black cultural expressions occurred in a larger context marked by the Pan-Africanist movements deeply identified with the realm of cultural production (as in the case of the Harlem Renaissance), and by the rise to stardom of several African-American figures and interpreters in the ever-increasingly important media and cultural industry of the period.

The increasing social value of Afro-Cuban artistic expressions illustrates Carl Schmitt's point that in the modern political order everything is "potentially political."[27] The primacy of the potential is illustrated by the two possible

---

24. On the segregationist practices of the early twentieth century, see Alejandro de la Fuente, "Race and Inequality in Cuba, 1899–1981," *Journal of Contemporary History*, vol. 30 (1995): 131–68.

25. Serafín Portuondo Linares was an eyewitness of the 1912 massacres. He authored *Los independientes de color* (The Independents of Color). For decades, the book was almost impossible to find. It was reissued in Havana in 2002 by Editorial Caminos, with a foreword by philosopher Fernando Martínez Heredia.

26. Robin Moore, *Nationalizing Blackness: Afrocubanismo and Artistic Revolution in Havana, 1920–1940* (Pittsburgh: University of Pittsburgh Press, 1998), 1 and 69. There is a long tradition in Cuba of former slaves, and even actual slaves, competing advantageously with whites for some semiliberal professions such as painting, crafting, cooking, and even dentistry. Sybille Fischer recounts how the number of well-remunerated positions held by freed slaves was a point of concern for the Cuban bourgeoisie almost throughout the nineteenth century. See Part I, devoted to Cuba, in Sibylle Fischer, *Modernity Disavowed: Haiti and the Cultures of Slavery in the Age of Revolution* (Durham, NC: Duke University Press, 2004).

27. Carl Schmitt, *The Concept of the Political*, trans. George Schwab (Chicago: University of Chicago Press, 1996), 22.

destinies of the politicization of cultural forms: some perceive cultural dissent as a stepping-stone toward the construction of a new hegemony while others see it as an inconsequential release valve alienated from the actual mechanisms of political change. As political demands acquire the ability to be not just coded but lived in the realm of culture, the political valence itself of these demands is weakened. In modernity, the upsurge of the new does not happen without a measure of annihilation. Signs labeled "cultural" circulate freely on condition of having been stripped of their original authorial force. Most of the time we behave unaware of this situation, in part because we have been thoroughly educated in the attitude of inhibiting the essential motives that sustain our cultural endeavors—for Freud this was the definition of culture: a process of sublimation of unviable urges.[28] Since the cultural codification of political antagonisms is by its very nature highly unstable, liberal societies developed early on supplementary mechanisms aimed at stabilizing its recurrent crises. Education—in the nineteenth century, a notion coextensive with properness and decorum—took as its task to enforce the fundamental tenets of the dominant culture. Education makes the rationality of political domination coextensive with the rationality of cultural authorization. Even if it was a commercially profitable expression, Afro-Cuban music was subjected to strict policing in the name of cultural property by white and Black censors alike. The most common criteria for censoring popular expressions was sensuousness; that is, the failure to produce the anesthetic stylization proper to art—proper to a bourgeois ideal of art. A revealing episode regarding this politics of anaesthetization took place in the 1980s when the socialist government opted for a public acknowledgment of *santeria*. A theatrical performance showcasing *candomblés* was organized under the supervision of the Conjunto Folklórico Nacional. Both performers and organizers were at pains to enforce into the public the role of spectators. (The santeros themselves favored this strategy since a "true" rite involved the risk that some of the public may fall into a trance.) In this way, the theatrical representation became the "cultural" representation of a cultural practice.

As the above example shows, the goal of anaesthetization is to prevent the emergence of contagion as a predominant logic in cultural communication. Contagion bypasses the dams built by consciousness, education, or decorum. Its logic partakes more of the asynchronous nature of enjoyment (which is always "recognized" retrospectively) than of the simultaneity proper of pleasure. With tedious predictability, all descriptions of the masses insist on their underlying linkage to the world of appetites and lack of restrain. Not even Freud can be excused in this respect. He, too, championed the exclusion of any form of communality grounded on contagion—although another word for it is solidarity. Inside this dominant framework, *santería* cannot be but the

---

28. This is the classical argument of Sigmund Freud's *Civilization and Its Discontents*, trans. James Strachey (New York: W. W. Norton, 2010).

most uncanny of guests. The taming of an original force and the anesthetic nullification of practice are all conditions that stand in open conflict with the religious rites described in *El Monte*. This is so because of the preeminence that Cabrera grants to the act of possession in "her" book. Let us consider one of the many stories retold in *El Monte*.

> Maria G. was in a hotel, just arrived in Havana from her home town. Not knowing anyone in the city, she did not dare to go out alone onto the streets. Her husband goes out to buy cigarettes ... when he comes back she was no longer there ... She had been stricken by a saint who had led her to a *toque de tambor* in honor of ... Yemayá. An hour later, a Black boy comes to the hotel to tell the husband, on behalf of Yemayá, that he should go to pick up his wife at a *tambor* that was being held in a house located on Figuras Street. (32)

Possession, which many observers mistook as a purely Haitian style of voodoo, has always represented an intractability to the eyes of educated society. Possession challenges the anesthetic threshold that disengages bodies and representations; and in so doing, it contravenes the fundamental disposition of modern anatomo-politics: that the body is a site for the production of a subject; that cultural indoctrination is, at bottom, an existential version of a juridical habeas corpus. Qua practice, possession remains difficult to reconcile not just with the disciplinary effects pursued by the state, but with the aims of bourgeois society at large. (Already the first Catholic priests to arrive in the Americas persecuted drug-induced religious trance with particular zeal.) There is in *santería* a ruination of property (often, the *santo* commands the person to distribute all his/her money freely) and an erasure of individual or personal traits—the saint commands the most repugnant acts to the tidy, the most vehement prodigality to the miser. The trance itself is profoundly inimical to the form of subjectivation proper of a liberal style of political identification.

It would be surprising that a scrupulous author like Lydia Cabrera failed to see the problematic status that the poetic of possession represents for a culture of reflexivity and self-appropriation. Her solution to this problem is as bold as it is far-reaching. Possession is ordinary! she cries. In a passage whose apparent matter-of-factness does not render it less enigmatic, Cabrera explains: "The reader unfamiliar with Cuba should know that for a saint to 'rise up into' someone or 'descend upon' someone or for someone to 'carry a saint' or to be 'stricken by a saint'... are all names used here for a phenomenon as old as humanity, known throughout all time and by all peoples, and which occurs incessantly here among us" (30). Possession is universal, only that some people had forgotten it! Indeed, possession is not far from the notion of interpellation developed in the 1970s by Louis Althusser. In the Althusserian story, individuals are interpellated into subjects by external mechanisms and procedures that they "live," however, as their own making. Althusser even uses the Christian act of kneeling and praying as the general blueprint of that disposition that allows ideology to possess the subject. Lacan—from whom Althusser borrows the basic elements of his theory of interpellation—sides with Cabrera on the question of the naturalness of possession. In his seminar on psychosis, Lacan says "As if we don't, all of us, all the time, have visions, as if we are never in the grip of phrases that just pop into our heads, sometimes brilliant, illuminating phrases that orientate us."[29] It is the function of the subject (and sometimes the ego) to evaluate, filter the discourse that comes from the Other. And is not this what the practice of possession reveals in Cabrera's description of the *santeria* rite—the trance that connects the subject to the Other with a minimum of egotistical mediation? The impossibility of reconciling possession and interpellation doesn't reside just in the fact that they answer to different formations of the Other, but on the most fundamental fact that they entertain a different relationship to enjoyment. What organized religion organizes is precisely a limit to enjoyment through the mechanism of sublimation. Althusser would have had a tough time modeling his argument about interpellation as stenciled on a religious command if he tried to use the religious ceremonies referenced by Cabrera. This is not so much because Afro-Cuban religion teaches the "wrong lessons," but instead because the mechanism of interpellation itself runs aground in possession. The gist of interpellation lies in an identification that connects the subject to the ideal of society. Its mechanisms are those of identification and projection, which Freud singles out as the fundamental procedures for the constitution of the ego. *Santería* rites, on the other hand, are based on an identification with a de-subjectifying force, to the point that a cancellation of the ego seems to be the mandatory psychological requisite for possession by the *santo*. Cabrera observes that "The ego of an individual who is possessed by the santo [a quien 'le da santo'] is withdrawn, ejected outside his body ... Proof of this, and most convincing for the black person, is that the 'horse' entirely loses consciousness of his or her habitual personality. He loses his head [le roban la cabeza]."[30] Joan Dayan spells the same fragmentation and annulment of a juridical sense of subjecthood in the case of Haitian voodoo: "It is as if the self is not so much annihilated as rendered piecemeal ... Each Iwa has a variety of character traits—speech patterns, body movements, food preference, or clothes—but he or she cannot express them except by mounting a horse."[31] In the end, *santería* presupposes a more or less complete abdication of any principle of autonomy. The entire narcissistic economy of the subject is emplaced in the *santo*, who satisfies his/her drives at the expense of the dominated subjectivity of the "horse."

---

29. Jacques Lacan, *The Seminar of Jacques Lacan. Book 3. The Psychoses 1955–1966* (New York: W. W. Norton, 1997), 110.

30. Cabrera, *El Monte*, 28.

31. Joan Dayan, *Haiti, History and the Gods* (Berkeley: University of California Press, 1998), 39.

All this does not mean that there is no place in *El Monte* to name the forces of subjugation, or for historical rememoration, or even for the articulation of emancipatory promises. However, these forms of testimony are always inscribed in another language, most of the time mocked as a foreign body that has crawled more or less inadvertently into a symbolic space that is fundamentally reactive to their principles.[32] At one point, the police break into a secret ceremony and take all those present to the police station. The possessed enter the premises dancing and talking cheerfully: "The police asked them their names:—Yánsa jekuá jei!-Alafia kisieco! Immediately the police let them alone: get these *morenos* out of here! Lákue lákua boni, said Yemayá, giving thanks."[33]

Why is it that the stories told in *El Monte* reach either slavery or racism only in an episodic form—to the point where slavery (*esclavitud*, or *trata*) is seldom mentioned in the text? We can invoke a myriad of reasons for this strategy. By focusing on religious ritual, Cabrera may be favoring that instance in the social-historical imagination in which the formative principle of identity comes from the Black tradition itself. What is proper to Blacks is not to fight for independence or to desire to become a citizen. Clearly, these are desires of white provenance, which does not mean that they cannot be appropriated by Blacks (just as they were at some point appropriated by whites). But the desires in question are not genealogically tied to the Black population. If republican ideas came from boats, they came from the boats coming from Paris, London, and Philadelphia, while the Egba Infa came from Africa or from Africa's outposts in the new world.

It is in light of this problematic of the possible inscription and memory of antagonism in Black popular religiosity that we should weigh a critical passage in *El Monte*, even if we are not yet at a stage in our analysis where the passage can take on its full meaning.

> It is interesting to note that most of the spirits that manifest themselves through so many black mediums—and through so many supposedly white mediums—are also spirits of Africans [negros de nación], of black slaves, actual Congos or Angungas, all of them "disincarnated" [desencarnados] at

---

32. One is reminded here of the exceptional mise-en-scène of Nicolás Landrián's short documentary "En un barrio viejo," where marching men and women representing the socialist mood of postrevolutionary Cuba are overlapped with shots of a religious popular ceremony. Toward the end of the short, the camera pans upward, revealing that the public house where the rite is taking place is profusely decorated with posters of the recently triumphal revolutionary movement and drawings representing heroes of the Cuban war of independence.

33. Cabrera, *El Monte*, 39.

the time of the slave trade and who express themselves like *bozales* [slaves from Africa who speak Spanish with difficulty].[34]

I do not know if in the vast archive of unintentional memories that constitutes the history of the body of labor in Latin America, we would stumble upon a more pristine example of repression and rememoration taking place in a single strike. This most oblique reference to history and slavery in *El Monte* calls to mind an observation made by Joan Dayan in her work on voodoo in Haiti. The religious elements of voodoo, Dayan writes, "must be viewed as ritual reenactments of Haiti's colonial past, even more than as retentions from Africa."[35] Cabrera herself makes no effort to underscore the crypto-political nature of these phenomena. She simply annotates this return of history in which possession exhibits or performs a recognizable political dimension, but she refuses to pursue the matter further. Doing so would imply taking a step back into the realm of distance and analysis. It would mean presenting the Afro-Cuban instead of facilitating what Cabrera hopes is an act of self-presentation. A historical analytic of possession—if indeed possible—would destroy its object.[36]

This much should be clear: Cabrera does not *have to* refer to slavery or racism. Perhaps her informants did not do so, and she never pressed the subject. Perhaps her testimonial drive led her to include in the text only those problems and events that fall into the sphere of consciousness of her informants. All this is entirely legitimate, and I am in no way faulting her for omitting these aspects. My point is simply that *El Monte* is a book about *the black population* of *Cuba*, and remains so despite Cabrera's claim that the practices she documents have spilled over to the white population. And being Black in Cuba means to have suffered the formative conditioning of slavery and the promises and betrayals

---

34. Cabrera. *El Monte*, 65. In the preface to *El Monte*, Cabrera says that all her informants are Creoles born in Cuba.

35. Dayan, *Haiti, History and the Gods*, xvi. For his part, in *Wizards and Scientists*, Stephan Palmié mentions two examples from Fernando Ortiz and Lydia Cabrera that also underscore how religious practice memorializes the traumas of slavery. Ortiz speaks of a practice of "abusing, beating, spitting on, or flogging the *nganga* object in order to 'drive it to work'"; Lydia Cabrera recounts how the onset of possession is marked by a ritualized march of the medium along the perimeter of the ritual space, termed "making a round of the sugar mill." Cited in Palmié, *Wizards and Scientists*, 174 and 176.

36. The episode seems to confirm Edward Kamau Brathwaite's opinion that in the case of cultures of African ancestry, the cultural sphere in general is included and determined by a religious affect that operates as the larger container of cultural propositions. Edward Kamau Barthwaite, "The African Presence in Caribbean Literature," in *Africa in Latin America: Essays on History, Culture, and Assimilation*, ed. Manuel Moreno Fraginals, trans. Leonor Blum (New York: Holmes and Meier, 1984), 103–44.

of emancipation. These conditions impose themselves on Cabrera, but not only as determinations of her "theme" or "area of study" but as determinations of her speaking persona. History and politics catch up with Cabrera regardless of her intentions, which does not mean that these instances are also and simultaneously the ones under which the message that was entrusted to her could be delivered.

Alejo Carpentier

Alejo Carpentier began to write *!Ecue-yamba-O!* in prison towards 1927 and published it six years later in Spain. His treatment of Black popular culture in this book falls somewhere in between Lydia Cabrera and Miguel Barnet. Like Cabrera, Carpentier seeks to preserve the cultural intractability of Black popular culture while, like Barnet, he wants to understand Black popular culture as *immediately* political—as ineluctably antagonistic. The novel has been considered a failure on many accounts and even Carpentier spoke with distress of his opera prima in an interview with Mario Vargas Llosa.[37] In the novel, Carpentier wants to be a witness to the initiation ceremonies of secret religious societies and, derivatively, to the persistence of another thinking (magical, even prelogical) able to provide a differential stress on the vogue of things Afro-Cuban in the period. But Carpentier, who always found it difficult to lend his voice to his characters, who raged against indirect discourse as one of the essential limitations of literature, falls into the trap of conceiving the world he wishes to unveil through an alienating lens.[38] Carpentier's depiction of the Black *ñáñigos* looked as an exercise in exoticism to some critics.[39] His knowledge of Black religious practices seemed incomplete, and his grasp of the vernacular languages weak—despite owning a copy of Ortiz's *Catauro de cubanismos* and enlisting the father of Latin American transculturation as a

---

37. To Vargas Llosa's observation that *!Ecue-yamba-O!* is difficult to find at the moment of the interview (1965), Carpentier retorts: "The first person who doesn't want to find this book is me." Mario Vargas Llosa, "Cuatro preguntas a Alejo Carpentier," *Marcha* (Montevideo), March 12, 1965: 31–2, 31.

38. The accusation of folklorization was leveled at almost every single author dealing with Afro-Cuban expressions in the early twentieth century. See Vera Kutzinski, *Sugar's Secrets: Race and the Erotics of Cuban Nationalism* (Charlottesville: University of Virginia Press, 1993), 145.

39. The *ñáñigos* are associated to the secret society Abakuá "an esoteric fraternity … whose members came from the province of Calabar in Nigeria and which was first established in the Cuban port of Regla in 1836." See Castellanos and Castellanos, *Cultura afrocubana*, vol. 3, 205.

consultant.[40] Finally, a persistent nationalism obliterated the possibility of an essential solidarity of a trans-Caribbean racial alliance, which is replaced by suspicion and distrust of Haitian migrants to Cuba. It is relatively easy for a contemporary reader to spot all the areas in which ¡Ecue-Yamba -O! stumbles according to its own principles. However, the language of failure itself fails. It doesn't account for the productivity of failure, and, for the same reason, it loses sight of the critical power of impotence.[41]

A recurrent criticism of ¡Ecue-Yamba-O! hinges on the fact that while Carpentier intended to deduce the political self-presentation of the Black popular from the cultural material itself, his treatment of the ñañigos deprived their figures of any political charge. Instead, he limited himself to formulas of considerable conceptual torsion. Popular characters—like Menegildo—appear bathed in a vitalism that is explicitly opposed to the abstraction represented by capital and empire. Carpentier always flirted with these proto-Bataillean ideas of excess and expenditure, but insofar as the ideas in question entail a rather extensive questioning of two of Carpentier's guiding ideas (Marxism and criollismo), they would only appear in his narrative in an episodic way. By and large, they go under; they are repressed, so to speak—but it is the essence of the repressed to be one with its return.

Haiti's Revolution

The Kingdom of This World (1949) was born from what Carpentier himself perceived as the shortcomings of his literary debut.[42] Situating the action of

40. Juan Marinello, a critic dear to Carpentier, objected to a hesitation, a methodical doubt in Carpentier's novel that make Blacks appear as object of a Western gaze and as subject of his own narrative; Juan Marinello, *Literatura Hispanoamericana: hombres, meditaciones* (Mexico City: Ediciones de la Universidad Nacional de México, 1937), 173.

41. Anke Birkenmaier proposes an ironic reading of the novel as an artifact that contains a sharp criticism of representation and derivatively of itself: "In the city, Menegildo and Longina's life is a farse and their friends are all actors or impostors: ... Atilana wants to be a medium ... but she is always rejected as a false medium ... Menegildo gets a job working in an amusement park. ... The city where Menegildo moves is packed with false names or names that designate absent things." See Anke Birkenmaier, *Alejo Carpentier y la cultura del surrealismo* (Madrid: Vervuert-Iberoamericana, 2006), 61. While Birkenmaier acknowledges that the novel is overwhelmingly committed to political and social causes, this fold in the criticism of representation is worth noticing in light of Carpentier's emphases on immediacy in his subsequent novel.

42. Alejo Carpentier, *El reino de este mundo*, in vol. 2 of *Obras completas de Alejo Carpentier* (Mexico City: Siglo XXI, 1989), all translations are mine; page numbers will be provided parenthetically in the text. Available in English as *The Kingdom of This World*, trans. Harriet de Onís (New York: Noonday Press, 1957).

his novel in Haiti allowed Carpentier to articulate a successful Black revolt of clear political intentionality that would include Black self-revelation in all its cultural recalcitrance.[43] In Haiti, Carpentier found the equation that looked so elusive to him in Cuba: a politics grounded in cultural forms of "both festivity and hedonism, replete with rituals of play and insubordination" and to which was added "a quest for political power," all "contained in a singular cultural and political formation."[44]

In the sixteen years that elapsed between *¡Ecue-Yamba-O!* and *The Kingdom of This World*, Carpentier became a devoted reader of ethnographic studies on Black Caribbean culture. In the famous foreword to *The Kingdom of This World*, Carpentier does not foreground his involvement with Haiti's Bureau de Ethnologie. Anke Birkenmaier documents the connection and shows how deep and transcendental it was in securing for Carpentier a view of Black insurgency and religiosity detached from his original surrealist moorings.[45] Carpentier's foreword instead refers the question of origins to his visit to the ruins of Sans Souci in 1943. I think that we should take Carpentier at his word here. That he consulted Moreau de Saint-Méry's *La descripción géographique de l'Isle de Saint Domingue* holds only philological value. What counts is the type of phantoms he had glimpsed at Sans Souci and that were able to take on a body through that reading. Like Cabrera after him, Carpentier positions himself as a listener to whom a secret may or may not be entrusted. By taking this step, he executes a gesture deeply inscribed in the phenomenality of the Haitian revolution itself. How many articles, fictions, historical books, and political studies have vowed to make the Haitian revolution *speak*? This project of linguistic reconstitution is no doubt determined by the fact that most of the leaders of the uprising were illiterate; that they spoke Creole; that their command of French was limited; and, lastly, by the fact that perceived as men almost at the threshold of civilization, few were interested in interviewing them or inquiring about their points of view. Moreover, in reading the historical accounts about Haiti produced in Europe, whether those in favor (a few) or those against the revolution (the majority), one is immediately struck

---

43. The Haitian revolution of 1791 had a powerful formative effect on Cuba, not only because Cuba positioned itself to replace Haiti as the foremost sugar producer, but also because from that point onward white planters and authorities would live in constant fear of a Black uprising like the one that had wiped out white power and lives in French Saint-Domingue.

44. I borrow this description about Brazil's "Workers Party" from Michael Hanchard, *Party/Politics: Horizons in Black Political Thought* (New York: Oxford University Press, 2006), 4. Hanchard's characterization of course applies to a very different context and also has a far larger programmatic emphasis than the one Carpentier had in mind in his novel.

45. Birkenmaier, *Alejo Carpentier y la cultura del surrealismo en América Latina*, 102.

by the absence of a language in which the events of the Haitian revolution could be narrated under a logic other than the simple mimicry of European historiography. The circulation of the Haitian revolution as desire often could only take its bearings from the language of those destined to be its enemies. How much this contradiction weighs on Carpentier can be glimpsed from a comparison between his account of the revolution and the one contained in of the early classical works on Haiti, C. L. R. James's *The Black Jacobins*.[46] Both texts share the same timeline and many sources. The Trinidadian historian published his book in 1938 in London, although Carpentier does not seem to have been aware of its existence at the time of writing his novel.[47] A concern about a Black agency clearly dominates both narratives. Furthermore, both of these leftist authors wrote their books about a country that was not the one in which they lived. James openly declared that *Black Jacobins* was written for a future African revolution. Carpentier did not make such a declaration, but surely he saw in *The Kingdom of This World* the continuation, the culmination, or perhaps even the recommencement of *¡Ecue-Yamba-O!* At any rate, it was a Cuban novel whose main characteristic was that of taking place for the most part outside of Cuba.

Despite these similarities, the two treatments of the revolution could not be more at odds. For James, the unquestionable hero of the revolution is Toussaint L'Ouverture. In a grandiose, Hegelian style, James considers the former slave the very incarnation of the revolutionary ideas that, from France, would shape the modern world. In a sense, Toussaint L'Ouverture represents the French revolution better than any other figure of his time. In him, the ideals of freedom, fraternity, and equality come closer to earthly realization than in any other figure of the revolutionary process. James quotes extensively the famous discourse in which Robespierre, Robespierre confirms the will as the most formidable force in political modernity.[48] Toussaint takes Robespierre's disposition to its farthest extreme. The actuality of Toussaint's spirit is one with his potentiality. He is possessed by this spirit of bridging realities and ideals all the time, every second of his life.

For Carpentier, on the other hand, the heroes of the Haitian revolution are men for whom that distance does not need to be bridged because it is not part of their existential purview: men like Mackandal or Boukman, who appear in the novel as true representatives of the anti-calculational spirit that Carpentier, like others, began to celebrate in the confluence of avant-garde primitivism and social revolution that characterizes the early twentieth century in Europe and

---

46. C. L. R. James, *The Black Jacobins: Toussaint L'Ouverture and the San Domingo Revolution* (New York: Vintage Books, 1989).

47. Victor Figueroa, "The Kingdom of Black Jacobins: C. L. R. James and Alejo Carpentier on the Haitian Revolution," *Afro-Hispanic Review* 25, no. 2 (2006): 55–71, 58.

48. Maximilien de Robespeire, cited in C. L. R. James, *The Black Jacobins*, 76.

its Latin American enclaves.⁴⁹ Although a figure like Toussaint would logically appeal to a writer like Carpentier, he relegates the portentous Black general to the role of a tertiary character who lacks much historical purchase. Carpentier, often acclaimed as one of the fathers of the historical novel in Latin America, confines history itself to a position of dubious authority. Certainly, history as timeline—as History 1—provides the general blueprint for *The Kingdom of This World*, but it does not explain the historical dynamic itself, whose force not only comes from elsewhere but is never entirely reducible to the historical *récit*.

An index of the preeminence that Carpentier grants to the historicity proper of popular traditions is the fact that the plot of *The Kingdom of This World* begins almost half a century before the Haitian revolution, with the exploits of Mackandal who, after the amputation of one arm, goes on to patiently collect and catalog poisonous herbs with which he will wage a one-man war against the plantation.⁵⁰ The line that goes from Mackandal to Ti Noël in the novel discloses a revolutionary affect that precedes its formulation in the dominant political grammar of the time and is also destined to outlive it.⁵¹ This intermittency (this tradition) is not only difficult to read, but difficult to understand. A tradition, unlike a history, holds a complicated relationship with the dimension of socialized time. Since its reality is not one of continuous existence, for a tradition to be binding, its founding instances need to be repeated and exposed, subjected to a sort of vote of confidence. Carpentier treats the Haitian revolution as that knot in the symbolic that allows the tradition to consist in a particular point in time. This is the role played in the narrative of the Haitian revolution by the pledge of Bois Caiman.⁵²

---

49. Carpentier was drawn to the possibility of an anonymous novelistic hero. In an interview he conducted with Sergei Eisenstein in Paris, Carpentier appeared impressed by Eisenstein's project of filming Karl Marx's *Capital* almost without actors. See Alejo Carpentier, "Con el creador del Acorazado Potemkin," in *El cine, décima musa*, ed. Salvador Arias (Havana: Ediciones ICAIC, 2011).

50. Carpentier seems to be following the historical record very closely here. Mackandal was a slave in the Lenormand plantation where he organized slaves for a potential revolt. He died after a failed execution depicted by Carpentier in his book. See Carolyn Fick, *The Making of Haiti. Saint Domingue Revolution from Below* (Knoxville: University of Tennessee Press, 1990).

51. In a visit to Haiti in 1943, Carpentier delivered a lecture in which he praised the Haitian revolution as the first Latin American revolution of an authentically popular nature and origin. See Birkenmaier, *Alejo Carpentier*, 103.

52. "A howl went up out of the storm. Next to Boukman, a bony, long-limbed negress was brandishing a ritual machete ... The machete suddenly buried itself in the belly of a black pig, which spewed forth guts and lungs in three squeals. Then, called on by the names of their masters, for they had no surnames, the delegates came forward one by one to smear their lips with the foaming blood of the pig, caught in a big wooden bowl ...Ti Noël, like the others, swore to always obey Boukman." The scene quoted here from

In one of the few essays devoted to a comparison between Carpentier's and C. L. R. James's accounts of Haiti's revolution, Victor Figueroa notices that "*El reino de este mundo* never loses sight of the fact that the solidarity among slaves that so impresses (C. L. R) James perhaps owed less to the ideals of the French Revolution than to a shared vision that found its expression in the rituals of voodoo."[53] The event of solidarity is rarely highlighted in historical narratives. Solidarity and its attendant forms of cultural expression (such as rumor or confidence) have often been debased on the grounds of their unreflective nature. In any event of solidarity, attention to strategy seems to be lacking. When it is not itself the sign of a calculation, solidarity brings all calculation to a halt. In this sense, solidarity appears as a practical declension of the ethical restraint of the political. If a long list of commentators has missed its importance, it is because they have taken solidarity as a means to an end, when instead it is altogether beyond the opposition of means and ends. The poetics of a minor politics, the nature and consistency of solidarity unavoidably changes when it is transposed to a larger stage where the moorings that link it to a given reality must be ideologically imagined instead of immediately felt.

Dessalines

The question has been asked, and it is worth repeating: given Carpentier's search for a point of coincidence between History 1 and History 2, why is it that he did not make Jean-Jacques Dessalines a central character in his novel? An illiterate slave, Dessalines commanded the Haitian troops that vanquished general Leclerc (whose wife Paulina organizes one of the main erotic subplots of Carpentier's novel), thereby securing Haiti's independence that Dessalines himself proclaimed in 1804. Dessalines rejected Henri Christophe's penchant for imitating Western mores and scolded Toussaint's Catholicism. He was a well-known adept of voodoo but he also massacred its practitioners. He became the nation's first president and later proclaimed himself emperor. More important, as Joan Dayan underlines, he is the only revolutionary leader to become a god in the voodoo pantheon. His traits as a deity closely follow the popular memory of his figure, which is at once redemptive and terrifying.[54]

The Kingdom of this World (51–2) is an almost exact repetition of the account provided by Jean Price-Mars in *Ainsi parla l'oncle: essais d'etnographie*, ed. Celucien L. Joseph (Port St. Lucie, FL: Hope Outreach, 2016), and also reproduced by C. L. R. James in *The Black Jacobins*.
    53. Figueroa, "The Kingdom of Black Jacobins," 64.
    54. Dessalines sealed Haiti's independence with a massacre of white men, women, and children, an act that contributed in great part to the ambiguity that surrounds his figure—at once inspiring and horrifying—in popular memory and voodoo rites. Dayan, *Haiti, History and the Gods*, 28.

Perhaps the presence of Dessalines in *The Kingdom of this World* is metaphorically marked by its portentous absence: his kingdom coincides with the span of time that Ti Noël spends in Cuba, a Cuba that is presented at every page as an afterthought to the slave rebellion. And it is not by chance that when Ti Noël returns to Haiti the first historical figure to pop up is none other than Dessalines himself. An old but free man, Ti Noël returns to "the land of the Great Pacts" where slavery has been abolished forever. He knew, the narrator tells us, "and all the French negroes of Santiago de Cuba knew—that Dessalines's victory was the result of a vast preparation in which had taken part Loco, Petro, Ogún Ferraille, Brise-Pimba, Caplaou-Pimba, Marinette Bois-Cheche, and all the deities of powder and fire, in a series of seizures [caídas en posesión] of such terrible violence that some men had been thrown into the air or dashed against the ground by the spells" (76–7).

When Ti Noël returns to Haiti, Dessalines has been dead for several years and Henri Christophe, self-proclaimed Emperor of Haiti, is building the impressive Sans Souci that according to Carpentier's own legend inspired the writing of the book. In the beginning, a fascinated Ti Noël falls for the pomp and extravaganza he sees in Sans Souci, where Black characters reenact all the luxury of a European court. However, soon he is forced to work in the construction of the fortress along with other poor peasants, women, and even children, whose bodies are unceremoniously discarded when they fall prey to an accident or simply die of exhaustion. Prisoner of another war of time, Ti Noël "began to lose heart at this endless sprouting of chains, this rebirth of shackles, this proliferation of misery, which the more resigned began to accept as proof of the uselessness of all revolt" (115). And it is only then, at the border of despair, that Ti Noël's kingdom of this world begins, in total dispossession.

After the revolt that ends Christophe's kingdom, Ti Noël returns to Monsieur Lenormand de Mezy's estate with a pile of disparaged objects he managed to steal from the plundering of Sans Souci. By then, little remains of the old mansion: only a section of the floor and the barely recognizable shape of a chimney. In this place, Ti Noël is his own king, and he lives in the happiness that only a truly carefree existence can provide, the same carefreeness that was denied to Henri Christophe in the ironically named palace of Sans Souci. It is difficult not to see that this is what freedom means for Carpentier: an unburdening of a person who is no longer caught in the narcissistic trap of his/her possessions and concerns about their preservation. The free people of Haiti inhabit their land as souls stricken by an oblivious saint. Retrospectively, this is the happiness that captivates the white French exiled in Santiago de Cuba following the revolt in Haiti.[55] Such is Carpentier's deep, fully anti-modernist translation of the Marxist idea that the liberation of the lower strata of society

---

55. "The strange thing was that the old colonists, divested of their fortunes and ruined, ... instead of lamenting were almost rejuvenated ... Those who had been unable

means the liberation of all. But in this formula, the word liberation remains completely unspecified, and one strongly senses that it did not mean the same in Marx's historicist narrative as it means for the almost cyclical narrative of the Black popular classes with whom Carpentier's political stance so forcefully identifies.

A Question of Language

The vindication of Afro-Cubanism undertaken by intellectuals like Cabrera, Barnet, or Carpentier—to which we can add other names, such as those of Nicolás Guillén or Fernando Ortiz—all have something in common: they are the vindication of Blacks as part and even representatives of the *bajo pueblo*.[56] This is the familiar mechanism through which Latin American populisms sought to offer a cultural supplement to the deficient integration of marginalized populations into the national community. It is in the shadow of this identification between the Black popular and the *bajo pueblo* that we should locate Fernando Ortiz's vehement assertion that "without the black, Cuba would not be Cuba."[57] We all understand what Ortiz means; his assertion is even intuitive. The simplicity of this formula has not prevented rivers of ink to be wasted in attempts to prove the point. Significantly, Ortiz poses the problem in terms of being, as if Blacks would allow Cuba to *be*. And even if he was correct, writing from the perspective of Cuba, standing on its very soil, it did not occur to him that the African diaspora was bringing to Cuba a type of cultural assertion destined, perhaps, to put into question the very system that ties meaning to substance. The nation form is acquainted with this problem. Nations *are not*, and this is why they need to be imagined. The nation's lack of being is both its curse and the source of its tremendous historical success. The nation continually exposes this lack only to cover it up in the dimension

---

to save anything reveled in their disorder, in their living day by day, in their lack of obligations" (Carpentier, *Reino de este mundo*, 74).

56. In his 1939 lecture, "Los factores humanos de la cubanidad," Fernando Ortiz evokes this image of the "bajo pueblo" (the people from below) as the specific site for the creation of a Cuban transcultural nation: "Blacks … created among the great masses of our people from below [bajo pueblo] a syncretism of equivalences, a syncretism so lucid and eloquent that it is sometimes tantamount to a critical philosophy." Fernando Ortiz, "The Human Factors of Cubanidad" (translation by Gonçalves and Morton slightly modified), 474.

57. Fernando Ortiz, *Etnia y sociedad* (Havana: Editorial de Ciencias Sociales, 1993), 136. The idea reappears profusely in Fernando Ortiz, for instance in the programmatic text, "Por la integración cubana de blancos y negros," *Ultra* (Havana, Cuba) 13, no. 77 (1943): 69–76.

of meaning. The nation builds a hypostasis of meaning insofar as meaning is the conclusion, the impossible *this* that according to a famous argument will always be denied to us because the relentless passing of time turns any de facto tautology (any identity of perception) into a myth.

A hypostasis is an efficacious fiction, to use Joseph Vogl's expression, that "informs the self understanding of societies, coordinates social and symbolic practices, and provides intuitively justified images or self-evident truths to determine how society functions and which options for action are available at any given time."[58] What the nation proposes is not that all meanings are reducible or redeemable in terms of the present configuration of the national culture, but instead that every symbolic is *in principle* reducible to the structuration of meaning—and that the historical apparatus of the nation-state provides the final form for any meaningful articulation whatsoever. The colonial Latin American state was grounded on a universalist theory of symbolization, and the independent republics never abandoned the belief that one of the main tasks of the state was to provide venues and models for symbolic identification. The voracious process of symbolization that starts in 1910 (coincidentally with the centennials of independence and the establishment of philology as the science of the national) targets the voice of the other as the foundation of a new cultural hegemony.

The rhetoric of the *bajo pueblo* does not put in doubt the fundamental transmissibility of the languages of the excluded to the protocols of recognition proper to the nation form. It would seem then that "without blacks, Cuba would not be Cuba" meant that through an act of cultural ventriloquism Cuba could appropriate the words, languages, and styles of Blacks for itself. Moreover, it could appropriate them because it has already done so—because Cuba will be unrecognizable without the contribution of the Black. However, Ortiz's proverbial intellectual honesty leads him to complicate his own argument. The 1923 *Un catauro de cubanismos* clearly argues for the centrality of Black popular culture (and more prominently of its voice) in the constitution of Cuban nationality.[59] However, the *catauro* itself is traversed by so many disputes about meaning, by such an anarchic etymology that the ideal unity of the nation is more unfounded than secured by this procedure. The necessarily unfinished, and in consequence antidisciplinary nature of Ortiz's book is emphasized by the word catauro itself (a small basket where different items are mixed) which suggests an avoidance of totalization and a distrust of meta-linguistic procedures. The catauro was not even alphabetically organized, an "oversight" that was "remedied" in the 1974 reedition that the Editorial de Ciencias Sociales de La Habana published shortly after Ortiz's death.

---

58. Vogl, *The Specter of Capital*, 37.

59. See for instance the preface to Fernando Ortiz, "Al lector," *Catauro de cubanismos: apuntes lexicográficos* (Havana: n.p., 1923), viii.

Similarly, Gustavo Perez Firmat observed that Ortiz's *Catauro de Cubanismos* works more through the dissemination of meaning than through its stabilization.[60] Ortiz delivers a philology that explicitly refuses to anchor words and expressions in specific meanings; and favors, instead, a linguistic playfulness marked by irony and mistrust of authority.

At the time in which all across Latin America, philology was taking charge of anchoring the history of the popular speaking subject into the grammar of a national expression, Ortiz makes a wager for an anarchic form of historicism. A substantialist ideology of language is the first casualty of Ortiz's encounter with something that appeals to him but whose unfolding demands the rejection of traditional ethnographic forms of access to cultural phenomena. What Ortiz discovers in the African inflicted popular parlance of his time is not so much a meaning as a sense, a directionality of language. In the cleavage between meaning and sense, it is clear that the force of diasporic consciousness tips the scales in favor of the latter.

At moments, it seems that the entire complexity of the African diaspora resolves itself into a ceaseless circulation of objects that become texts, gestures that convey meanings, layers, and layers of signs that are simultaneously open and inscrutable. While the mythology of foundation that presides over the idea of the nation lives in need of anchoring gestures characterized by the clarity of a voice and a fullness of intentionality, the conviction that "without blacks, Cuba would not be Cuba" proposes an eccentric foundational model, since the voice animating it is mediated and made possible by solidarities born in a murmur, in secret and double coding.[61]

It is apposite to evoke at this point Hortense Spiller's notion of a "pattern of dispersal" into which captive persons were forced "beginning with the Trade itself, into the horizontal relatedness of language groups, discourse formations, bloodlines, names, and properties by the legal arrangements of enslavement."[62]

---

60. Gustavo Perez Firmat, "The Philological Fictions of Fernando Ortiz," *Notebooks in Cultural Analysis*, 2: 190–207. In a similar fashion, Anke Birkenmaier argues that Ortiz's work in these two books exceeds the simple refutation of an authoritative etymology of popular languages and points, instead, to a questioning of the historical underpinnings of the philological method itself. It is just not the case that Ortiz distrusts etymologies, but rather that he is more interested in disclosing the "twisted, 'zigzag-like" nature of the construction of meaning. Anke Birkenmaier, "Entre antropología y filología. Fernando Ortiz y el Día de la Raza," *Antípoda. Revista de Antropología y Arqueología*, 15 (2012): 205.

61. Although the work is somewhat dated, it is interesting to recall here Henry Louis Gates Jr.'s ethnography of double meaning in *The Signifying Monkey: A Theory of African-American Literary Criticism* (New York: Oxford University Press, 1988).

62. Hortense J. Spillers, "Mam's Baby, Papa's Maybe. An American Grammar Book," *Diacritics*, vol. 17, no. 2 (1987): 75.

The idea that slavery created a generalized destitution of language as symbolic and contractual tool is an affirmation that can be found in almost every single critic or historian of slavery. What the archive of the expression of diasporic consciousness invites to ponder is that this disaster of meaning became constitutional. And this is so in a fashion that may exceed the space of Latin America and concerns, according Achille Mbembe's expression, Black reason at large.

> Still today, as soon as the subject of Blacks and Africa is raised, words do not necessarily represent things; the true and the false become inextricable; the signification of the sign is not always adequate to what is being signified. It is not only that the sign is substituted for the thing. Word and image often have little to say about the objective world.[63]

The disaster of meaning is the most recurrent, the most easily verified destiny of the word in the whole extension of the African diaspora. Such disaster of meaning—the ruin of the subsumptive force of language—does not enforce silence, but invites more language. It even proliferates language and signification in excess to any economy of communication. Carpentier is onto something when he packs *The Kingdom of This World* with omens, signs, and fore-messages whose full meaning is only open to the initiated. These messages travel and endure, surviving beyond the constant suspicion of authorities and slave owners. Already on their estates, the masters lived in perpetual terror of an impending meaning suspected in gestures, rhythms, or glances. Is it not telling that in *The Kingdom of This World* no event goes unannounced and no character is ever entirely surprised, even when the blows of fate are just seconds away? (Poor King Christophe, so imbued in his mimicry of European mores that he realized a second too late that the music played by the imperial band carried the overtones of his dismissal.)

This over-coding of reality, this becoming sign of an existence whose underside is the utter problematization of "the facts of perception" (Mackandal's spectral flight from death/his actual death), is not just a literary rendering but a malaise that affected the order of the believable in its entirety. In *Freedom's Mirror*, Ada Ferrer recounts that three weeks after Boukman's insurrection, a shortage of pigs in the markets of Havana sent shivers of terror through the colonial authorities.[64] Although no news from the rebellion in Saint-Domingue was supposed to reach the shores of Cuba, details of the Black uprising rapidly spread to all corners of the Caribbean—not by magic, but by the simple fact that the network of slave exploitation overlapped inch to inch with the network

---

63. Mbembe, *Critique of Black Reason*, 13.
64. Ada Ferrer, *Freedom's Mirror. Cuba and Haiti in the Age of Revolution* (Cambridge: Cambridge University Press, 2014), 5.

of mercantilism. Planters and authorities knew that drums and immemorial gods had come together at Bois Caiman to provide a literal inspiration to those bodies that the island capitalists had tried to empty of any signification by imposing the first large-scale biopolitical regime of modernity. The sacrifice at Bois Caiman had developed into the pervasive presence of an-other language whose unreadability always "meant" the same: the impossibility of exhausting the notion of the slave by their instrumental use in exploitation.[65]

In *Haiti and the Gods*, Joan Dayan underlines Dessalines's complex, almost maddening relationship to language and signs. He is not only responsible for renaming the country in an attempt to erase the island's lexical subordination to European conceptualism, but also suggested that Haitians should be called "Incas or children of the sun," memorializing Tupac Amaru's 1780 uprising.[66] For all his antipathy to the zealous Catholicism of a L'Ouverture, Dessalines ended up crowning himself king and mimicking the most ridiculous aspects of European court life. He passed proclamations using the language of the French republic he abhorred. Fully conscious of the nature of this unshakable symbolic yoke, already an emperor, Dessalines took pride in the perverse practice of referring to himself as Duclos, the name of his former master.[67] And as Michel-Rolph Trouillot notices in *Silencing the Past*, King Christophe was playing dice with fate when he named Sans Souci, the palace adjacent to La Citadelle where Ti Noël toiled to the verge of disbelief. Like the possessed who speak in broken Spanish, Sans Souci evokes an echo too close to Dessalines to be ignored. The palace could not possibly be named after Colonel Jean Baptiste Sans Souci, an African slave known for his uncompromising stance against European powers and culture. As Rolph Trouillot retells the story, some ten years before the construction of the fortress, Christophe invited Sans Souci to a conciliatory meeting and had him murdered.[68]

65. In a chapter suggestively titled, "An Excess of Communication," Ada Ferrer narrates the finding of "a rosette or cockade (*escarapela*) carried by the black insurgents ... [that] consisted of three discreet images: a small heart made of seeds ... a *fleur de lis*, and the word *Constitution*" (*Freedom's Mirror*, 55). Ferrer notes that the seeds were "perhaps similar to the one that would later become a traditional representation of the voodoo deity Erzulie" (55).

66. Dayan, *Haiti and the Gods*, 22.

67. Carpentier does not fail to notice how heredity and disinheritance play against each other in the pledge of Bois Caiman, where the call of an ancestral language is combined with the counting of leaders who have lost their names at the hands of their masters.

68. In *Silencing the Past* Michel Rolph Trouillot retells the story of Colonel Jean Baptiste Sans Souci, a principled military officer who was summoned by Henri Christophe, who eventually killed him. See Michel Rolph Trouillot, *Silencing the Past: Power and the Production of History* (Boston, MA: Beacon Press, 1997).

Not all those who listen to this pilgrimage of signs are in the same position to understand their meaning (that is, to construct their meaning since all understanding is a construction). What happens to the signifier "Cuba" when it is exposed to a perpetual parade of signs that seem to live in the expectation of a meaning that never arrives? This nagging doubt inflicts the thinking itself of ethnographic difference and touches on what I have just called "the facts of perception." The text in which Ortiz issued his proclamation of an identity between Cuba and the Black allows us to visualize the complex economy that, many years later, will authorize Lydia Cabrera to doubt the authority of her own voice:

> Already at the beginning of my research, I realized that like all Cubans, I was confused. I was confronted not just with a curious black masonic cult, but with a vast, complex web of religious vestiges (supervivencias religiosas) originating in different and remote areas -and enmeshed in them there was a wealth of lineages, (linajes) languages, music, instruments, dances, songs, traditions, legends, art, games and local philosophies (filosofías folklóricas). Indeed, I stood before the portentous and immense detritus of the many African cultures that were brought to Cuba -cultures which were utterly unknown in academic circles. And all this material presented itself in convoluted ways since it was transplanted from one side of the Atlantic to the other with chaos as its only method. Through four centuries, the piracy of black people milled the forests (montes) of black humanity of Africa, decimating them and delivering its product, admixed and confused, upon the land of Cuba -ship after ship brought with it branches, roots, flowers and seeds extricated from all the forests of Africa.[69]

In this context, let us hear Joan Dayan retelling the story of the day she was introduced to the *oungan* who was to serve as her guide into the world of voodoo. He greeted her by saying: "Salam Alechem" (peace be with you). Wondering why he spoke Arabic to her, Dayan asked what language that was. "He answered 'ce langaj' which means 'a secret language with its sources in Guinea, used by initiates.'"[70] The creole expression "ce langaj" takes the Arabic expression "Salam Alechem" as a sign-object rather than as representative of an intended meaning; and this is why although he was asked for a translation the ougan answered on the plane of reference rather than on the plane of discourse. Stephan Palmié recounts a similar situation on the occasion of the visit of Nigerian *santería* scholar Wande Abimbola to Salvador, Bahia in the 1970s. While Abimbola testified to the "strong attachment and respect whichthe

---

69. Fernando Ortiz, "Por la integración cubana de blancos y negros," *Estudios Afrocubanos*, Havana (1945–6): 216–29.

70. Dayan, *Haiti, History and the Gods*, xv.

eople from Brazil still have for the Yoruba divinities," he was dismayed by the evidence that the devotees did not understand the meaning of the liturgical texts, which hampered their access to their own religious repertoire.[71]

When sign-objects are elicited to produce the effects of signs of intended meaning, it is not the intentionality of the subject that is lacking but intentionality itself as that other scene in which the hesitations of our hearsay may come, if only fictitiously, to a rest. In its obstinacy, the use of Arabic or of any other sign-object in the rituals of *santería* and voodoo introduce a positive moment of reference and enunciation that can be and has been linked to phenomena like syncretism or collage. However, it is also evident that words and signs lend themselves here to other inflections that go well beyond their mere instrumental use in communication. The dissemination of meaning constitutes the symbolic matrix that diasporic consciousness imposed upon many cultural sites and practices with the force of a destiny. If these signs are always so disposed to appear and disappear, adapting themselves to the most variegated contexts, always retaining a sort of orphanhood that makes of them ready material for new articulations, it is because they circulate in despair of finding a master code able to build a home for them outside of diasporic longing. In them, the plasticity of their expressions is one with the melancholy of their loss.[72]

Firmas, or *anaforuanas* (*vévés* in the French-speaking Antilles), refer to a group of ideographic symbols used by the practitioners of *santería* and voodoo. They are ubiquitous in Cuba, Haiti, and Brazil. Carpentier included reproductions of these signs both in the first and the 1975 edition of *¡Ecue-Yamba-O!* The anaforuana is a derivation of the Nsibidi writing system that was used in Africa at least since 2000 BC.[73] Lydia Cabrera is credited with collecting and cataloging the largest number of anaforuanas, over 2,000. Cabrera does not treat them as messages but as liturgical objects of high symbolic power. As symbols, anaforuanas point to a commerce with a beyond that can be equally transcendental (the dwelling place of the gods) or historical (the African point of origin of this system of writing). Cabrera notices that anaforuanas do not behave like phonetic writing, not only because they are not the transcription of a voice, but also because new combinations are infrequent. In *Hegel, Haiti, and Universal History*, Susan Buck Morss reflects on the Haitian vévés as silent

---

71. I am drawing here from a report by Stephan Palmié in *The Cooking of History*, 61–3.

72. The topic of the return to Africa or the genealogy of the *santería* pantheon to Africa are widespread features among the adepts of the religion. As I have suggested repeatedly, these cultural expressions should be subjected to a double reading: on the one hand, they represent a utopian longing that speaks in the language of lack and loss; on the other, they are adaptative discourses directed to the most immediate conditions of cultural understanding and creativity.

73. See Jorge Castellanos and Isabel Castellanos's discussion of the anaforuanas in *Cultura afrocubana*, vol. 3, 306–13.

signs, fragments of "hollowed out" meanings that barely survived (if life can still be said to be one of their attributes) the horror of a profound natal alienation. In the Haitian ritual, the vévé is painted with flour on the floor and its form is slowly yet inexorably erased by the rhythmic movement of the ritual's dancers.[74]

If in a radical Hegelian fashion we admit that the final instance of all meaning and thinking is the figure of God itself, it is no doubt instructive that the descendants of the Yorubas (the term is shorthand for a missing identity whose utter deconstruction by Stephan Palmié resounds, however, with the structure I am recounting in these paragraphs) should acknowledge a supreme God to whom all other deities are subordinated.[75] Variously called Olodumare, Oloru, or Olofín, this omnipotent God created the cosmos only to ignore his work. Leaving his creations behind, he now lives on the underside of the sun without concerning himself with the lives of its followers.[76] This is the story of the dancing feet and the vévé all over again. My question is directed to the impasse as the cipher of the structure. What is it that the ritual dance performs? Is it the fatality of historical amnesia or the revelation of a symbolic arrangement that we may call Haitian, Cuban, or Caribbean and of which Edouard Glissant will have given us a gripping dialectic in his *Poetics of Relation*?[77]

If *El Monte* is the forerunner of testimonio (but also its impossible conclusion), this is not so because Cabrera lends her voice to her informants or because she discovers and reasserts an entire spectrum of life: it is, overwhelmingly, because she sequesters the conditions of reception from any normative context of understanding. Cabrera raises the question of belief in her text: do I, Cabrera asks, believe the claims of my informants? The reader can almost see her shrugging, dismissing the question as fundamentally wrongheaded. It may be that one day, in the whole trajectory of a discourse that unfolds in history but is not identical with it, the question could be raised about the truth of these practices and of the truth in general of events that cannot possibly be, as Stephan Palmié puts it, "exhausted in the literalism implied by such terms as *belief, plausibility,* or *rationality*."[78] Meanwhile, I do not want the necessary imprecision of my language to be taken for a transcendental recourse. I risk more than what I can reasonably prove by saying that what we see acting here under a form of an obstinate memory going back to a world that it never knew is the trace of the entire process of natal alienation. In any event, I think that something that touches on the epochal and irreducible

---

74. Susan Buck Morss, *Hegel, Haiti, and Universal History* (Pittsburgh: Pittsburgh University Press, 2009), 127.

75. See the opening chapter of Stephan Palmié's *The Cooking of History*.

76. Castellanos and Castellanos, *Cultura afrocubana*, 3, 18–19.

77. Edouard Glissant, *Poetics of Relation*, trans. Betsy Wing (Ann Arbor: University of Michigan Press, 1997).

78. Palmié, *Wizards and Scientists*, 3.

experience of slavery itself is responsible for this symbolic damnation that does not survive in memory without being subject to a steady process of rewriting and dissemination.[79]

History and Haiti

Like so many texts centered on the African diaspora, Susan Buck Morss's *Hegel and Haiti* is plagued with meditations about broken chains of meaning, evidence of symbolic short-circuits, and laments over severed intentionalities and catastrophes of sense. Yet, it is also a text that remains, if not utopian, at least optimistic. *Hegel and Haiti* delves into the possibility of including the lost voices and canceled intentions through operations of which the book itself wants to be an exemplar. This strategy of pulling the experience of the Black diaspora into the clearing of history (into a History 1 made multiple) is one of the explanations for the centrality of Hegel in the book. Buck Morss pits Hegel, the master of any tarrying with the negative, against what I have just referred to as symbolic damnation. The optimist in Buck Morss tells us that the project of universal history, once Hegel's rallying call for an emancipated humanity, may still be adapted, corrected, and made inclusive, especially in the case of Blacks, whose historical experience has punctuated—as Buck Morss's book shows—the day-to-day thinking of the German philosopher. By abolishing the heterogeneous barrier that seems to separate History 1 from the multiple histories of the African diaspora, the irrational core of history can be made to signify once again. A world that signifies is a world that makes sense. It is one step closer to redemption. In another phenomenology, written over a century after Hegel's, Martin Heidegger doubts the possibility of such redemption being ever possible. In Chapter 3 of *Being and Time*, "The worldhood of the World," the world itself is perceived as a system of signs, or as Heidegger writes, of references and assignments. These references do not constitute an infinite series (the iron to be cast in order to melt the mineral that will be used to build a road on which cars will travel, and so forth). The way in which every object of the human world refers to every other comes to a stop in the "for the sake of which" it was produced. The unity of all assignments is provided by Dasein itself as the final addressee of all these multiple references. But the system of involvements crumbles under its own weight. Once the question of all reference is understood as a slide towards a final destination,

---

79. The notion of natal alienation was popularized by Olando Patterson, *Slavery and Social Death: A Comparative Study* (Cambridge, MA: Harvard University Press, 1982). Frank B. Wilderson III recasts and radicalizes the notion in *Red, Black and White: Cinema and the Structure of U.S. Antagonisms* (Raleigh, NC: Duke University Press, 2010), 20–1.

the analytic of finitude places death in all its meaninglessness as the ultimate source or fate of any symbolic construction. Insofar as death is the last "for the sake of which" and in itself lacks any signification for Dasein "the totality of involvements ... collapses into itself."[80] This collapse does not bear the stamp of damnation because it is only in terms of failure, of its possibility and even of its certainty, that Dasein can reach a modicum of authenticity. Perhaps this Heideggerian model of culture as a related series of "for the sake of which" is closer to the symbolic structure of diasporic consciousness than the restitutive model insinuated in the Hegelian dialectic of the tarrying with the negative. For what is the semiotic of the evanescent that structures *santería* and Black popular religiosity if not a sustained mourning for the missing links of a chain that knows itself defunded *ab initio*? Is not a catastrophe of meaning what is remembered continuously, and yet rarely named, in the disseminating force of the diasporic expression? This catastrophe, whose distinct historical index is the slave traffic, is not just a concern of the Black diaspora, in a certain sense, it eviscerates the European logos from within. As Achille Mbembe writes:

> Everytime it confronted the question of Blacks and Africa, reason found itself ruined and emptied, turning constantly in on itself, shipwrecked in a seemingly inaccessible place where language was destroyed and words themselves no longer had memory. Language, its ordinary functions extinguished, became a fabulous machine whose power resided in its vulgarity, in its remarkable capacity for violation, and its indefinite proliferation.[81]

In the hermeneutics of *Being and Time*, death represents the catastrophe of meaning. It represents, also, meaning's secret core. Death appears not as the external limit of meaning but as its condition of possibility. It was Hegel (who "talked a lot about slavery," as Buck Morss informs us) who popularized the expression "Absolute master" to refer to death. But death or irreparable symbolic loss is itself subjected to a dialectic in the last great thinker of the enlightenment. Such is the gist of one of the most famous passages in the *Phenomenology*, in which Hegel makes of Spirit the supreme power able to look at death in the face; a power that, in tarrying with the negative, sustains the totality of existence so that things can, after all, hang on in the symbolic. The exact phrasing is: "This tarrying with the negative [the power of Spirit as combination of understanding and reason] is the magical power that converts

---

80. Martin Heidegger, *Being and Time*, trans. John Macquarrie and Edward Robinson (Oxford: Basil Blackwell, 1978), 231.

81. Achille Mbembe, *Critique of Black Reason*, 13. One is reminded here of the tortuous reasoning that leads Roberto Schwarz to postulate the notion of a misplaced idea in the context, precisely, of an analysis of the end of slavery in Brazil. See *Misplaced Ideas: Essays on Brazilian Culture*, ed. John Gledson (London: Verso, 1992).

it [the negative] into being."⁸² The powerful moral of the story may obscure the intrusion of another discourse strange to Hegelian language, an unlikely word indeed: *Zauberkraft*; that is, the magical, the supernatural, or (why not?) witchery. Even a superficial rereading of this sentence confirms the syntactical centrality of the word in the passage: "This tarrying with the negative is the magical power (Zauberkraft) that converts it [the negative] into being." It is not my intention to charge Hegel with practicing a form of conceptual voodoo, but merely to show how deep the crisis of any symbolic runs in the absence of some remedial hypostasis of meaning. In the shadow of a trauma that it refuses to name as much as it refuses to forget, this hypostasis of meaning is precisely what is denied to diasporic consciousness, or what diasporic consciousness denies itself.

---

82. G. W. F. Hegel, *The Phenomenology of Spirit*, trans. A. V. Miller (Oxford: Oxford University Press, 1977), 19 (the bracketed explanations are mine).

Chapter 5

JOSÉ MARÍA ARGUEDAS: CAPITALIST ACCUMULATION AND NOVELISTIC MODE OF PRESENTATION IN THE ANDES

Progressive Peru expected a great deal from José María Arguedas. These expectations were grounded on the unique position of a writer-anthropologist who, despite being a Spanish-speaking creole, was educated by Indians and said to have had Quechua as his first language. The two professions that Arguedas knew in his life, fiction writer and anthropologist, were part of the nation's design to reduce ethnic and cultural conflict through some form of narrative synthesis. However, his books were rarely greeted with unanimous critical acclaim. *Yawar Fiesta* (1941) bewildered many readers, and it will take years for *The Fox from Up Above and the Fox from Down Below* (1971) to acquire the ultra-canonical status that it enjoys today. *Todas las sangres* (1965, from now on *TLS*) tops the list when it comes to critical discomfort. The novel was labeled reactionary by some readers appalled by the sympathetic treatment of the ruthless *gamonal* Don Bruno and the most lukewarm picture of Don Fermin, Don Bruno's industrialist (hence supposedly more progressive) brother. To compound problems, the indigenous people in the novel seemed at first to be simple pawns in the power games between Don Bruno and his brother, although they start gaining consistency as the novel progresses. It was not altogether surprising then that when on June 23, 1965, the Instituto de Estudios Peruanos organized a roundtable to celebrate the publication of the novel, a group of prominent sociologists and anthropologists ditched *TLS* in the name of ideas that were considered simultaneously scientific and politically progressive.

In the 1960s, the synthesis of which Arguedas was supposed to be a messenger did not exclude but rather demanded an intensification of class struggle. At the time of the publication of *TLS*, many people believed that Peru was on a revolutionary path not unlike the one which, in Cuba, had shocked all of Latin America. Some readers may have expected *TLS* to make a decisive contribution to this manifest historical road—and there are reasons to believe that Arguedas himself saw his novel under this light. The criticism that befell the novel at the roundtable dashed this perception and renewed the particular tension that often pitched Marxism and indigeneity against each other in the cultural tradition of the continent.

Mostly ignored as a literary nuisance at the time, the roundtable claimed an enormous retrospective value and has been revisited by several scholars in recent years. Most of the speakers who questioned Arguedas's novel, sometimes in very harsh terms, were not literary critics but intellectuals of leftist convictions. As Irina Feldman summarizes the situation in a recent book:

> The progressive Marxist intellectuals aspired to use what were considered the modern tools of analysis, moving away from the caste system, founding their reflection in strictly economic categories. They desired to show that the Peruvian poor as a culturally homogeneous social group were ready to enter as a working class in the industrialized reality of the modern nation.[1]

Against this abstraction, Arguedas sustained the reality of his own encounter with the Andean world. His resentful answer to his critics is well known: "If *Todas las sangres* is not a testimonio, then I have lived for nothing; I have lived in vain or have not lived."[2] Arguedas did not ignore—he highlights, as Feldman shows—the proletarization of the indigenous masses. But his numerous and tortuous reminders of the indigenous traits of the Andean population frustrated the social scientists, in part because they could not see how such traits carried any significance for the social function of their bearers. As the roundtable progressed, Arguedas was forced to take refuge in a language of art and testimony, leaving the terrain of the political to his critics. And on this terrain, the critics felt quite at home, since both the language of politics and the language of progress they incarnated share a similar streamlining of reality, a streamlining in which whatever plays a function of obstacle is either insignificant or pathological.

Some of the participants in the roundtable were Arguedas's personal friends. He expected an intellectual sympathy from them that did not materialize. In retrospect, it is possible to describe the exchange at the roundtable as a form of disagreement, a word that, in the specific intonation given to it by Jacques Rancière, has the advantage of highlighting that the core of this dispute lies in the almost inexistent distance running between realism that continued to be the poetics of reading of the critic and irrealism that increasingly became the poetics of production of the engaged writer. This was a surprising outcome. After all, Latin American writers and critics have constituted a tight socius throughout their history. Often, they belonged to the same class, attended

---

1. Irina Feldman, *Rethinking Community from Peru: The Political Philosophy of José María Arguedas* (Pittsburgh: University of Pittsburgh Press, 2014), 75.

2. Quoted in Guillermo Rochabrún, *¿He vivido en vano? La mesa redonda sobre todas las sangres del 23 de Junio de 1965* (Lima: IEP, 2011), 38.

the same schools, and shared the same anxieties about the backward-looking nature of their societies. They befriended each other and exchanged drafts and ideas at conferences and private meetings. Leftists, cultural Marxists of sorts, they were committed intellectuals long before Jean Paul Sartre popularized the term. For the critics, it was the desire to uncover the Latin American truth that turned their heads toward developmentalism as a general ideological ideal that could acquire in some cases a socialist tonality. In practical terms, the kernel of the disagreement between critics and writers is (or was) that while for the former cultural differences and exclusion were a sociological and political problem that could be addressed and transcribed in the positive languages of the social sciences, for the latter they became a conundrum that challenged the very definition of the political and the ultimate ground of the social.

Cornejo Polar has discussed this rift as "an acute although understated contradiction … between a programmatic form of historical thinking that seeks an alternate future reality" and a literary discourse that carries "a valorization of traditional traits of the indigenous people," and which can even find "a re-iteration of the past" appealing and politically expedient.[3] What Cornejo perceived as a conflict peculiar to Peru and anchored in residues of colonialism is rehearsed as a more widespread rift between the culture of the humanities and the culture of the social sciences in the work of Immanuel Wallerstein. In the introduction to the volume that he coedited with Richard Lee, *Overcoming the Two Cultures: Sciences and the Humanities in the Modern World-System*, Wallerstein and Lee map the slow and long-winded separation between sciences of fact (which will lead to the creation of the social sciences) and discourses unwilling to renounce the dimension of value (which will lead to the conformation of the humanities).[4] They write:

> The word "culture" in the phrase "two cultures" refers to the fact that scholars do their research, writing, and teaching on the basis of underlying epistemological presuppositions, which they use but seldom expound. To say that there are two cultures (in the structures of knowledge) is to say that scholars tend to group themselves in two different, indeed often opposing, camps with regard to the set of epistemological presuppositions they employ and believe useful and/or correct to employ. (1)

---

3. AntonioCornejo Polar, "La Novela indigenista: Una desgarrada conciencia de la historia," LEXIS, vol. 4, no. 1 (1980): 77–89.

4. Richard E. Lee and Immanuel Wallerstein, *Overcoming the Two Cultures: Sciences and the Humanities in the Modern World-System* (New York: Routledge, 2016). In the same volume, Richard Lee revisits the two-cultures hypothesis and writes that throughout history only modernity "has created two antithetical, contradictory epistemological bases for the production of knowledge, one excluding human values a priori and one in which human values are an inseparable component" (30).

While the idea of two cultures is simple, the problem lies in the translatability (or lack of it) between both realms. Wallerstein revisits the question in the afterword that he writes for the volume *Immanuel Wallerstein and the Problem of the World*.[5] In a short piece that betrays a certain impatience with his humanist colleagues, Wallerstein describes the divide in these terms:

> For many people in the humanities, the social sciences are simply one branch of the sciences and attitudes toward the social sciences tend to reflect the classic divide between the two cultures. We humanists write about the concrete particular, which we seek to "understand." You social scientist pretend to write about "systems," which probably don't exist and in any case are reified versions of reality.

Wallerstein acknowledges that this picture exaggerates "the term of this debate ... but not by much."[6]

The description of two mutually exclusive processes of truth formation that have persisted through modernity begs the idea that since the world is unreachable, what matters in the last instance is the form of its presentation. World here doesn't mean the immediate context of existence but rather the chain or sequence of effects that stand for the efficacy of the totality. For our historical juncture, notices Fredric Jameson "Neither society nor what is called cultural or aesthetic experience are ... stable substances that can be studied empirically and analyzed philosophically."[7] Simply put, the chain of effects cannot be reconstructed in the scale of verification from which our ideas of truth have been historically born. The notion of verification itself is entirely dependent on a mutual commensurability between subject and phenomena. Such immediacy has become more and more complicated since the onslaught of the colonial era and became utterly improbable in the twentieth century. As Hanna Arendt pointed out in her discussion of technology, science makes "the body's natural sense of the universe [increasingly] irrelevant."[8] The mediations that characterize our globalized world introduce questions of verisimilitude that are in principle irreconcilable with the horizon of embeddedness popularized by art, literature, and existential phenomenology in the early twentieth century. The tension between knowledge and experience has momentous consequences for literature whose very impulse is transformed as modern

---

5. David Palumbo-Liu, Nirvana Tanoukhi, and Bruce Robbins eds., *Immanuel Wallerstein and the Problem of the World: System, Scale, Culture* (Durham, NC: Duke University Press, 2011).

6. Ibid., 224.

7. Fredric Jameson, *The Antinomies of Realism* (London: Verso, 2013), 6.

8. Hanna Arendt, "The Conquest of Space and the Stature of Man," in *Between Past and Future* (New York: Penguin Classics, 1954), 268.

expression increasingly embodies a "growing contradiction ... between a phenomenological description of the life of an individual and a more properly structural model of the conditions of existence of that experience."[9] From this situation alone, we can measure the exorbitance of Arguedas's project in *TLS*: it seeks to be an embodied account of the totality of its world.

First Image of Todas las sangres

TLS resembles the great nineteenth-century European realist novel in its scope, in the vast mosaic of people depicted in its pages, and in the parables of existence through which its main actors pass. Even a quick summary of the novel's main actions would take pages. Arguedas himself claimed that his novel contained "the totality of Peru," and Cornejo Polar spoke of its "unusual and disproportionate range."[10] There is, however, a fundamental difference between *TLS* and canonical realist writers. For them, realism could reflect a totality because that totality was already given in the hegemonic view of the time. In Arguedas, the totality is the result of an artful and controversial literary operation. Many critics have called *TLS* schematic and simplistic, noticing an eerie lack of verisimilitude in its pages. Characters and discourses are brought together artificially and made to reflect on and weigh each other up. The list includes: a ruined landowning class and the upstarts from that class, like the Cholo Cisneros, who needs to recur to primitive forms of exploitation of indigenous labor to make his hacienda profitable; the dignified *señores* who abhor working with their hands, so they go out to pick up the potatoes that save them from starvation under the cloak of the night; the communal Indians who go to work at a distant mine wary of the temptation of money or alcohol; the consortium Wisterth Bozart, so fantasmatic that it only becomes visible through its representative Cabrejos; the stubborn *varayoks* who accept stoically any punishment armed with the fanatical belief that endurance will lead them to acquire rights in the end; a fair-minded woman like doña Matilde, who looks at the world as a place to which she simultaneously belongs and does not belong; and a middle man like her husband, Don Fermín, whose mind is made of the practicalities of money but whose skin still trembles under the effects of the old codes that Don Bruno and his Indians recognize as the stuff of their life. The great accomplishment of *TLS* lies in building a common ground for the coming together and mutual interaction of characters and social groups that otherwise would have nothing to tell to each other.

9. Fredric Jameson, *Postmodernism or, the Cultural Logic of Late Capitalism* (Durham, NC: Duke University Press, 1993), 247.

10. Cited by Antonio Cornejo Polar in *Los universos narrativos de José María Arguedas* (Buenos Aires: Losada, 1974), 187.

These characters are not literary devices as much as embodiments of meaning and history. So, when using the theoretical vocabulary of his time, Cornejo Polar calls the novel dialogical, this designation is still insufficient to account for the lack of consideration with which Arguedas piles up in a single movement those isolated elements that a more historiographically minded sociology would organize around the labels of the dominant, the emergent, and the residual. Sensing this conceptual insufficiency, Cornejo adds that the characters of the novel should be called, as a matter of fact, speakers; and that their different speeches are more than personal stances. They bring about "a plurality of truths." For Cornejo, this "dialogical organization" stamps *TLS* "at a deep structural" level.[11] However, Cornejo does not further inquire into this surprising structure. For my part, I call them monads, entities who are not explicated by the context, but who instead bring their ground along with their presence to bear on the novelistic structure. While these monads influence each other, they also represent intractable positions that do not find echoes or answers in the dialogical structure of the novel. In my view, this structure is one in which the novel does not realistically reproduce the relationships among the monads so much as it stages them.[12] The world stage is not just a metaphor here, but a constructive principle for a text that asks itself an ambitious question: how can an overdetermined reality be presented in the sequential nature of a text?

In *TLS*, the self-presentation of the monads works according to a declamatory logic. Even when we are privy to the thoughts of a character, the verbal performance suggests an exteriority of meaning deployed in characteristic theatrical fashion. As he witnesses the Indians taking his father Don Andrés Aragón de Peralta to the cemetery, Don Bruno "thinks," "My God, they bury him as an Indian. I hope Fermín doesn't become furious, that he doesn't lose his mind, said Don Bruno in his consciousness and he looked at his brother" (30). Another instance of this theatrical quality emerges in the relationship between Don Fermín and the engineer Cabrejos in charge of exploiting the mine. Cabrejos is a spy of the Wisther-Bozart international. Don Fermín knows that Cabrejos is a spy and Cabrejos knows that Don Fermín knows. They even have open conversations about this situation. This open exteriorization of their relationship does not bring any new information to the reader, and it doesn't even add drama to the plot (both men are quite nonchalant about the situation). Don Fermín comes very close to declaring that they should press on with their roles for the benefit of the spectacle.[13]

---

11. All direct or oblique quotes in this passage from Cornejo Polar, *Los universos narrativos*, 191.

12. Mabel Moraña underlines this formal characteristic of the novel: "Meaning is to a great extent *acted*, staged (puesto en escena), dramatized ..." Mabel Moraña, *Arguedas/Vargas Llosa. Dilemas y Ensamblajes* (Madrid: Iberoamericana Vervuert, 2013), 111.

13. In a different sense Don Fermín and Cabrejos embody or allegorize two ideals, the constitution of national capital (that Arguedas seems to defend) and the presence of

The exceptional fourth chapter of *TLS* represents the most consummated version of this dialogism of monads. The chapter itself begins in the style of stage directives: "In the great corridor of Don Bruno's rancho-house, three men of different ages, dressed in riding apparel with their vicuña ponchos still on, encircled the owner of The Providence" (178).

These four men of different ages represent three historical stages in the development of agribusiness in the highlands. Cisneros is rich but Indian, Aquiles is white but impoverished, and Don Bruno introduces himself as neither rich nor poor, but as someone whose authority is consecrated "by the laws of feudal inheritance" ("*herencia señorial*") (186). That each monad brings with them the ground for their existence is reflected in the language they speak or fail to speak. Cisneros swears, Don Bruno oversees the conversation from the heights of tradition, Aquiles, who has lost his ground on the highlands, has no words or discourse. The third visitor, referred to as "the almost old" (casi viejo) tries to mediate between the parts, although he resents the changes in the highlands.

Since the ground that determines him in this conversation is quite different from the turmoil of feelings and emotions that marks his presence in the novel, the often contradictory and passionate Don Bruno appears uncharacteristically phlegmatic and aloof. The conversation centers around the nature of reality and the world, and of what in it may hold the function of cause, and hence be open to narrativization. To Don Bruno's references to caste and feudal inheritances, the Cholo Cisneros replies:

- What of caste?! Those times are gone. The one with money, the one with more money, that is the one in control; that is the señor. I will show you … I have influence. With my money, I made the state representative, and even the senator (190).
- The senator is a great landowner.
- Yeah, but he spent the money of the Cholo Cisneros.
- He will deal with you as a Cholo, my friend. Don't harbor any illusions. Try if you will. If you want to smash a nobody, he will help you. But the Aragon de Peralta are not ruined, and they have been señores for a long time, like the senator … Try. I already have shown you excessive tolerance.[14]

The heart of the disagreement between Cisneros and Don Bruno is of a temporal order: are the times of caste really past? What constitutes effective causation in this world: rank? tradition? money? domination? In other words, under what laws does the present appear and authorize (or rebuke) a claim to

international, nihilizing capital (that Arguedas clearly abhors). But the two functions, staging and allegory, do not exist at the same level.

14. José María Arguedas, *Todas las sangres* (Lima: Horizonte, 1983), 194.

action? The conversation is inconclusive. In the end, the notion of present time ("those times are gone," Cisneros claims) is not enough to decide what in this world carries a function of cause. The theatrical mode of presentation holds together the most disparaged materials in a way that makes them coextensive but also, more importantly, that presents them under a form of mutual determination that is not schematized through novelistic time. Staging allows Arguedas to claim that traditions or ideas that can be considered dated still hold essential purchase in the Andes or that some of them can be revitalized. In this sense, staging can be characterized as the presentation of totality under conditions of heterogeneity.

TLS bears its totalizing ambitions already in the title. Cornejo Polar's well-known argument is that the novel represents an expansion of the author's circle of increasing awareness about the determinations of national life in the early 1960s.[15] But the objections raised at the roundtable already indicates that the notion of totality lends itself to a form of synchronization that will fatally rule out as fabled any element that cannot be correlated with the dominant perception of the "state of the world," a perception upon which the social scientists of the 1960s imagined as having almost unrestricted jurisdiction. Henri Favre, clearly conflates experience and temporality in his famous refutation of Arguedas's construction of the indigenous in the novel: "I have lived for two years in Huancavélica ... and did not find Indians, but only exploited peasants."[16] For Favre the subject of immediate experience and scientific truth are correlative and commensurable. For his part and starting with the title of his novel, Arguedas vows to interrogate the effective totality beyond any easy measure of verification. The title not only refers to "all," but it also indicates that this totality is both fluid and composite. As in the case of *Deep Rivers*, the title alludes to an existence that is not so much subterranean as fluid and beyond the mere purview of the present. By the same token, a totality cannot be dated and still be a totality. It is only a residual Hegelianism (the belief that the new configurations sublate the old ones) that gives credibility to this operation. But this does not mean that we should abandon Hegel's reflection on totality altogether since so much of it can serve our argument against the platitudes of positivism. Hegel famously said that "the truth is the totality." This is the phrase that Theodore Adorno mischievously turned around as "the totality is the false." In Hegel, totality means a notion able to gather all the effective determinations that go on to constitute a reality. We can adapt this definition to the universe of *TLS* in which the issue of totality emerges conflated with the question of heterogeneity, lending the whole novel an air of strangeness that has not ceased to disorient its readers.

15. Cornejo Polar, *Los universos narrativos*, 178.
16. Guillermo Rochabrún, ed. *La mesa redonda sobre "Todas las sangres"* (Lima: Pontificia Universidad Católitca del Perú, 2000), 57.

Literature is as a subtle tool to grasp the totality of determinations. But the totality of determinations cannot be synchronized with the tool that aims at representing this totality. That the problem was present to Arguedas seems unquestionable to me. In his posthumous novel, one of the foxes declares, "The word must shatter (desmenuzar) the world." Frances Barraclough's admirable translation is not entirely felicitous at this point, since the Spanish "desmenuzar"—flake, shred, scrutinize—has connotations that are more analytic than merely destructive. The same Fox emphasizes a few lines later: "The word is more precise, and that's why it can be confusing."[17] The word brings into the world more legibility, but it is a legibility to which we can scarcely accommodate our own reified perceptions of reality. Still, the fundamental disposition of the writer toward the world has to pass through an analytic sifting of the materials, discourses, and ideologies that pre-exist the literary intervention. On his speech of acceptance of the Garcilaso de la Vega Prize, Arguedas says: "It was by reading Mariátegui and later Lenin that I found a permanent order in things."[18] The ultimate question here is how this "permanent order of things" finds as an embodiment a delirious novel like *The Foxes* or a seemingly contradictory text like *TLS*?[19]

Beyond Heterogeneity

It is a common place to describe Arguedas's literature in terms of heterogeneity. *TLS* marks a new turn in the confrontation between literature and the heterogeneous, insofar as in the novel heterogeneity is both surpassed and amplified. It is surpassed because some characters cross the line and go to live a life (or death) on the other side: don Andrés Aragón de Peralta, whom the

---

17. Both quotes in José María Arguedas, *The Fox from Up Above and the Fox from Down Below*, trans. Frances Horning Barraclough (Pittsburgh: University of Pittsburgh Press, 2000), 52–3.

18. José María Arguedas, discourse of acceptance of the Garcilaso de la Vega award. Included in *The Fox from up Above*, 270.

19. Arguedas's ethnographic writings are often equally concerned with questions of embodiment and presentation. In "La sierra en el proceso de la cultura peruana," one of the essays selected by Angel Rama for the compilation of Arguedas's ethnographic work, Arguedas quotes Dilthey (the great philosopher of life) to suggest that something akin to the power of Greek tragedy, in which characters embody exterior reality, is necessary to do justice to the drama of the coming into historical maturity of the Andes. More importantly, Arguedas is led to raise the question of presentation even while accepting the dominant Hegelian logic of civilizational evolution. See José María Arguedas, *Formación de una cultura nacional indoamericana*, ed. Angel Rama (Mexico: Siglo XXI, 1989), 9.

Indians buried as one of their own or his wife, considered upon her burial an "Indian in death." The most significant case of this surpassing of heterogeneity is, of course, Rendón Wilka who represents in Arguedas's eye the plasticity of the indigenous people. But heterogeneity is also amplified because the overcoming of heterogeneous barriers does not result in a more intelligible world, but rather in the fact that the non-dialectical overcoming of heterogeneous relations gives way to hybrid and unstable constructions of meaning. Let us look at an exchange between Cabrejos, the engineer in charge of the mining exploration, and Rendón Wilka, the leader of the Indians borrowed in mita by Don Fermin: "I already told you. Don't fuck with me, Rendón. Whoever knows that the sugar-mills give toxic aguardiente to their Indians cannot believe in Pachamama." "That's right chief. This is how it is. For you, chief, there is no *mamapacha*, sure there is not. But in my inside clearly speaks the waterfall" (83).

This dialogue gives an idea of the unity in disjuncture that is *TLS*. But what is really important in this dialogue is that Rendón and Cabrejos are destined to meet. Nothing represents the determination toward the totality in the novel better than these chance-like groupings of characters and worldviews. Where does the push for unity come from? Or better expressed, why is it that the totality of conditions of Peru would be incomplete—it would be false—if were not to include this push for unity? I think that the novel leaves little doubt about this: it comes from capitalism itself, and inside capitalism from the process of accumulation, which is from beginning to end what seems to be at play in the novel. It is in the name of accumulation that Don Bruno and Don Fermin disregarded their filial obligation and stripped their ailing father of his lands; it is because of a lack of accumulated capital that Don Fermín has to ask Don Bruno for his Indians in *mita*; it is in his revulsion for accumulation itself that Don Bruno identifies money as the soul enemy of his spiritual Indians and forbids them to accept a salary. Finally, it is the perspective of the productive mine of Aparcora (whose exploitation like that of the Indians form a clear reference to what Marx called primitive accumulation) that brings all the dramatic elements of the narrative together. This push for unity is also a push for synchronization and in that sense, it addresses the question of the presentation of the totality in ways that are different from and perhaps even antithetical to the theatrical mode of presentation.

Arguedas novelizes the contradictions brought about by the process of capitalist accumulation in the Andes and represents them according to the temporal axes proper to both the novel form and the cumulative temporal style of capitalist recording.[20] However, this literary synchronization brings together onto the same plane and postulates as an effective totality a vast assemblage of

---

20. Commenting on Melisa Moore's book *En la encrucijada. La literatura y las ciencias sociales en el Perú, lecturas paralelas* (Lima: UNMSM, 2003), Mabel Moraña notices that Arguedas's "kaleidoscopic" form of presentation remains unacceptable for the social sciences since it implies "a simultaneity which does not result from an organized temporal synthesis." Mabel Moraña, *Arguedas/Vargas Llosa*, 113.

characters who, insofar as they carry their ground with them, do not submit entirely to the ground provided by the linear account of capital/history/story. The theatrical presentation of the world, meanwhile, does not simply stage the same antagonism that the novelistic form presents diachronically. In a very important and profound sense what counts as antagonism for one style of representation does not count as antagonism for the other. This is so because it is the framework of presentation that confers an antagonic value to this or that element of its conglomerate.

The difference and even contradiction I have outlined between staging and narration structurally rehearse the opposition between abstract symbolic subsumption and the project of embodiment that in the first chapters I traced back to the work of the nativist avant-garde. As a result, the cipher of the relationship of *TLS* to reality must be located not at the level of meaning (a successful or failed accomplishment of its intrinsic realist tendencies) but rather at the level of narrative form. The question of the form of the novel as a clue for Arguedas's own perception of Andean reality was first raised by Alberto Escobar under the heading of a "polyhedron." As the word suggests, Escobar sees the novel as a fragmented surface. However, any fragmentation can be understood as a result of the violent shattering of an original, perhaps organic unity or as the coming into visibility of a multiplicity of determinations. The first option would underscore the dissolution of a world (a trait certainly present in the novel) and the growing crisis of embeddedness so dear to Arguedas's narrative.[21] In this perspective, Arguedas would be a writer reduced to an impotent form of nostalgia, forever carrying with him the repressed perspectives of an indigenous endurance, and who only reluctantly makes room for history and capitalist development in the narrative—painting it with ominous and abject colors. Nevertheless, there is also in the novel an equally uncontestable movement forward that impels all characters into a unified scenario. It is then a matter of establishing if the words and notions that we possess (nostalgia, reality, realism) are enough to account for the fragmentation at stake, or if other notions are necessary; notions able to draw a different genealogy for these fragments or to refute their fragmentary character altogether.

---

21. One of the most poignant examples of this ethics is Arguedas's "Llamado a algunos doctores" ("Appeal to Some Intellectuals,") composed shortly after the round table on "Todas las sangres." In this poem, Arguedas writes: "They say that we no longer know anything, that we are backward, that they will exchange our heads for better ones./ They also say that our heart is not in trune with the times, that it is full of fears,/of tears, like the heart of the calandria, like the heart of a great bull whose/throat is cut, and fo this we are considered impertinent." José María Arguedas, *Obras Completas,* vol. 2 (Lima: Horizonte, 1983), 253.

The Theater of Accumulation

The theatrical mode of presentation accomplishes more than the simultaneous staging of monads proceeding from different temporalities. Precisely because these monads bring their ground with them, staging also works as a criticism and dismantling of the reifying force of formal subsumption—since it is clear that this formal relationship is the only one that capital can entertain with respect to the heterogeneous. The formally subsumed appears to history as a leftover whose ground or context slides into inexistence. Only the writer's words can vivify it. The coming forward of monads who "speak their truth" introduces a passionate attachment to the perspective of the subsumed rather than—as it is almost invariably the case—to the perspective of the subsuming agency. Inhabiting the "now-then" is a prerogative of literature that remains difficult to read from a critical standpoint insofar as criticism has to adopt the perspectives of capital and narration for its grounding. But in all this reasoning, we are assuming too readily that capitalism is per se synonymous with the temporalization of action that we also attribute, without much further ado, to the narrative form as well. In *Limits of Capital*, David Harvey offers a clear example of this diagrammatic imaginary that ties capital to historicism, when he writes that "capitalism is dynamic, expansive, revolutionary."[22] This historicist narrative was subjected from very early on to a counter-imaginary that exposed destruction as the constant underside of development. Walter Benjamin delivered one of its most lasting formulations under the figure of the Angel of History: "Where we perceive a chain of events, he sees one single catastrophe which keeps piling wreckage upon wreckage."[23] This double-sided view of accumulation is already present in Marx, in the section titled "the so-called primitive accumulation" where one of the main effects of the "enclosure of the commons" is a landscape of ruins and depopulation. However, it is possible to read a tremor in the linear logic of accumulation even inside the scientific (rigorous, Harvey calls it) rather than merely historical exposition of accumulation. The famous first line on "The Commodity" in *Capital* reads "The wealth of those societies in which the capitalist mode of production prevails appears as 'an immense collection of commodities.'" "Immense" is an adjective that brings to mind questions of measurement and intelligibility. The German word is *ungeheuren*. It is a word in line with a whole saga of the immeasurable through which the romantics attempted to find an equivalence for the new dimensions of experience, both inner and outer. Actually, the adjective appears sometimes to denote the monstrous, the colossal, the unlimited.[24] The

---

22. David Harvey, *The Limits of Capital* (London: Verso, 2007), 156.

23. Walter Benjamin, *Illuminations*, ed. Hanna Arendt, trans. Harry Zohn (New York: Shocken Books, 1968), 257.

24. Howard Caygill notices that in a context not unlike the one I am exploring here, Clausewitz uses the expression "ungehueren Wirkungen," to designate the "monstruous

ungeheuren (vast, immense, or monstrous) nature of capitalist production immediately brings up in Marx the problem of the presentation of this totality or "collection." Although in this opening line Marx speaks of societies in the plural, once he begins the analysis of the commodity, and especially the analysis of accumulation, he proposes to remain in the limits of the nation alone as a way to reduce the empirical noise that would threaten the theoretical clarification of the matter at hand. This is not the only reduction that Marx operates in the chapter. Constant reduction (not unlike the reduction of positions to monads in *TLS*) is necessary since the object to be delimited constitutes the technical horizon of the description. Without the reduction, the simultaneity of commodities would appear as ontologically maddening as the simultaneity of planes through which Arguedas presents the totality of the Andes in *TLS*. Marx is clear about this character of appearance of a simultaneous manifold that needs to be organized in some analytic fashion. The wealth of societies just appears, pops up before our eyes. This is the way Marx stages the analysis. Historicization is always already a secondary feature. There is a pre-givenness of the world that Marx punctuates by using *Erschein* as the verb that sustains the visibility of the commodity form, rather than any of the verbal forms associated with presentation or representation—as some translations of *Capital* into English actually suggest. Thus, *Capital* confronts the reader with a dichotomy between a mode of presentation that seeks to control the variables of the analysis and the actual form of existence of the world of commodities that is itself uncontrollable. The question of how to stage the theater of commodities is an essential rhetorical problem in the opening volume of *Capital*. Marx himself treats accumulation as a theater of shadows in which essential relationships are exhibited, represented, and rehearsed: "Exchange value cannot be anything other than the mode of expression, the 'form of appearance' of a content distinguishable from it."[25] (In his notorious exegesis of the pair *Vorstellung-Darstellung* in Althusser's reading of Marx, George Hartley does not fail to notice that *Darstellung* means also "theatrical representation.")[26] Accumulation itself is progressive or narrative only at a second degree (as turned into capital). However, at any synchronic stage, the process is characterized by a complex assemblage of production/destruction whose outcome, properly recoded, can be "creative," (Schumpeter) or profitable once money secures the commercial fungibility of all existence. Progressive—readable—accumulation happens only as a recoding over of the original scene

effects" of the French revolution. Howard Caygill, *On Resistance. A Philosophy of Defiance* (London: Bloomsbury, 2013), 20.

25. Karl Marx, *Capital: A Critique of Political Economy*, vol. 1, trans. Ben Fowkes (New York: Vintage Books, 1977), 127.

26. George Hartley, *The Abyss of Representation. Marxism and the Postmodern* (Durham, NC: Duke University Press, 2003).

of production, which is not inherently cumulative.[27] This is, of course, Fernand Braudel's thesis, for whom capitalist accumulation results from a constant process of abstraction and reification that recodes the multiple into some form of linearity.[28] If this is the case, it should be possible to propose a loose isomorphic relationship between theatrical simultaneity and the simultaneity that presides over accumulation as a dystopic (rather than utopian or organized) process of coding existence. With isomorphic, I am not suggesting that *TLS* mimics the always conflictive and non-linear form of the capitalist process of accumulation in Peru. This may be true or not, but nothing is gained by saying that chaos resembles chaos. If the isomorphism in question holds any interest, it is insofar as accumulation is the light that illuminates whatever comes into focus in the narrative. In other words, insofar as capitalism is what brings together and binds the different kaleidoscopic elements of this narrative, it has also a power of disclosure even when a transparency of being is essentially inimical to its essence. Capitalism cathects. The capitalist development of the highlands is necessary because life itself has ceased to be one of its attributes. With the exploitation of the mine, "we would come back to live in the eyes of the world" says Don Fermín—actually in the eyes of capital and by means of capital. Here too, the eye through which I see God is the same eye through which God sees me.[29] This is life in the dimension of subsumption, but Arguedas says that another life exists. Literary critics found the naive expressionism of Arguedas's characters disconcerting. But one may speculate if part of the critical discomfort does not originate in an inversion in which the characters appear in terms of their content (to which no expression can ever correspond) rather than in terms of a cognizable "form of appearance" that would correspond to them in the subsumptive logic of capitalist attribution of being. It is this tautology of capitalism (verisimilitude is tautological at heart) that Arguedas's characters ruin with their overly theatrical, earnest, and over the top commitment to expression. Capital illuminates them and they perform poorly in the eyes of capital; is this not, in the last instance, what the roundtable confusedly and involuntary articulates?

Capital illuminates. It sanctions, gives birth, and visibility to the full extension of the sayable and the visible even when it remains exterior to the whole universe of phenomena that come to life in the perspective of its rays. In the Braudelian perspective, this exteriority of capital to markets (and to the

---

27. Left to itself, capitalism would degenerate into anarchic production. This is the thesis admirably argued by Richard Ohmann in *Selling Culture. Magazines, Markets and Class at the Turn of the Century* (London: Verso, 1998).

28. Fernand Braudel, *The Wheels of Commerce. Civilization & Capitalism 15th-18th Century*, vol. 2, trans. Siân Reynolds (Cambridge: Harper & Row, 1988).

29. Barthes evokes these lines by Angelus Silesius to describe an undifferentiated gaze in *Le Plaisir du texte* (Paris: du Seuil, 1973), 29.

scene of production in general) would be a constitutive limit of capital—the one that neo-liberalism intends to incorporate as a productive moment of reproduction itself. In one of those conversations that are as a matter of fact speeches in a forum, Don Fermín insults Cabrejos by describing him as a figure of "bad capital," a vampire-like form of excising life:

> In you, [Rendón] smelled the emptiness, the nothingness that covets power, blind in order to kill and devour. In the United States or in England, you would not be such a rare monster. Here … you are like a man who needs to kill in order to borrow a soul, since by itself, your nature is incapable of harboring a spirit. (164)

The theatrical form claims that the world is conceivable from a vantage point other than the centrifugal point at which all equivalences can be expressed by an absolute supernumerary. What sustains the isomorphic principle is, however, the work of visibility itself, the task of presentation that, I claim in a perhaps heretic Heideggerian fashion, should be attributed to the capitalist principle of accumulation. As Reiner Schurman put it: "Phenomena are phenomena for epochal principles."[30] Of course, Heidegger would have never sustained that capital constituted an epochal principle, the "honor" was instead deferred to technologies and machines—and yet Deleuze and Guattari thought that capitalism itself is nothing but a machine or an assemblage of machines.

The emergence of capital as a dominant hegemon (the revocable principle that allows things to be, to be seen, to be perceived) coincides or overlaps with the total dissolution of previous forms of donation. In this sense, it is significant that Don Bruno "lends" his Indians to Don Fermín and that he vehemently identifies interest and profit with soul corruption. The principle of illumination inaugurated by the decline of the sovereign paradigm and its replacement by an elusive supernumerary ("The one with money is the one in charge") does not throw a particularly intense light. Some characters, like Rendón Wilka, remain enigmatic and in the shadows, his potentiality for being much higher than what he actually becomes. The theatrical mode of presentation remains ambivalent regarding how it is going to harness the singularity of the monadic to the impetus of the historical at large.

Mapping in Fragmentation

One can hear echoes of Hegel in Fredric Jameson's argument that since social relations are intrinsically opaque, they need to be "figured" or represented.

---

30. Reiner Schurmann, *Heidegger on Being and Acting: From Principles to Anarchy*, trans. Christine-Marie Gros (Bloomington: Indiana University Press, 1987), op.cit, 41.

For Jameson, literature makes available to many a reflection of their own conditions of life through a sensible and interpersonal form.[31] However, each cycle of capitalist accumulation and each mutation in how capitalism goes about the business of colonizing the world introduces new forms of opacity and consequently, different demands on the task of mapping in which literature is always and necessarily implicated. The axes of the reproduction of capital and the axes of the reproduction of life trace two divergent lines.[32] This is an immediate effect of "monopoly capitalism," whose apprehension is often limited to how imperialist ventures encroach and endanger local economies of life and meaning. Remarkably, the disorienting effect of capital accumulation is as intense in the center as it is in the periphery:

> The experience of the individual subject—traditionally, the supreme raw material of the work of art—becomes limited to a tiny corner of the social world ... the truth of that experience no longer coincides with the place in which it takes place. The truth of the daily experience of London lies, rather, in India, Jamaica or Hong Kong; it is bound up with the whole colonial system of the British Empire that determines the very quality of the individual's subjective life. Yet those structural coordinates are no longer accessible to immediate lived experience.[33]

After acknowledging that this creates a paradox in which if individual experience is authentic it cannot be true, and if a scientific view results true, it will not coincide with individual experience; Jameson finds a respite to this problem in national allegories. Allegory may be able to express the absent cause through "distorted and symbolic" means. In this way, these figures can reach "the ultimate realities" that evade experience on a daily basis. Is not a failure to allegorize the Andean world what his critics resented about Arguedas's novel at the roundtable? The notion of cognitive mapping does not aim at an accurate reproduction of the conditions of life under capitalism, but rather at a figuration that could allow certain groups to act on the bases of an assumed and shared knowledge of what the current world is about. In other words, the quest is for an operational notion of social truth able to ground political and social agency.

---

31. Jameson writes, "All thinking today is also, whatever else it is, an attempt to think the world system as such." Fredric Jameson, *The Geo-Political Aesthetic. Cinema and Space in the World System* (Bloomington: Indiana University Press, 1992), 4.

32. Does the actual subsumption of life into capital cancel this dichotomy? Or is the ground of life and of the subject located in an alternate location refractory to capitalist colonization? In other words: do the symbolic and its rationalizations overlap with the totality of existence? How one answers the first question will depend on how one feels about the second.

33. Jameson, *Postmodernism*, 411.

Although their objections were couched in a positivist language of "what can be seen or observed in the highlands," what his critics objected to Arguedas at the roundtable was the lack of such operational truth.

It is disputable that the notion of mapping advanced by Jameson can elude the traps of realism that the same Jameson denounces in his most recent work on the concept. Allegory implies a hermeneutic circle in which the mapping that the novel is supposed to provide has as its condition of possibility a reader who is more or less already acquainted with the map. Mapping seems to designate a hegemonic operation consubstantial to the idea of recognition—that is grounded on a previous submission to the general aesthesis of a time. This is precisely the function of mapping contested (rather than "not achieved") by Arguedas in *TLS*—and in some sense in all his literary works. That Arguedas produced the "wrong allegory" in the eyes of his critics does not mean that allegorical recourse is absent from the pages of *TLS*. On the contrary, there are several instances in the novel when Arguedas attempts to allegorize a desirable political and ideological alliance that would make viable the presence of his indigenous characters in an anti-imperialist crusade. One of the political questions of the novel is indeed, what is the place of the indigenous people in this projected national coalition. This question is sustained, not refused, solved or idealized in the novel. This is another way of saying that Arguedas does not foreclose the dimension of the future or the role of historicity upon the constitution of particular subjectivities, even if his method of exposing the effect of time upon substance bewildered so many of his readers.

Nietszchean Huayco

Arguedas thought that the whole of Peru was in this novel. However, the totality is given through a remarkable paradox since the place where all determinations are gathered is an isolated region of the Peruvian highlands. Characters travel to San Pedro de Lahuaymarca or are born there. Lima and the coast are mentioned, but we know about what transpires there in that style that the Greek tragedians called obscene—by indirect means, outside our view. Through this narrative strategy, *TLS* seems to take on the paradox described by Jameson, seeking simultaneously to be the totality of determinations and the singularity of life. Something that *TLS* makes clear is that although the truth may be the totality, this totality does not have as a correlate a singular spiritual development, but rather a plurality of monads whose interactions cannot be really subsumed by any unified narrative. So, the question of the totality should be thought in terms other than the dialectic between staging—which accommodates the plurality—and historical streaming—which schematizes and sacrifices singularity in favor of a destinal meaning. Arguedas has at least three words to think on the simultaneous uprooting and continuity of cultural traditions: *Yawar mayu*, *lloqlla* and *huayco*. These are—as Althusser says of

Marx's use of *Darstellung* "metaphors ... which are already ... almost perfect concepts."[34] It is important then not to translate them too quickly, but rather respect, as much as possible, the horizon of their unfolding.

Regarding these terms, William Rowe writes:

> Among the symbols that embody the rupture of barriers, there are two that are especially salient: the *yawar mayu* and the *huayco*. A powerful symbol in Arguedas's production, the *yawar mayu* connotes an overflowing force that gathers within it all uprooted elements. It is a tragic force, but one that also signals a regeneration.[35]

In my reading, the *huayco*, the *lloqlla* and the *yawar mayu* are not symbols, but rather, metaphors that are almost concepts. The symbol is an intuition. It names certitude about an immediate access to a meaning or a suprasensible ideal. The simplicity of the expression is supposed to match the self-contained nature of the essential. But there is nothing simple in the *huayco* or the *yawar mayu*. They are compounds of time and meaning that, modeled after natural phenomena are relatively free of the weight that for centuries had tied intelligibility to the double valence of the eidos as both form (idea) and transcendence (ideal).

Arguedas himself explains the *yawar mayu* as "the bloody river, for in Quechua that is what we call the first flash flood of the rivers that carry the juices developed on the mountaintops and in the abysses by insects, sun, moon, and music."[36] *Yawar Mayu* is the river of blood that runs through Don Bruno when he suffers in his flesh the contradictions that history accumulated in the Andes for centuries. A character who witnesses the moment Don Bruno kills Cisneros says that a river of blood ran through the *gamonal's* eyes. This is why Feldman, who also reads these metaphors as concepts, invites an identification of the *Yawar mayu* with Walter Benjamin's pure (unalloyed) violence: the violence that stands outside the separation between law and justice's means and ends. The *huayco* and the *lloqlla* have similar connotations. They are carriers, figures of remembrance, containers of experience in their own right. These notions act as a transindividual (or better metasubjective) conditions. They point to a possible dialectic that will be implicated but not entirely determined by the volitional structure of its actors.

There is also a figural aspect that should not be overlooked. The *huayco*, the *yawar mayu*, and the *lloqlla* are rivers. They run from the highlands to the coast. The movement, Arguedas writes in one of his essays, "must

---

34. Louis Althusser and Etienne Balibar, *Reading Capital*, trans. Ben Brewster (London: Verso, 1990), 192.

35. William Rowe, "Deseo, escritura y fuerzas productivas," in *El zorro de arriba y el zorro de abajo*, ed. E.-M. Fell (Mexico: Colección Archivos, 1992), 336.

36. Arguedas, *Fox from Up Above*, 83.

follow and does follow from East to West, as is commonly said, from the past to the present, from stillness to dynamism."[37] Thus understood, the *huayco* is the concept of the historical. Not surely of a history understood along the traditional lines of positivism and historicism, but rather along the lines of what, in his discussion of Nietzsche, Michel Foucault exhumes as *wirklich histoire*, actual history. Foucault says that what Nietzsche found most troublesome in the idea of history was the silent inclusion of a supra historical perspective that is "always already teleological," ready to ground its judgments and perspectives "on an apocalyptic objectivity."[38] I don't think it farfetched to speculate that the presentation of multiple monads developing in time is grounded in Arguedas in a thinking of the historical for which the transitory nature of time weighs much more than its apocalyptic resolution. The resolution in Arguedas is not of a humanist nature (the *yawar mayu* and the *llolla* are not personifications in any sense), but neither is Nietzsche's effective history, since it comes to replace an overtly narcissistic exercise on the temporal with a history impossible to appropriate or reappropriate by any spirit (or subject) whatsoever.

To say that *huayco* is the notion of the historical does not mean that *huayco* and history think or intend the same region of being. The dazzling nature of Arguedas's concept lies precisely in the way that it limits (not always, not absolutely) any possible act of translation. Neither is it a matter, then, of establishing a superiority of the *huayco* over the Western notion of the historical or to propose a lax equivalence between *huayco* and *wirkliche historie*. History is a concept that allowed us to think many, marvelous things: from the notion of a history of everydayness to the bizarre idea that history has its secretaries. *Llolqla, huayco* and *yawar mayu* are concepts that allow us to think other things. I can sense and suggest what these may be, but not fully or completely know. A few preliminary indications are possible just by attending to what Arguedas himself says in his novels. *Huayco, yawar mayu, lloqla* are all fluid metaphors. They open nonsubsumptive possibilities that allow for disclosures and articulations that would result foreclosed in a cumulative, dialectical historical perspective. They are not themselves subject, but subjects can use them as mirrors of their fate. They are forms of recording (or reflection) despite being tumultuous, and they ignore the sharp separation between the human and the natural, between the sensible quality of the *res extensa,* and the disincarnated thinking of reason. And Arguedas plays them anytime that a traditional or dominant form of indicating causality and connection faltered or felt incomplete.

---

37. The passage of clear Hegelian overtones is found in "La sierra en el proceso de la cultura peruana" (10).

38. Michel Foucault, "Nietzsche, Genealogy, History," in *Language, Couner-Memory, Practice,* selected Essays and Interviews by Michel Foucault, ed. Donald F. Bourchard (Ithaca, NY: Cornell University Press, 1977), 139–64.

Perhaps *TLS* is like a *huayco* and not a kaleidoscope; perhaps the fluid and not the fragment is the essential way in which the novel intends its world. In this perspective, *huayco* would be a mode of presentation of the totality and a specific contribution to the criticism of history as an ontology of formal subsumption. With it, Arguedas provided us not only with a powerful image so we can steal a glance at the question of "how the other thinks," but more decisively a concept able to implicate us—his readers—in the always necessary task of forging new words for the unveiling of the real as the precondition for the construction of a world in which the subject can feel one step closer to home.

Chapter 6

PSYCHOTIC VIOLENCE:
CRIME AND CONSUMPTION IN THE
APOCALYPTIC PHASE OF CAPITAL

> No one pays attention to these killings, but the secret of the world is hidden in them.
> —Roberto Bolaño, *2666*[1]

For three consecutive years, between 2009 and 2011, Ciudad Juárez was ranked as the most violent nonwar zone in the world. At that time, "images poured out of the desert ... with visions of beheadings, car-jackings, child assassins, abandoned houses, extortion ... the bodies of raped and murdered women dumped in public spaces."[2] The violence hounded working women with particular tenacity. A description from Sergio González Rodríguez, the Mexican journalist who produced the first extensive media research on Juárez, evokes images of generic and inexorable cruelty: "The victims were abducted from the streets ... and taken by force into safe houses where they were raped, tortured, and murdered at stag parties or orgies."[3] Marcela Lagarde y de los Rios notices that the modality of the victims' deaths speaks of their subtraction from any form of social bond, even that of hatred: "Humiliated, tortured, mutilated, ... they were killed in cold blood and their bodies were left in the street, in the desert, or in open spaces."[4] The citizens of Juárez became accustomed to seeing

---

1. Roberto Bolaño, *2666*, translated by Natasha Wimmer (New York: Picador, 2009), 348.
2. Alice Driver, *More or Less Dead: Feminicide, Haunting, and the Ethics of Representation in Mexico* (Tucson: University of Arizona Press, 2015), xii.
3. Sergio González Rodríguez's inaugural investigation, *Huesos en el desierto* (Barcelona: Anagrama, 2010) was partially translated as *The Femicide Machine*, trans. Michael Parker-Stainback (Los Angeles: Semiotext(e), 2012), 72–3.
4. Marcela Lagarde y de los Rios, "Preface: Feminist Keys for Understanding Feminicide. Theoretical, Political, and Legal Construction," in *Terrorizing Women: Feminicide in the Américas*, ed. Rosa-Linda Fregoso and Cynthia Bejarano (Durham, NC: Duke University Press, 2010), xv.

their faces in the multitude of flyers that cover the streets of the downtown, insistently asking: Have you seen her?

Aberrant, pathological, and unprosecuted, the violence against women put into circulation a new word in the Spanish vocabulary: *feminicidio*—a crime committed not against a person but against a category. Certainly, deaths of men are numerically higher in Ciudad Juárez than those of women; however, unlike women, "men are not killed *because* they are men."[5]

The deepest risk here concerns promoting a vision of the feminicides in terms of a generic and ahistorical notion of violence. In any discussion of this term, Walter Benjamin's "Critique of Violence" often comes readily to mind. The teratology of death that surrounds narco-violence in Mexico—especially regarding the feminicides—exceeds all the oppositions that Benjamin deploys in his text for thinking violence, whether those of natural versus historical violence or of law-preserving versus lawmaking violence. Benjamin himself provides the clue for such incommensurability when, in the opening paragraph of the essay, he spells out the parameters of his investigation as "that of expounding [the] relation [of violence] to law and justice."[6] The violence of Juárez relates to the order of the law only negatively. It is not an ordinary type of violence, but a psychotic violence.

The expression "psychotic violence" is not meant to suggest a psychological profile. It says nothing about the perpetrators of this violence. Psychotics are rarely violent.[7] Why, then, label this violence "psychotic?" The characterization was suggested to me by the complex network of social and political activism that arose in Juárez as a communal response to the crimes. This activism displays an ever renewed attempt to infuse a symbolic dimension in a reality that is perceived as senseless and inimical to communication. In reaction to the crimes, writes Marcela Lagarde y de los Rios, "A particular culture … emerged … constituted by literary and poetic, pictorial, sculptural, musical, photographic, theatrical, filmic, and other artistic creations."[8] Kathleen Staudt notices that "at the border, anti-femicide activists have communicated, silently and loudly, with the use of symbols … They painted names and colors in

---

5. Rosa-Linda Fregoso and Cynthia Bejarano, "Introduction: A Cartography of Feminicide in the Americas," in *Terrorizing Women: Feminicide in the Américas*, ed. Fregoso and Bejarano (Durham, NC: Duke University Press, 2010), 7.

6. Walter Benjamin, "Critique of Violence," *Reflections: Essays, Aphorisms, Autobiographical Writings*, ed. Peter Demetz, trans. Edmund Jephcott (New York: Schocken Books, 1978), 277.

7. Bruce Fink, *A Clinical Introduction to Lacanian Psychoanalysis: Theory and Technique* (Cambridge, MA: Harvard University Press, 1999), 77. On the other hand, the word "psychosis" has emerged constantly in reports profiling perpetrators of sexually aggravated assaults. See for instance, Lagarde y de los Rios, "Preface," xiii.

8. Lagarde y de los Rios, "Preface," xii.

crosses, dresses, and public signs … Victims' mothers and activists repeated stories, showed pictures, and gave personal testimonies at rallies, creating vivid memories with personal names and faces attached to them."[9] This emphasis on communication likewise permeates academic, journalistic, and political writings on the crimes. Counterintuitively, bodies that have been stripped of any signification, tossed outside of the networks of state, family, and community, are perceived as containing a message or hiding a meaning. Julia Estela Monárrez Fragoso contends: "It is possible to read the mutilated bodies as 'signs' that circulate socially."[10] Rita Laura Segato joins a long list of commentators who see in the barbaric, anomic crimes a form of writing: the feminicides are "messages sent by a subject/author who can be identified, located, and profiled only by rigorously 'listening' to these crimes as communicative acts."[11] For his part, Sergio González Rodríguez writes: "Messages, wounds, marks, mutilation, and torture have been inscribed in those bodies."[12] Against the anomie of the crimes, their lack of expression, and their anchorage in an evil without passion, activists and analysts proceed to a restitution of the absent socius and a strengthening of the binding character that the law seems to have lost in its confrontation with a reality that only recognizes as its limit the dissolution of every limit.[13]

In its uttermost generality, psychotic violence is a violence without other: an act performed *as if* the other didn't exist—actually performed in the utter indistinction between reality and the *as if*. By "other," I mean simultaneously these others who are present before me in an everyday sense (what Freud called the *Nebenmensch*: fellow human beings) as well as the binding system of habits and cultural and political beliefs that allow human beings to build a common world—what Lacan termed the big Other. It is because the other answers my call that I know that my relationship to the Other is adjusted to intangible and yet forceful parameters. When the avenues to the Other are blocked, so are the paths of empathy.

Far from being a Mexican exceptionality, psychotic violence is the predominant type of violence in the world today, and it is always spectacular

---

9. Kathleen Staudt, *Violence and Activism at the Border: Gender, Fear and Everyday Life in Ciudad Juárez* (Austin: University of Texas Press, 2008), 19.

10. Julia Estela Monárrez Fragoso, "The Victims of the Ciudad Juárez Feminicide," in *Terrorizing Women: Feminicide in the Américas*, ed. Rosa-Linda Fregoso and Cynthia Bejarano (Durham, NC: Duke University Press, 2010), 60.

11. Rita Laura Segato, "Territory, Sovereignty and Crimes of the Second State: The Writing on the Body of Murdered Women," in *Terrorizing Women: Feminicide in the Américas*, ed. Fregoso and Bejarano (Durham, NC: Duke University Press, 2010), 80.

12. González Rodríguez, *Femicide Machine*, 13.

13. González Rodríguez speaks of the "central concern" in Juárez as "the reconstruction of the political and economic fabric of a city, devastated by the symbiosis between local power, drug traffickers, and US interests," *Femicide Machine*, 25.

since it emerges in the place of something that can no longer contain it. Psychotic violence is the violence of the drone that kills, like all machines, innocently; it is the violence of the summary executions of Black people by the police; it is also the more democratic execution committed by the mass shooter, who likewise kills without reason and discernment. It is more and more the violence that assaults us from the pages of newspapers, the characteristic psychopathology of our everyday life—a violence tied to an irrepressible passage to the act and to a massive failure of symbolization. What is privative about Juárez are its outer forms. But even these forms are bound to repeat themselves in all areas in which strong institutional restraints—or what is left of them—are unable to facilitate the transition from local conditions of existence to the exposure to neoliberal globalization as an experience of unrestricted global war.[14]

The State and the Exception

According to Amnesty International, 373 women were killed or disappeared in the Ciudad Juárez area from 1993 to 2003 (the year range is arbitrary; there were crimes before and after these dates). According to the United Nations, the number for this period was 328; according to the Attorney General of the state of Chihuahua it was 110; and according to several nongovernmental organizations, the figure was no less than 500. Faced with unreliable state data, Julia Estela Monárrez Fragoso conducted her own investigation. By her estimate, 382 killings or disappearances involving women and girls were registered in Juárez between 1993 and 2004.[15]

A perverse uncertainty predominates regarding the number and pathologies of the crimes. Are they (relatively) few, as reported by the State of Chihuahua, or are they more than what is usually believed, as several NGOs and private investigations claim? Even acknowledging different ranges in dates, how can the counts be so disparate? And why so many different attempts to count? A striking element throughout the bibliography and cultural production surrounding the feminicides is the impossibility of actually establishing what

---

14. Rita Laura Segato is one of the many commentators who place the Ciudad Juárez crimes in a global perspective. In her book *La guerra contra las mujeres* (Madrid-Buenos Aires: Traficantes de Sueños, 2016), she writes, "The humble dead women of Juarez ... awaken and lead us to the most lucid reading of the transformations experienced by the world today, as it becomes more terrifying and inhospitable by the second" (52). On globalization and global world see Carlo Galli, *Political Spaces and Global World*, ed. Adam Sitze, trans. Elisabeth Fay (Minneapolis: University of Minnesota Press, 2010).

15. Julia Estela Monárrez Fragoso, *Juárez, Trama de una injusticia: Feminicidio sexual sistemático en Ciudad Juárez* (Ciudad Juárez, Mexico: Colegio de la Frontera Norte, 2009), 93.

type of phenomena and what sets of facts are mobilized by the crimes.[16] The crisis of the real reached such proportions that in 2009 the Inter-American Commission on Human Rights rejected as unreliable the data presented by the Mexican authorities on the feminicides.[17] The contradictory versions; the inability to solve at least one case of forced disappearance of women and children; the grotesque involvement of the police in the illegal trafficking of drugs and human beings; and finally the impotence of efforts to construct a conceptual framework with regard to the feminicides bespeaks a profound crisis in the function of the state as a guarantor of truth in a country where the relationship between the state and truth is a particularly strong one, insofar as the drive to count the uncounted and to represent the unrepresented constituted the pillar of the social order built after the demise of the Porfirian oligarchy.

Once the state relinquishes its role as the arbiter of the real, it is not clear what other functions are left to it. In the case of Juárez, this uncertainty led police agencies to a renewed disavowal of their own function through what many activists have called a revictimization of the victims. Families denouncing a kidnapping or a disappearance often found the authorities uncooperative or unconcerned. Police and state agencies claimed that the victims were gang members (when they were women working 10-hour shifts); that they came from dysfunctional families and marriages (an indirect admission of the perceived threat represented by the assertiveness and economic independence of many migrant women); or that they lived lives on the margins of law and society (as if such a trait, even when true, would excuse the aberrant crimes). In this way, relatives and victims met a common fate at the hands of state officials, "treated unjustly, with contempt, paternalism, lack of professionalism, negligence, and violence."[18] For a while the mass media collaborated with this picture that lent the madness a veneer of rationality, but public uproar forced it into a different position.[19]

16. In the introduction to the third edition to *Huesos en el desierto*, González Rodríguez notices the big variations in the number of victims according to different sources and wonders about the generic indetermination of his own text.

17. González Rodríguez, *Femicide Machine*, 77.

18. Lagarde y de los Rios, "Preface," xii.

19. Prejudices and unprofessionalism alone are not enough to explain police inattention to the crimes. The inaction of the authorities should also be seen in light of some stupefying statistics about the bribery of state representatives in areas of heavy drug trafficking. According to José Z. García, "at one point 90 percent of the police officers, prosecutors, and judges in Tijuana and the state of Baja California were on the Arellano Félix payroll ... and the cartel pays up to US 1 million a week in bribes to law officials." José Z. García, "Security Regimes on the U.S.-Mexico Border," *Transnational Crime and Public Security: Challenges to Mexico and the United States*, ed. John Bailey and Jorge Chabat (La Jolla: Center for U.S.-Mexican Studies/University of California, San Diego, 2002), 322.

The reduction of the voice of the state to one murmur among others (and not the most credible of them) determines that all the different discourses about the feminicides exist at the same level. No discourse can take preeminence over the others. This fact alone explains the freedom with which interventions, analyses, and texts move easily between the fictional and the legal, the sociological and the hypothetical, or the critical and the testimonial. All of them navigate with equal rights an amorphous discursive space. By the same token, the lack of the state's answers to the crimes contrasts with the multiplication of discourses that seek not only to denounce and expose the murders, but more important, to uncover their subtending logic; to deduce their motives and conditions of possibility; in the end, to understand them in such a way that a challenge to their continuous perpetration may become thinkable.

However, these many forms of struggle and redress confront the dissolution of the sphere of the political as perhaps their most formidable obstacle. Reality as a shared construction dissolves as state and society alike are caught in the grip of a paralyzing lack of an epistemology of the present. In this situation, "appearances and perceptions have displaced mechanisms of the past that once offered meaning within a collective coexistence."[20] The dominance of neoliberal injunctions has exacerbated (if not in good part created) this cognitive-political impasse.[21]

In the Order of Causality

Scholarly work on the feminicides displays two emphases. The first underlines the role of misogyny and the historically subordinate position of women as the fundamental condition behind the propagation of the crimes and of the violence against women.[22] The second seeks to clarify the socioeconomic and structural conditions that favor or frame a landscape of violence of which the feminicides are just a part. Marcela Lagarde y de Los Rios summarizes the first perspective when she attributes the crimes to "the patriarchal, hierarchical,

---

20. "Photographer Julián Cardona on Juárez and the Limits of Photography," (interview) in Alice Driver, *More or less Dead. Feminicide, Haunting and the Ethics of Representation in Mexico* (Tucson: University of Arizona Press, 2015), 26–31.

21. For Sigmund Freud, one of the distinguishing features of psychosis (he used the word schizophrenia) was the rejection of reality. See "Psycho-analytic Notes on an Autobiographical Account of a Case of Paranoia," *The Standard Edition of the Complete Psychological Works of Sigmund Freud*, translated by James Strachey (London: Vintage, 2001), 12:1–82.

22. A distinction should be made between the criminal assault on women by gangs and organized groups and the crimes committed against women in the domestic sphere or in the context of family relationships.

and social organization of gender."[23] This approach heavily contextualizes the feminicides in a set of institutional strictures such as family, education, and security. Its strategy often consists of demanding state recognition for the plight of women and the instrumentation of measures to address it. It does not ignore that there is an always changing shape of social domination that exacerbates and reinscribes patriarchal strategies in ever evolving ways, but its focus is primarily institutional.[24] No other discourse has done more to reshape social and state practices that bear decisively on violence against women and the institutional frameworks to address it. Its effectiveness can be seen in three specific efforts: to identify the types of violence exerted upon women, which has led to specific forms of prosecution and prevention;[25] to raise challenges to Mexican legislation, thanks to which the latter now recognizes gender violence as a distinctive sphere requiring its own forms of protection;[26] and to stress the global implications of the discourse on human rights, which is a particularly important perspective both in Mexico and the larger Latin American context where human rights violations have been a constant of the late Cold War period.[27]

The second, socioeconomic, perspective, which sees the feminicides as the result of the precarization of life under neoliberalism, is best represented by Sergio González Rodríguez's *The Femicide Machine*. The Mexican journalist

23. Lagarde y de Los Rios, "Preface," xix and xi.

24. Julia Estela Monárrez Fragoso points to the widespread reification of women and to the pressure of neoliberal globalization on the production of consumable identities as fundamental to the renewed forms of gender subjection. Fregoso, "The Victims of the Ciudad Juárez Feminicide," 61.

25. Lagarde y de los Rios comments that when victims had been sexually assaulted, initial police investigations took into account a victim's gender only "as one more item of information," Lagarde y de los Rios, "Preface," xv.

26. The characterization of feminicide as a specific type of crime entered Mexico's legislation in 2004 and three years later was also adopted by the legislature of the state of Chihuahua.

27. Although Mexico was the first Latin American country to typify femicide as a crime, an important ruling by the Inter-American Commission on Human Rights (IACHR) found the country in violation of international agreements on human rights for failing to adequately investigate the murders of Juárez. An account of the OAS ruling and comparison to other legislations in Latin America can be found in Patsilí Toledo Vásquez, *Femicidio/Feminicidio* (Buenos Aires: Ediciones Didot, 2014), 91–139. See also Ana Elena Badilla, *Femicidio: más allá de la violación del derecho a la vida; análisis de los derechos violados y las responsabilidades estatales en los casos de femicidio en Ciudad Juárez* (San José, Costa Rica: Instituto Interamericano de Derechos Humanos, 2008). On the case of the cotton field murders, see the web page of Grupo de Acción de Derechos Humanos (NGO), https://grupodeacciondhh.org.

does not ignore the weight of misogynistic attitudes in the crimes, but he sees that misogyny intensified and renewed by the reshaping of economic and social relationships in the northern frontier. Misogynistic attitudes are aggravated by the emergence of an independent and sexualized type of women against the background of a generalized crisis of masculine social roles.[28]

González Rodríguez also calls attention to the role of spatiality in the disintegration of traditional forms of sociability, pointing to the material changes suffered by the living texture of the city as one of the agents of the dislocation to which the crimes attest. These material transformations are part and parcel of the anxiety about symbolization betrayed in Juárez' activism.[29] For González Rodríguez, the decomposition of social space served as a precondition for the decomposition of socially validated forms of symbolic efficacy. Juárez's integration within the scope of NAFTA—an integration that preceded the 1992 agreement by decades—accelerated the city's exposure to global economic flows that completely reshaped its contours. González Rodríguez summarizes: Capital "was given free rein to play God with the landscape," and a flow of unregulated investments turned the city into "an almost unimaginable" space. A forceful neoliberal splintering of social space led to the multiplication of slums, and squatting in uninhabitable buildings became the norm. Traditional communities were exposed to rapid disintegration, and new communities were born already uprooted and fragile. The main agent of these changes was the maquila, which since 1965 began to exert an almost uncontested power in decisions regarding the overall planning of the city.[30]

---

28. Leslie Salzinger, *Genders in Production: Making Workers in Mexico's Global Factories* (Berkeley: University of California Press, 2003), 17.

29. Lacan "borrows" the notion of the symbolic and of symbolic efficacy not from de Saussure's "semiology," but from Levi-Strauss's studies of the spatial distribution of dwellings in indigenous villages.

30. The history of Juárez as a future neoliberal enclave began just after the middle of the twentieth century, with the passage of the 1965 legislation that paved the way for the maquila industry. For decades the presence of the maquilas grew in the desert. But by 2004, Juárez had over three hundred factories and more than 200,000 workers, more than half of them women. The city is home to important American and international corporations such as Bosch, Electrolux, Lexmark, Foxconn, Boeing, and Siemens. Unlike the United States, where these companies are careful to dissociate themselves from causes that can be deemed politically incorrect, the transnational corporations in Juárez have done virtually nothing to alleviate the conditions leading to the city's horrendous crimes. For González Rodríguez they have done just the opposite, spreading working conditions that strip their employees "of every political status and reduce them completely to naked life." (*The Femicide Machine*, 23). For a similar observation, see Diana Washington Valdez, *Harvest of Women: Safari in Mexico; the Truth About Mexico's Bloody Border Legacy* (Burbank, CA: Peace at the Border, 2006), 15.

In his novel *2666*, Roberto Bolaño does not fail to notice the preeminent role of biopolitically determined zones of abandonment in the geography of the crimes. In the novel, the criminals disseminate the bodies of the murdered women in dumpsters, wastelands, deserts, and other deeply anomic spaces. The unimaginable city and the zone of abandonment are the counterfigures of a foreclosed act of imagination.[31]

González Rodríguez's insistence on the fundamental solidarity between crime and neoliberalism dismantles the neat oppositions in the global economy of desire in terms of "countries of homeostasis" and "countries of jouissance."[32] When Charles Bowden gave the title *Juárez. Laboratory of our Future* to his famous journalistic and photographic exploration of the feminicides, he implied that it was only a matter of time before the techniques, the anxieties, and the world-forming conditions active in Juárez will fully emerge in the first world. For González Rodríguez what unites machine and crime is not a direct causality but a trait: the compulsive automatism that governs economic calculation and pathological violence alike. Between the maquiladora-machine and the city-machine there is a sympathy but also an ontological abyss. The maquiladora-machine is planned, self-regulated, serviced, and well connected to the world in accordance with the rules of post-Fordist global exchange. A female worker in a maquila travels from one of the most advanced facilities in the world to one of its the poorest and worst-serviced urban environments during the time that it takes for the buses (owned and operated by maquila companies) to deposit her in the outskirts of Ciudad Juárez. This is the limit of the maquila involvement with the city, and this limit makes the maquila unimpeachable.

The War against Women

In her book *La guerra contra las mujeres* (The War against Women), Rita Laura Segato conjoins the emphasis on historical gender-based violence and the violence derived from the present configuration of capital. For Segato, the feminicides actualize violence against women as a historical constant whose anthropological and juridical roots Segato aims to clarify. In Juárez, police investigations of the feminicides are often misled by an inertia over the political status of women. A true valuation of crimes with strong sexual markers remains difficult to apprehend for a "collective imaginary in which sexuality and law pertain to separate and irreconcilable spheres" whereby

---

31. On this point see Sergio Villalobos-Ruminot, *Heterografías de la violencia. Historia. Nihilismo. Destrucción* (Buenos Aires: La Cebra , 2016) 212–13.

32. Colette Soler, "The Body in the Teaching of Jacques Lacan," the English translation of this conference can be found in https://jcfar.org.uk/wp-content/uploads/2016/03/The-Body-in-the-Teaching-of-Jacques-Lacan-Colette-Soler.pdf.

sexual matters are considered part of the "private, intimate, and domestic order" and the law pertains to "the public sphere of universal and general interest" (88). Thus, crimes against women (especially when sexually marked) are a priori located outside the sphere of the social and the political and are instead prosecuted—or ignored—as crimes related to questions of domesticity or passion; that is to say, as pertaining to a sphere that has always functioned as a threshold for the law and its application. So, "even as the contemporary feminicides are carried out in the midst of the clamor, spectacle, and score settling of parastate wars, they never manage to emerge from their private capture in the imaginary of judges, attorneys, media editors, and public opinion in general" (23).

To the juridical prejudice that allocates women to the domestic sphere, Segato opposes the well-documented fact that the female body is tied to sovereign punishment. Wars, invasions, raids, and counterterrorist operations are pervasively marked by sexual violence against women. By an interpretive inversion, it is possible to understand the crimes of Juárez as a sign of an epochal mutation in the notion of sovereign power itself and, more specifically, of sovereignty's disengagement from the figure of the state in favor of its inscription on the obscene side of capitalist accumulation. One of Segato's most far-reaching speculations is that "a second state" emerges from the shadow of a weakening state.[33] Like the first (legal) state, the second state likewise relies on sovereign punishment for its operation—although this punishment is no longer an attribute of the law. Segato sees the criminal gangs of the deterritorialized spaces of global capitalism as the armed forces of the fantasmatic second state. In Juárez, where the relation between the second state and the first state becomes one of contamination rather than competition,[34] the city's criminals want to be recognized as the purveyors of a new power. Their crimes are signed, and what the signatures say is that the crimes were committed by people wielding the "capacity for cruelty and the power over death that high-risk enterprises require."[35]

New Maladies of the Soul

One can be hardly surprised by the somber tone in which Segato casts the question of the model subject of late capitalism in *The War against Women*:

---

33. Ibid., 75. Sayak Valencia makes a similar argument in *Capitalismo gore* (Madrid: Melusina, 2010).

34. However, Sayak Valencia says that in the 1990s "narco traffickers developed prerogatives proper to the state, such as the creation of infrastructure, labor positions, and schools." Valencia, *Capitalismo gore*, 41.

35. Segato, *La guerra*, 43.

Today the psychopathic personality would seem to be the personality structure best equipped to operate functionally in the order of the apocalyptic phase of capitalism. The psychopathic profile, with its ineptitude for transforming hormonal excess into affect and emotion; its need to constantly intensify stimuli to achieve their effect; its definitively non-linking structure; its indifference toward its own pain and—consequently, and even more so—that of others; its alienation, its encapsulation, and its unrootedness from both its own landscapes and collective ties; its instrumental and objectified relation to others ... seem indispensable for operating in an economy organized to the extreme by dehumanization and the absence of limits.[36]

The reference to the "psychopathic personality" is not intended as a clinical description, but nor as a metaphor. It is instead a border concept that invites us to take notice of a historical intimacy with the pathological.[37] Different as their realities may be, the first and the third world brush elbows around the psychopathology of their everyday life. Daniel Koren, a practicing analyst, was describing his urban educated patients, not murderous gangs when he characterized the contemporary collective mentality in terms of "an extraordinarily lax palette of clinical traits," marked by "rejection of symbolic inheritance and of social authority, sexual indifference, inconsistency of the body, augmentation of narcissistic impulses."[38]

Nothing of this seems to constitute a novelty. Already in his 1979 *The Culture of Narcissism*, Christopher Lasch—a historian by training— characterized some of the behaviors arising from consumerist self-absorption as pathological.[39] Slavoj Žižek, who wrote an enlightening introduction to the Croatian translation of Lasch's book, generalizes Lasch's observations and argues that Lasch's pathological narcissism has become a form of living the social link—a new ethic.[40] It is to this new ethic that J. A. Miller points to with the introduction of the expression "ordinary psychosis" to conceptualize the

---

36. Segato, *La guerra*, 101–2. See also Valencia, *Capitalismo gore*, 45–6.

37. Todd McGowan offers a description of this model subject that does not stray much from Segato's own words: "The superego commanding enjoyment and the epoch of global capitalism exist in a symbiotic relationship. Those who are under the sway of the command to enjoy become perfect global capitalist subjects." *The End of Dissatisfaction? Jacques Lacan and the Emerging Society of Enjoyment* (Albany, NY: State University of New York Press, 2003), 34.

38. Daniel Koren, "Destinos del padre," in *Freud: A cien años de Tótem y Tabú (1913-2013)*, ed. Néstor A. Braunstein, Betty B. Fuks, and Carina Basualdo (Mexico: Siglo XXI, 2013), 59.

39. Christopher Lasch, *The Culture of Narcissism: American Life in an Age of Diminishing Expectations* (New York: W.W. Norton, [1979] 1991).

40. Slavoj Žižek, "'Pathological Narcissus' as a socially Mandatory Form of Subjectivity," the English version of Žižek's introduction to the Croatan translation of

analytic landscape summarized by analysts like Koren. The idea that the most terrible of mental afflictions could become "ordinary" could not fail to have seismic consequences in the relationship between culture and psychoanalysis. Surely ordinary psychosis is not a full-fledged psychosis, but in a text that predates Miller's intervention by a couple of years Julia Kristeva was struck by patients exhibiting new " 'maladies of the soul' ... that are not necessarily psychoses, but that evoke the psychotic patient's inability to symbolize his unbearable traumas."[41] In Miller, ordinary psychosis names a series of partial and contingent disengagements of the subject from the symbolic, thereby comprising a peculiar form of "discontent" that takes the social link itself as its point of inflection. The partial disconnections from the regulative function of the law are covered up with substitutes (*suppléance*) of the law.[42] These substitutes are not free-floating symbolic elements accessible to all. They and their performance are socially disaggregated in such a way that an increase of economic means guarantees better access to better functioning substitutions.[43]

What is the law invoked here? It is any law whatsoever. It is the law insofar as it divides the subject, blocking his/her path toward an imaginary restitution of a mythical sense of completeness. The law simply says that the subject cannot exist in the dimension of the all. Freud called this limit the "pleasure principle." Certainly, he also spoke of a beyond the pleasure principle. Lacan located the mythical land of jouissance in that beyond, and he even made of transgression a form of access to that forbidden territory. But there is not such territory. Jouissance is not desire for evil. It is simply the desire to go beyond the limit, the limit drawn by the law on the bases of a conception of the good. The only reason why we can argue that we live in societies of enjoyment (Tod McGowan) is because the domination of the market has left us in a geography without any limit to transgress.

Lasch's book can be accessed in the internet at Zizek - 1986 - Pathological Narcissus as A Socially Mandatory Form of Subjectivity | PDF | Id | Narcissism (scribd.com).

41. Julia Kristeva, *New Maladies of the Soul*, trans. Ross Guberman (New York: Columbia University Press, 1995), 9.

42. Miller's first references to "ordinary psychosis" occurred in several conference talks and were later expounded in Jacques Alain-Miller, "Ordinary Psychosis Revisited," *Psychoanalytical Notebooks* 19 (2013): 139–67.

43. As for those without means, quite often they are the target of selective medicalization, which represents "a form of diffused governance that substitutes everyday commonsense categories and practices for rational and technical ones so as to vitiate the moral and political meaning of subjective complaints and protests." Joao Biehl, Byron Good, and Arthur Kleinmann, introduction to *Subjectivity. Ethnographic Investigations*, ed. Biehl, Good, and Kleinmann (Berkeley: University of California Press, 2007), 3.

According to analytic wisdom, the subject receives his/her point of orientation from a myth. Already in the 1950s, Lacan noticed the close connections that the dimension of the law keeps with the sense of the real. In *Seminar III*, he established a gnoseology of psychosis that relates it to the failure of the subject to inscribe in his/her unconscious the signifier of the law—what Lacan calls the name or no of the father.

> Everything that abounds in our literature, the fundamental principles on which we agree, imply it—in order for there to be reality, adequate access to reality, in order for the sense of reality to be a reliable guide, in order for reality not to be what it is in psychosis, the Oedipus complex has to have been lived through.[44]

Most of the time, Lacan's references to Oedipus are in fact references to castration. Paraphrasing him, we can say that in order for reality to be a reliable guide, castration has to have been lived through. The fact that the subject cannot "have it all" opens the possibility of searching for the lost happiness in a world constituted in such a way that the subject can ramble through it in search of his/her (improbable) satisfaction.

In stark opposition to this old ethic, we live in a world in which satisfaction is guaranteed—without anyone turning particularly happier on that account. Happiness—Lacan says in *Seminar XI*—is what happens. It is the happy encounter—the *bonheur*—with something that we are in no way predestined to encounter. The happiness offered by the market, on the other hand, is necessarily preprogrammed: the subject can have it all on condition that he/she ascribes to the idea that all there is to have is present in the horizon shaped by the total sum of the commodities of the contemporary globalized world. This strategy is powerless before the pregnancy of the real, but the logic of the market has found an unexpected ally in the discourse of modern science—which has wrested from religion and the humanities the traditional function of instilling existence with meaning. Once science assumes the place of authority in modernity, questions about existence (about the cohesiveness of the symbolic) circuit back to the dimension of the market where they are dealt with in terms of imaginary identifications and fulfillments. Slavoj Žižek calls this process "answers without questions." The flood of new consumer items "masks the empty place" from which desire emerges and creates a saturated field where the "impossible" desire (which is also the desire for the impossible) "can no longer be articulated."[45]

---

44. Jacques Lacan, *The Seminar of Jacques Lacan, Book III: The Psychoses 1955–1956*, trans. Russell Grigg (New York: W. W. Norton, 1997), 198.

45. Žižek, " 'Pathological Narcissus' as a Socially Mandatory Form of Subjectivity." This essay is the introduction to the Slovenian translation of Lasch, *The Culture of Narcissism*. The English version of Žižek's introduction is taken from Zizek - 1986

The importance of an "outdated" book like *Totem and Taboo* for our own time lies in the fact that the system of prohibitions it sketches allows us to read, as in a negative, the key injunctions that are promoted by consumer society and monopoly capitalism and which contribute to the distinctive features of our own discontent in civilization. To the centrality of prohibition, consumer society opposes the constant encouragement of satisfaction in all orders of life; to the traditional (Weberian) emphasis on deferral and restraint, the market opposes a sense of immediacy that has weakened our ability to tolerate waiting time and has increased our impatience with everything pertaining to an order that demands maturation or patient elaboration. Finally, the function of symbolic substitution or inheritance becomes increasingly irrelevant for a culture in which the general crisis of knowledge as a means to an end, and the ceaseless, yet also superficial, renewal of its codes of production, makes ever more superfluous the transmission from parents to children of any set of skills or even convictions.[46]

In 2016, the Museo de la Tolerancia in Mexico City organized an exposition on the feminicides that included a wall of "pesquisas" (pictures of missing girls) by Teresa Margolles. One of the most impacting images of the exhibit was that of the "to-do-lists" of the departed girls, which delineate plans to complete high school, read Plato, undertake vocational studies, be nice to people, paint a room, or change the curtains. These to-do lists, in their reliance on patience, waiting time, and maturation, are the exact reverse of the dominant relationship of the narcissistic pathological personality to time. The plans speak of goals that cannot be accomplished in solitude, or outside a mediation that is unknown to a morality for which satisfaction is the greatest good regardless of the modalities of its enjoyment: a morality sanctioned by the times in which no limitation of enjoyment can entertain any degree of social validation.[47]

The structure of contemporary servitude is unlike that of any other in history because it contains the freedom of the subject as its main premise. Under this structuration, the positive and enhancing function of the law withers away. It is often said that the Lacanian father (his name and his "no") inscribes the law of the signifier in the subject. The only thing that the name of the father inscribes is the signifier of lack in the Other—the possibility of an absence against whose background, symbolic circulation, absence and presence (and along with them reality) become possible. By stating a limit, the law gives to the subject the measure of his/her desire and the possibility of his/her defiance.

- Pathological Narcissus as A Socially Mandatory Form of Subjectivity | PDF | Id | Narcissism (scribd.com).

46. Todd McGowan, *The Real Gaze: Film Theory after Lacan* (Buffalo, NY: SUNY Press, 2008), 51.

47. Charles Melman, *Novas Formas Clínicas no Início do tercero Milênio* (Porto Alegre, Brazil: CMC, 2003), 65.

Transgression, that formidable engine in the unfolding of civilization, is the result of the interdicting function of the law. But transgression itself becomes a problematic notion once all that is left to a culture is to innovate.

In 1972, Lacan explicitly connected psychosis (the idea that there is no limit, the blind assertion of the all) and capitalism when he defined the latter as "forclusive of the things of love."[48] This statement has been read as indicative of capitalism's animosity toward the social bond and the work of symbolization. There is a second aspect not to be missed. Love—Lacan writes in Seminar X—is that force by which jouissance condescends to the level of desire.[49] The removal of limits favored by capitalism results in a delirious constitution of subjectivity grounded on a perpetual erosion of any sense of common reality, and on an increasingly problematic relationship between the rights of the subject to enjoy and the rights of enjoyment to ignore any limit. In this talk, Lacan advances the formula of the discourse of the capitalist as a variation on the discourse of the master. Like the structure of psychosis, the discourse of capitalism proclaims that having it all is not only possible but as a matter-of-fact constitutes a sort of mandate for its subject. The ability of the discourse of the capitalist to block the imaginary of castration inherent to the construction of the symbolic hinges not so much on the possibility of hindering the paternal function but in disavowing the role of the paternal metaphor in the creation of a signifier of lack. It is not the name of the father that capitalism colonizes, but the signifier of lack in the Other. And in the same way that the absence of a welcoming space in the other leads the subject of psychosis to an alienating plenitude of meaning, the systemic obturation of any lack by the discourse of capitalism psychoticizes its modelic subject of consumption by constantly forcing him/her to oscillate between frustration and acting out.

The persistence of A as the destination of the subject's identification shows that a fundamental reference to the law remains the operational content of identification, but this space is now colonized by a discourse proclaiming that satisfaction must be unrestricted in principle. The neuroses of the Freudian subject originated in the impossibility of living up to the standards marked by socially recognized forms—Dora didn't know what it meant to be a woman, and little Hans couldn't be a son because he lacked an efficacious father. The contemporary subject must orient itself in a world where these ideals have been eroded if not have entirely disappeared.[50] There is no notion of woman to which

48. Jacques Lacan, "Du discours psychanalytique," in *Lacan in Italia 1953–1978/En Italie Lacan* (Milan: La Salamandra, 1978), 33.

49. Jacques Lacan, *The Seminar of Jacques Lacan*, Book X: Anxiety, 1962–1963, trans. A. Price (Cambridge: Polity Press, 2016), 179.

50. Although these ideals were unachievable by definition and tortured the subject for its shortcoming to measure up to the symbolic standards of the time, the discourse of the master/capitalist instilled in everyone the idea that unfulfillment is the result of a personal failure after the liberalization of the social has left us eye to eye with the object

the Doras of the present could submit their inquisitions, and the figure of the paternal—as a keyword for authority at large—is in tatters in all imaginable registers.

Anne Dufourmantelle summarizes the situation in the following terms: In our time, "the law ... appears so degraded it names only something prohibited that has been already transgressed without ever having been interiorized."[51] Something—Dufourmantelle continues—needs to be minimally respected (must work as a limit), or otherwise "the chaos of the drives threatens with invading it all."[52]

At this point, it is apposite to notice that the activism of Juárez does not conjure only the absent symbolic pact but also evokes the dimension of the law as that which should not be transgressed. A certain assertion of the political value of taboo is regularly involved in discourses about Juárez. In *More or Less Dead*, Alice Driver criticizes Charles Bowden's *Juárez: The Laboratory of Our Future* for publishing actual photos of murdered men and women. The book in question—which was published in English in 1998 with texts by Noam Chomsky and Eduardo Galeano—was never translated into Spanish due in part to the graphic nature of its material. The implicit censorship of Bowden's book looks like a displaced and delayed attempt to instantiate a prohibition. If Bowden's book can be said to be taboo, that would imply, out of necessity, the existence of a regulative rule—which, according to the market, no longer exists, as the crimes of Juárez confirm with pathological zeal. Something similar can be said of Sergio González Rodríguez's decision to print white pages in those sections of *The Femicide Machine* showing captions of absent photos. While the decision is unobjectionable, it is still possible to read it as a compensatory gesture pointing to the instantiation of a taboo as another strategy that seeks, like so many others in Juárez, to reconstitute the absent socius and the law as the binding manifestation of the symbolic pact.

Supplements of the Law

What is to be done? What is to be done is to make a call for politics, for the imagination about the future that appears foreclosed by capitalist discourse. This is urgent. But what is urgent is not necessarily what we should do first.

---

of our desires. The reconversion of this feeling gives rise to a strange ethics by which "individuals feel guilty not for violating moral inhibitions by way of engaging in illicit pleasures, but for not being able to enjoy." Slavoj Žižek, "Pathological Narcissus."

51. Anne Dufourmantelle, "Totém y Tabú: Una lectura," in *Freud: A cien años de Tótem y Tabú (1913–2013)*, ed. Néstor A. Braunstein, Betty B. Fuks, and Carina Basualdo (Mexico City: Siglo XXI, 2013), 35.

52. Ibid., 36.

Urgency itself, insofar as it is a trademark of consumerism's inability to sustain waiting time and the time of maturation, may well be one of our enemies. What is to be done is to introduce a pause, a split second of reflection, and not let the urgency to act lead us into an act without consequences.

Why is it that something needs to be done? Because something is constantly "being done!" It so happens that, sensing this problem, society—and especially in its first world instantiations that are subsequently spread as "solutions" to the rest of the world—has embarked on a mad proliferation of substitute law foundations, supplements of the law in Miller's sense, which aim to reinforce the subjective configuration of the present at the site where that configuration seems to be giving way. If, as I said, one of the most salient aspects of public mourning in Juárez has passed through the cultural instantiation of an absent symbolic, I can now venture the idea that in first world locations the withering of symbolic law is registered in the proliferation of norms that have become more a matter of etiquette than of self-examination.

All times have known norms. But not all times have lived in the shadow of their constant debasement in the form of ready-mades whose most disquieting power is that of divesting the subject of even a semblance of freedom. This scenario is easily verifiable in the multiple totemic arrangements of our times and in the most extreme forms of identity politics, where the assertion of the self often goes hand in hand with a perplexing difficulty to recognize the place of others. The withering of symbolic law affects, fundamentally, the dimension of language, where it takes the form of an increasing dominance of holophrases over the creative function of speech.[53] Linguists have characterized the holophrase as a congealed unit of meaning, one that is useful for starting or ending a conversation. Lacan used the holophrase to describe the gluing together of the subject and his/her statement. Already in *Seminar III*, he noticed that Dr. Schreber used language in such a way that did not open to any dialectic. For us, the holophrase takes the form of an urge to say the right thing. Saying the right thing has one characteristic: the statement doesn't need to be revised. In *RSI*, Lacan connects the decline of authority to the decline of the reading function.[54] The name of the father is just a statement offered up to the interpretive force of his children. The decline of reading—the push towards a message delivered from ambiguity—is the decline of freedom itself.

---

53. Holophrases are common in all languages as locutions that do not demand a meditated answer—greetings, speech acts of congratulations or condolences are often holophrases. When the distance between S1 and S2 congeals, the subject is holophrased (*s'holophrase*). Jacques Lacan, *The Seminar of Jacques Lacan, Book XI: The Four Fundamental Concepts of Psychoanalysis*, trans. Alan Sheridan (New York: W. W. Norton, 1998), 237.

54. Jacques Lacan, *The Seminar of Jacques Lacan, book XXII: RSI, 1974–1975*- unpublished seminar, available at http://staferla.free.fr/S22/S22.htm.

In the holophrase, the statement nullifies the force of enunciation. The said absorbs any saying. The statement cancels any singularity. For the subject of the watchword and the holophrase, all true decisions have been made for him/her.[55]

This detour through language is intended as a reminder that academic knowledge, the knowledge of the humanities, is not exempted from this decline of decision. Some time ago and in the context of a discussion of postcolonialism, Ray Chow referred to Thomas Elsaesser's observation that certain postcolonial contexts are impregnated by an attitude that "turns the machinery of surveillance ... into an occasion for self-display."[56] The targets of Chow's criticism are certain forms of identity politics that understand themselves too easily in terms of the master discourse they otherwise seek to undermine. Chow prefaces her discussion of the traps of identity with an epigraph from Roland Barthes, in which the French thinker characterizes fascism not as an interdiction on language, but instead as an incitement to say "the correct thing" in the eyes of the fascist. It is in light of this interpretation that we should read the somber tonality of Chow's criticism of the objectification of the colonial other "for a good cause":

> The machines of surveillance here are not war airplanes but the media—the networks of communication, which, in the academic world, include the classroom, conferences, publications, funding agencies and even letters of recommendation. With the large number of students (rightly) devoted to the constructions of difference, and of publishers (rightly) seeking to publish new, unexplored materials, fascism had reasserted itself in our era.[57]

Chow's observation is not empowering—but it has the virtue of locating the problem in the same coordinates through which the militants of Juárez tackle the unspeakable nature of a psychotic violence. One thing to be done is to reject the supplements of the law that represent the extinction of personal and social responsibility in the bonfire of a renewed form of positivism.

If, as Reiner Schürmann says, action follows being—meaning that whenever a time is provided with a key for its self-understanding (be it God, progress, spirit, final cause or sufficient reason) a modality of action follows—what then

---

55. Tod McGowan notices, "This complacency with the social order, however, is not experienced as complacency but as defiance ... we think we are challenging authority at precisely the moment we are most wholly following its directions. This is why political conservatives increasingly see themselves—and paint their conservatism—as rebellious," *End of Dissatisfaction?* 39.

56. Ray Chow, *Ethics after Idealism: Theory-Culture-Ethnicity-Reading* (Bloomington: Indiana University Press, 1998), 30.

57. Ibid., 30.

do we know?[58] We know that consumer society feeds on a crisis of community, on the production of a hypernarcissistic subject, on a destruction of inheritance, on the weakening of delay (and hence on a rejection of unproductive social time devoted to activities without ends). It feeds on an injunction to enjoy without limits (and hence without other, in an economy of pure sadism that can very well be passive). We know that in the absence of a regulative law "the chaos of the drives threatens to invade everything."[59] We know that the law (not just as prohibition but as decision about one's own desire) is tied to the arbitrariness of language and to the always enigmatic message of a paternal function that invites and demands a subject of reading as its correlate. What action follows from all that knowledge? Should we call for the reinstitution of a waning paternal authority? It certainly looks bizarre if a quest that began with the evidence of misogyny and the widespread abuse of women would end up postulating a return to patriarchal authority as a fix for the psychopathologies of late capitalism.[60] Likewise bizarre would be a nudge toward nostalgia for the old good days lived under the devastating oppression of always unachievable ideals.[61] Instead, it is a question of pondering how the democratic gains of our time can be decoupled from a systemic loss of freedom at the level of our existential possibilities.

We have found it very difficult to attend simultaneously to the rise of feminism on the one hand and to the internal combustion of the old patriarchal order on the other. But this is precisely the possibility that our present opens—a possibility that, moreover, is not merely reformist but truly revolutionary. This is the possibility embraced by Julia Kristeva, someone who is also troubled by the implications of the subject's perverted relationship to the law even though she is the author of a refined psychoanalytic theory that seeks to grant a symbolic role to the figure of the mother. It is by differentiating between paternal function and the symbolic that Kristeva can imagine a possible way out of the reiteration

---

58. Reiner Schürmann, *Heidegger on Being and Acting: From Principles to Anarchy*, trans. Christine-Marie Gros (Bloomington: Indiana University Press, 1987), 13.

59. Dufourmantelle, "Totém y Tabú," 36.

60. This is the prototypical right-wing solution to social discontent. As Slavoj Žižek writes, conservative positions call "for the restoration of the 'strong' paternal law as the only defense against the destructive potential of today's all-pervasive narcissism." Slavoj Žižek, *Irak. The Borrowed Kettle* (London: Verso, 2004), 103.

61. Lacan not only warned our present about the risks involved in a foreclosure of the cultural form of the name of the father (see ... *Or Worse, The Seminar of Jacques Lacan, Book XIX*, trans. E. R. Price (London: Polity Press, 2018)); he also sided without hesitation with the vindication of jouissance implied by the downfall of the universe of ideals. See *The Seminar of Jacques Lacan, Book XX, Encore. On Feminine Sexuality. The Limits of Love and Knowledge*, trans. Bruce Fink (New York: W. W. Norton, 1999).

of paternal law as the exclusive form of the law's inscription.[62] It is by departing from this assumption of a possible overcoming of symbolic domination while avoiding the risk of a psychotic rupture that she asks:

> What is our place in the order of sacrifice and/or language? Since we no longer wish to be excluded from this order, and we are no longer satisfied with our perpetually assigned role of maintaining, developing, and preserving this sociosymbolic contract as mothers, wives, nurses, doctors, teachers, and so forth, how might we appropriate our own space, a space that is passed down through tradition and that we would like to modify?[63]

Kristeva is placing more at stake in these sentences than the soft tone of her language may lead us to believe. She is talking not so much about women enjoying the same rights (or privileges) as men, but of modifying tradition as a phenomenal product of the symbolic, since it is in this phenomenality and not somewhere else that the conditions of possibility and actuality of patriarchal domination are inscribed. For Kristeva, opening this space of possibilities requires an act of political (and perhaps also poetic) invention. It cannot be achieved through the amplification of rights or recognition, because such strategies depend on the simple inversion and displacement of a sense of subordination.

Needless to say, this possibility of overcoming the most damning aspects of the symbolic structuration of society appeals to an array of progressive forces. It is a project that has the potential to stop neither at the frontier of class nor at that of race or nationality. It holds universal appeal at a time when the patriarchal demand is ostensibly reaching the pinnacle of its decline.

Language and Juárez

We speak better and more convincingly with our eyes fixed upon those forms of the world whose reflection gives us back a consistent image of our own selves. The Juárez of the crimes (because there are other Juárezes) is not such a place. It is, however, the place to which we must return in order to face a deficiency of words as a condition of our own discourse.

---

62. Kristeva writes: "It is difficult, if not impossible, for women to adhere to the sacrificial logic of separation and syntactic links upon which language and the social code are based, and this can eventually lead to a rejection of the symbolic that is experienced as a rejection of the paternal function and may result in psychosis." *New Maladies*, 213.

63. Ibid., 212.

How to understand and begin to talk about this violence (and what for)? What can be gained by dealing with facts only obliquely, proceeding through the commentaries of texts, testimonials, reports of activists and scholars; meditating on their repeated gestures, their blockages and breakthroughs? Have we not gotten to the end of language and its uses? It is not only that language falls short of its task, but that in addressing what it cannot address language becomes a mockery of itself, a waste, a redoubling of the impotence in the face of injustice that is one of the trademarks of our times. This pessimism about the possibilities of language, this hard to endure powerlessness of discourse, is in itself an essential aspect of the system that has produced the crimes of Ciudad Juárez. The activism around Juárez presents itself—unmistakably—as a fight for language.

I don't think it is too much of a stretch to venture that Roberto Bolaño felt the same trepidation before he embarked on writing "The Part about the Crimes" in *2666*, facing the impossibility of talking responsibly about the crimes and the unavoidable responsibility of talking. It is to this dilemma that "The Part about the Crimes" owes its dry style that has frustrated so many readers. In *Formas comunes*, Gabriel Giorgi reads the 106 forensic reports with which Bolaño tries the patience of his readers as representing the brutal staging of a state discourse in a position of indifference vis-a-vis "the life that it abandons."[64] For Giorgi, the apparent indifference of these pages has given us a clearer map, a far better idea, of the general context for the Juárez crimes than could be achieved through any "engaged" type of prose. Insofar as Bolaño positions himself in this biopolitical perspective he does not relate to the victims of Juárez under any form of redress. As a matter of fact, redress is a logical impossibility in this case, because the body of the victim is isolated from any social signification by the forensic gaze that, according to Eyal Weizman, is the increasingly dominant gaze of the state when confronted with the unwanted residue of its biopolitical functioning.[65]

The forensic gaze rejects the partition between life and death as a matter of principle. It deals only with corpses. In *Being and Time*, Heidegger—whose aversion to a merely biological treatment of the human is well known—makes

---

64. Gabriel Giorgi, *Formas comunes: Animalidad, cultura, biopolítica* (Buenos Aires: Eterna Cadencia, 2014), 199.

65. Weizman notices that "within the field of war-crime investigation, a methodological shift has recently led to a certain blurring. The primacy accorded to the witness and to the subjective and linguistic dimension of testimony, trauma, and memory—a primacy that has had such an enormous cultural, aesthetic, and political influence that it has reframed the end of the twentieth century as 'the era of the witness'—is gradually being supplemented (not to say bypassed) by an emergent forensic sensibility, an object-oriented juridical culture immersed in matter and materialities, in code and form, and in the presentation of scientific investigations by experts," Eyal Weizman, *Forensic Architecture: Violence at the Threshold of Detectability* (New York: Zone Books, 2017), 4.

a distinction between the perished and the deceased, pointing out that only the latter reflects the dignity of Dasein. Biological or empirical death and the cessation of life in an individual can never coincide, since every Dasein—whose being is made of existential possibilities—is necessarily more than itself.

In *2666*, where a forensic-like style delivers the bodies to statistical insignificance, the projective dimension of existence disappears. The capture of the dead body in a scientific, medical network evacuates a priori any vestige of meaning or expressivity. But it also represents, and in accordance with a variety of registers or necessities (juridical, biological, professional), a merely transitory status of the body. The forensic body is the body in abeyance—not only temporarily separated from its possibilities in an existential sense but also severed from the networks of meaning that seek to welcome it into a human form of death. The severing of the deceased from their sociohistorical attributes confirms the nature of modern biopolitics as a reduction of the human entity to mere life, a life that, when absent, reveals itself as mere death, as perished body rather than as departed. Sometimes Bolaño annotates that no one reclaimed the body. In these cases, the body in abeyance is released without having transitioned to a human death. Reclaiming anonymous bodies is one of the most ubiquitous—non juridical—forms of redress in Juárez. The sense-giving praxis of the city's activism is the obverse of forensic language. Insofar as culturally meaningful forms of redress target the biopolitical suspension of the symbolic pact, their ultimate object is the social in its totality—and not just the forgetting of the victims. The limits of their remedial power remain, however, the limits of discourse and praxis to reconstitute the space of the commons as the space of political efficacy. How this is to be done is a question that installs itself with more and more force as the first decades of the new century pass by.

Bolaño places a literary character as a placeholder for the reader's melodramatic expectations. Bolaño names him Lalo Cura. It is, according to both Lalo and the author, a fitting name. A thug turned police apprentice, Lalo is intrigued with particular intensity by the feminicides. He reads some police manuals in hopes of gaining a technical advantage that he can harness to the resolution of the crimes. In the end, however, no crime is solved, no identity restored, no trace vivified. One murder after another is closed without consequences in the archives of the law. Should we then conclude that madness is our destiny?

In a perspicacious reading of *2666*, José Ramón Ruisánchez shows that the justice that is unavailable in the perspective of forensic language emerges insidiously, indirectly, and without much fanfare in other parts of the novel. Ruisánchez reads the stories that surround "The Part about the Crimes," which he calls "the most risky of the parts in *2666*," as existing in an economic relation with other stories of justice and struggle. There is in Bolaño, Ruisánchez says, "a banality of evil but also a banality of the good, a good that has nothing exceptional about it," a good that just happens in the randomness of human affects. "The Part about the Crimes" would be "completely unreadable" (would not make sense) "without the apparently subsidiary stories of those who struggle, fall in love, and fail in Santa Teresa."[66] Is there a banality of the good? In her often contentious exchange with Gershom Scholem, Hannah Arendt argues that evil is always banal and only the good has deep roots.[67] If Arendt is right, where can we locate in the horizon of *2666* the depth of the good that so randomly traverses its pages? While I sympathize with Ruisánchez's idea of reading Bolaño beyond prophecy and utopia, I am forced to wonder if that random good that makes the world consist (and makes "The Part about the Crimes" readable) is not language itself under that form of indetermination that is literature's historical mission to represent.

Why should language and stories incarnate such a function? Because the unresolved jouissance of our present targets not only the anthropological ground of the law (and hence of freedom) but its structural foundation as well. It is apposite here to return for a moment to the landmark essay that Jacques Derrida published in 1992 under the title "Force of Law." I am interested in the centrality Derrida ascribes, starting with his title, to the notion of "force." What is this force in the text? Without entering into the long genealogy presupposed by this question, I would say that this force emerges from the law's fundamental insufficiency, from which it issues a call for a decision. Subjective responsibility—be it ethical, political, or aesthetical—is only imaginable if the law offers a space of undecidability as the ground of its own possible instantiation.[68] In the end, what is biopolitics if not the vehement censorship of that undecidability—that is, of any meaning that, originating in the body, would be able to attest to a destiny of the physical other than its capture in the senseless networks of science?

In Bolaño's *2666* language is the utopia of Juárez, but one that operates under incredible and increasing constraints. The rarefaction of discourse resulting from those constrains deeply concerns literature in its status as a discourse that, in principle, "can say everything."[69] At a time of "the overcoming of any symbolic activity by actions" and "the proliferation of pathologies of the act";[70]

---

66. José Ramón Ruisánchez, *La reconciliación: Roberto Bolaño y la literatura de amistad en América Latina* (Mexico City: UNAM, 2019).

67. Hanna Arendt, letter of July 24, 1963, in *The Correspondence of Hannah Arendt and Gershom Scholem*, trans. Anthony David, ed. Marie Luise Knott (Chicago: University of Chicago Press, 2017).

68. Jacques Derrida, "Force of Law: 'The Metaphysical Foundation of Authority,'" in *Deconstruction and the Possibility of Justice*, ed. Drucilla Cornell, Michel Rosenfeld, and David Carlson (New York: Routledge, 1992), 3–67.

69. Jacques Derrida, "This Strange Institution Called Literature: An Interview with Jacques Derrida," in *Acts of Literature*, ed. Derek Attridge (New York: Routledge, 1992), 37.

70. Diana Malamud, "Una imagen NO vale más que mil palabras," in *Psicoanálisis y cultura*, ed. Ricardo Mauro (Buenos Aires: Lugar, 2017), 129.

at a time of symbolic deficit and anemic metaphoric mediations, literature—a practice that is more and more domesticated, put in its place—still encapsulates the dimension of the word that remains to be fully expropriated by the forces of a neoliberal causation. Such expropriation is a constant possibility. It is one of the things that is being done. Its goal is not to silence us and render us mute, but to deliver us into the fold of an inconsequential word.

WORKS CITED

Ades, Dawn. *Art in Latin America. The Modern Era. 1820–1980.* New Haven, CT: Yale University Press, 1989.
Adorno, Theodore. *Aesthetic Theory.* Translated by R. Hullot-Kentor. Minneapolis: University of Minnesota Press, 1997.
Agamben, Giorgio. *The Man without Content.* Translated by Georgia Albert. Stanford: Stanford University Press, 1999.
Agamben, Giorgio. *The Open: Man and Animal.* Translated by Kevin Attel. Stanford: Stanford University Press, 2005.
Alighieri, Dante. *The Divine Comedy.* Translated by C. H. Sisson. New York: Oxford University Press, 2008.
Alonso, Carlos. *The Spanish American Regional Novel. Modernity and Autochthony.* Cambridge: Cambridge University Press, 1989.
Althusser, Louis, and Etienne Balibar. *Reading Capital.* Translated by Ben Brewster. London: Verso, 1990.
Arendt, Hanna. "The Conquest of Space and the Stature of Man." In *Between Past and Future,* 265–80. New York: Penguin Classics, 1954.
Arendt, Hanna. *The Correspondence of Hanna Arendt and Gershom Scholem.* Translated by Anthony David. Chicago: University of Chicago Press, 2017.
Arguedas, José María. *El zorro de arriba y el zorro de abajo.* Edited by E.-M. Fell. Mexico: Colección Archivos, 1992.
Arguedas, José María. *Formación de una cultura nacional indoamericana.* Edited by Angel Rama. Mexico: Siglo XXI, 1989.
Arguedas, José María. *The Fox from Up Above and the Fox from Down Below.* Translated by Frances Horning Barraclough. Pittsburgh: University of Pittsburgh Press, 2000.
Arguedas, José María. *Obras Completas,* vol. 2. Lima: Horizonte, 1983.
Arguedas, José María. *Todas las sangres.* Lima: Horizonte, 1983.
Arias, Arturo. "Algunos aspectos de ideología y lenguaje." In *Hombres de maíz.* Edited by Gerald Martin, 553–69. Madrid: ALLCA XX, 1996.
Arias, Arturo. *La identidad de la palabra: Narrativa guatemalteca a la luz del siglo XX.* Guatemala: Artemis-Edinter, 1998.
Arias, Salvador. *El cine, décima musa.* Havana: Ediciones ICAIC, 2011.
Arroyo, Jossiana. *Travestismos culturales: literatura y etnografía en Cuba y Brasil.* Pittsburgh, PA: Instituto Internacional de Literatura Iberoamerica, 2003.
Asturias, Miguel Angel. *Hombres de maíz.* Edited by Gerald Martin. Madrid: ALLCA XX, 1996.
Asturias, Miguel Angel. *Men of Maize.* Translated by Gerald Martin. New York: Delacorte Press/Seymour Lawrence, 1975.
Badilla, Ana Elena. *Femicidio: más allá de la violación del derecho a la vida; análisis de los derechos violados y las responsabilidades estatales en los casos de femicidio*

en Ciudad Juárez. San José, Costa Rica: Instituto Interamericano de Derechos Humanos, 2008.
Badiou, Alain. "Democratic Materialism and the Materialistic Dialectic." *Radical Philosophy* 130 (2005): 20–4.
Badiou, Alain. *Lacan. Anti-Philosophy 3*. New York: Columbia University Press, 2018.
Bakhtin, Mikhail. "Epic and Novel." In *The Dialogical Imagination*. Edited by Michael Holquist, 3–40. Austin: University of Texas Press, 1982.
Barnet, Miguel. *Biografía de un cimarrón*. Havana: Instituto de Etnologia y Folklore, 1966.
Barnet, Miguel. *Biography of a Runaway Slave*. Translated by W. Nick Hill. New York: Pantheon Books, 1968.
Barnet, Miguel. *Cimarrón: Historia de un esclavo*. Madrid: Siruela, 2000.
Barthes, Roland. *Camera Lucida: Reflections on Photography*. Translated by Richard Howard. New York: Hill and Wang, 2000.
Barthes, Roland. *Chambre claire. Note sur la photographie. Ouvres Completes*. III. Paris: Du Seuil, 1980.
Barthes, Roland. *Le Plaisir du texte*. Paris: Du Seuil, 1973.
Baucom, Ian. *Specters of the Atlantic. Finance Capital, Slavery, and the Philosophy of History*. Durham, NC: Duke University Press, 2011.
Bazin, André. "The Ontology of the Photographic Image." In *What Is Cinema?* Translated by Hugh Gray, 9–16. Berkeley: University of California Press, 2005.
Bellini, Giussepe. "Nota Crítica." In *Tres Obras: Leyendas de Guatemala, El Alhajadito, El señor Presidente*. Miguel Angel Asturias, 3–7. Caracas: Biblioteca Ayacucho, 1977.
Benjamin, Walter. "Critique of Violence." In *Reflections: Essays, Aphorisms, Autobiographical Writings*. Edited by Peter Demetz. Translated by Edmund Jephcott, 277–300. New York: Schocken Books, 1978.
Benjamin, Walter. *Illuminations*. Edited by Hanna Arendt. Translated by Harry Zohn. New York: Shocken Books, 1968.
Berger, John. *Understanding a Photograph*. Edited by Geoff Dyer. London: Penguin, 2013.
Berumén, Miguel Angel, and Claudia Canales. *México. Fotografía y revolución*. México: INAH-Conaculta, 2009.
Beverley, John. *Latinamericanism after 9/11*. Durham, NC: Duke University Press, 2011.
Biehl, Joao, Byron Good, and Arthur Kleinmann. "Introduction: Rethinking Subjectivity." In *Subjectivity. Ethnographic Investigations*. Edited by Biehl, Good, and Kleinmann. Berkeley: University of California Press, 2007.
Birkenmaier, Anke. *Alejo Carpentier y la cultura del surrealismo*. Madrid: Vervuert-Iberoamericana, 2006.
Birkenmaier, Anke. "Entre antropología y filología. Fernando Ortiz y el Día de la Raza." In *Antípoda. Revista de Antropología y Arqueología* 15 (2012): 193–218.
Bleichmar, Daniela. *Visual Voyages. Images of Latin American Nature from Columbus to Darwin*. New Haven, CT: Yale University Press, 2017.
Bolaño, Roberto. *2666*. Translated by Natasha Wimmer. New York: Picador, 2009.
Bolton, Richard. "Introduction. The Contest of Meaning: Critical Histories of Photography." In *The Contest of Meaning: Critical Histories of Photography*. Edited by Richard Bolton, ix–xix. Boston: MIT Press, 1992.

Boscán, Guillermo Yepes. "Asturias, un pretexto del mito." In *Hombres de maíz*. Edited by Gerald Martin, 675–89. Madrid: ALLCA XX, 1996.
Bosteels, Bruno. *Marx and Freud in Latin America*. Durham, NC: Duke University Press, 2013.
Bourdieu, Pierre. *Photography: A Middle Brown Art*. Translated by Shaun Whiteside. Stanford: Stanford University Press, 1990.
Bowden, Charles. M. *Juarez. The Laboratory of Our Future*. San Francisco: Aperture, 1998.
Brathwaite, Edward Kamau. "The African Presence in Caribbean Literature." In *Africa in Latin America: Essays on History, Culture, and Assimilation*. Edited by Manuel Moreno Fraginals. Translated by Leonor Blum, 103–44. New York: Holmes and Meier, 1984.
Braudel, Fernand. *The Wheels of Commerce. Civilization & Capitalism 15th-18th Century, vol.2*. Translated by Siân Reynolds. Cambridge: Harper & Row, 1988.
Braunstein, Néstor A., Betty B. Fuks, and C. Basualdo, eds. *Freud: A cien años de Tótem y Tabú. (1913-2013)*. Mexico: Siglo XXI, 2013.
Brecht, Bertolt. *Journals. 1934–1955*. Translated by John Willet. London: Routledge, 1995.
Brotherston, Gordon. "The Latin American Novel and its Indigenous Sources." In *On Modern Latin American Fiction*. Edited by John King, 60–77. New York: Noonday Press, 1987.
Brizuela, Natalia. *Fotografía e Império: paisagens para um Brasil moderno*, Translated by Marcos Bagno. Sao Paulo: Companhia Das Letras, 2011.
Buck Morss, Susan. *Hegel, Haiti, and Universal History*. Pittsburgh: Pittsburgh University Press, 2009.
Butler, Judith. *Gender Trouble: Feminism and the Subversion of Identity*. New York: Routledge, 1990.Cabrera, Lydia. *El Monte. Igbo. Finda. Ewe Orisha. Vititi Nfinda (Notas sobre las religiones, la magia, las supersticiones y el folklore de los negros criollos y el pueblo de Cuba)*. Miami: Ediciones Universal, 1995.
Campbell, Collin. *The Romantic Ethic and the Spirit of Modern Consumerism*. London: Blackwell, 1987.
Campobello, Nellie. *Cartucho, and My Mother's Hands*. Translated by Doris Meyer and Irene Matthews. Austin: University of Texas Press, 1988.
Canales, Claudia. "La densa materia de la historia." In *México: Fotografía y revolución*, ed. Miguel Angel Berumen, 51–118. México City: Conaculta, 2010.
Carpentier, Alejo. "Con el creador del Acorazado Potemkin." In *El cine, décima musa*. Edited by Salvador Arias. Havana: Ediciones ICAIC, 2011.
Carpentier, Alejo. *Ecue-Yamba-O y otros escritos afrocubanos*, vol. 1, *Obras completas*. Mexico City: Siglo XXI, 2001.
Carpentier, Alejo. *El reino de este mundo*, in vol. 2 of *Obras completas de Alejo Carpentier*. Mexico City: Siglo XXI, 1989.
Carpentier, Alejo. *Entrevistas*. Edited by Virgilio López Vermus. Havana: Letras Cubanas, 1985.
Carpentier, Alejo. *The Kingdom of This World*. Translated by Harriet de Onis. New York: Noonday Press, 1957.
Carpentier, Alejo. "On the Marvelous Real in America." In *Magical Realism: Theory, History, Community*. Edited by Lois Parkinson Zamora and Wendy B. Faris.

Translated by Tanya Huntington and Lois Parkinson Zamora, 89–108. Durham, NC: Duke University Press, 1995.

Castellanos, Jorge. *Pioneros de la etnografía Afrocubana: Fernando Ortiz, Rómulo Lachatañeré, Lydia Cabrera*. Miami: Ediciones Universal, 2003.

Castellanos, Jorge, and Isabel Castellanos. *Cultura afrocubana*, vol. 3, *Las religiones y las lenguas*. Miami: Ediciones Universal, 1983.

Castellanos Moya, Horacio. *Senselessness*. Translated by Katherine Silver. New York: New Directions, 2008.

Caygill, Howard. *On Resistance. A Philosophy of Defiance*. Bloomsbury, London: 2013.

Chakravarty, Dipesh. *Provincializing Europe: Postcolonial Thought and Historical Difference*. Princeton: Princeton University Press. 2007.

Chandler, Nahum. *The Problem of the Negro as a Problem for Thought*. New York: Fordham University Press, 2014.

Chow, Ray. *Ethics after Idealism: Theory–Culture–Ethnicity–Reading*. Bloomington: Indiana University Press, 1998.

Clifford, James. "On Ethnographic Surrealism." In *The Predicament of Culture*. Cambridge, MA: Harvard University Press, 1988.

Cornejo Polar, Antonio. "La Novela indigenista: Una desgarrada conciencia de la historia." LEXIS IV, no. 1 (1980): 77–89.

Cornejo Polar, Antonio. *Los universos narrativos de José María Arguedas*. Buenos Aires: Losada, 1974.

Coronado, Jorge. *Portraits in the Andes: Photography and Agency, 1900–1950*. Pittsburgh: University of Pittsburgh Press, 2018.

Damisch, Hubert. "Cinq notes pour une phénoménologie de l'image photographique." *L'Arc* 21 (1963): 34–7.

Dayan, Joan. *Haiti, History and the Gods*. Berkeley: University of California Press, 1998.

De Andrade, Carlos Drummond. *Alguma Poesía*. Rio de Janeiro: Pindorama, 1930.

De la Fuente, Alejandro. *A Nation for All: Race, Inequality, and Politics in Twentieth-Century Cuba*. Chapel Hill: University of North Carolina Press, 2001.

De la Fuente, Alejandro. "Race and Inequality in Cuba, 1899–1981," *Journal of Contemporary History* 30 (1995): 131–68.

Debroise, Olivier. *Mexican Suite: A History of Photography in Mexico*. Translated by Stella de Sá Rego. Austin: University of Texas Press, 2001.

Derrida, Jacques. *Archive Fever. A Freudian Impression*. Translated by Eric Prenowitz. Chicago: The University of Chicago Press, 1995.

Derrida, Jacques. "Force of Law: 'The Metaphysical Foundation of Authority.'" In *Deconstruction and the Possibility of Justice*. Edited by Drucilla Cornell, Michel Rosenfeld, and David Carlson, 3–67. New York: Routledge, 1992.

Derrida, Jacques. *Specters of Marx. The State of the Debt, the Work of Mourning & the New International*. Translated by Peggy Kamuf. London: Routledge, 2006.

Derrida, Jacques. "This Strange Institution Called Literature: An Interview with Jacques Derrida." In *Acts of Literature*. Edited by Derek Attridge, 33–75. New York: Routledge, 1992.

Derrida, Jacques. *The Truth in Painting*. Translated by Geoffrey Bennington and Ian McLeod. Chicago: University of Chicago Press, 1987.

Didi-Huberman, Georges. *Devant le temps. Histoire de l'art et anachronisme des images*. Paris: Les Editions de Minuit, 2001.

Didi-Huberman, Georges. *The Eye of History. When Images Take Positions*. Translated by Shane B. Lillis. Cambridge: MIT Press, 2018.
Didi-Huberman, Georges. *Images in Spite of All: Four Photographs from Auschwitz*. Translated by Shane B. Lillis. Chicago: University of Chicago Press, 2008.
Driver, Alice. *More or Less Dead: Feminicide, Haunting, and the Ethics of Representation in Mexico*. Tucson: University of Arizona Press, 2015.
Du Bois, W. E. B. *Black Reconstruction in America. 1860–1880*. New York: Simon and Schuster, 1992.
Dufourmantelle, Anne. "Totém y Tabú. Una lectura." In *Freud: A cien años de Tótem y Tabú. (1913–2013)*. Edited by Nestor Braunstein, B. Fuks, and C. Basualdo, 33–50. Mexico: Siglo XXI, 2013.
Echevarría, Bolivar. *El materialismo de Marx*. Mexico: Editorial Itaca, 2010.
Eisenstein, Sergei, dir. *¡Qué Viva México!* San Francisco: Kino Lorber, 1931.
Feldman, Irina. *Rethinking Community from Peru: The Political Philosophy of José María Arguedas*. Pittsburgh: University of Pittsburgh Press, 2014.
Ferrer, Ada. *Freedom's Mirror. Cuba and Haiti in the Age of Revolution*. Cambridge: Cambridge University Press, 2014.
Ferrer, Ada. *Insurgent Cuba: Race, Nation, and Revolution, 1868–1898*. Chapel Hill: University of North Carolina Press, 1999.
Figueroa, Victor. "The Kingdom of Black Jacobins: C. L. R. James and Alejo Carpentier on the Haitian Revolution." *Afro-Hispanic Review* 25, no. 2 (2006): 55–71.
Fick, Carolyn. *The Making of Haiti. Saint Domingue Revolution from Below*. Knoxville: University of Tennessee Press, 1990.
Fink, Bruce. *A Clinical Introduction to Lacanian Psychoanalysis: Theory and Technique*. Cambridge, MA: Harvard University Press, 1999.
Fischer, Sibylle. *Modernity Disavowed: Haiti and the Cultures of Slavery in the Age of Revolution*. Durham, NC: Duke University Press, 2004.
Folgarait, Leonard. *Seeing Mexico Photographed. The Work of Horne, Casasola, Modotti y Alvarez Bravo*. New Haven, CT: Yale University Press, 2008.
Foucault, Michel. "Nietzsche, Genealogy, History." In *Language, Counter-Memory, Practice*. Selected Essays and Interviews by Michel Foucault. Edited by Donald F. Bourchard, 139–64. Ithaca, NY: Cornell University Press, 1977.
Fregoso, Rosa-Linda, and Cynthia Bejarano, eds. *Terrorizing Women: Feminicide in the Américas*. Durham, NC: Duke University Press, 2010.
Freud, Sigmund. *Civilization and Its Discontents*. Translated by James Strachey New York: W. W. Norton, 2010.
Freud, Sigmund. "Fetishism." In *Sexuality and the Psychology of Love*. Edited by Phillip Rieff. New York: Collier Books, 1963.
Freud, Sigmund. "Psycho-analytic Notes on an Autobiographical Account of a Case of Paranoia." In *The Standard Edition of the Complete Psychological Works of Sigmund Freud*. Translated by James Strachey. London: Vintage, 2001.
Furst, Lilian R. *Realism*. London: Longman, 1992.
Galli, Carlo. *Political Spaces and Global World*. Edited by Adam Sitze .Translated by Elisabeth Fay. Minneapolis: University of Minnesota Press, 2010.
García, José Z. "Security Regimes on the U.S.-Mexico Border." In *Transnational Crime and Public Security: Challenges to Mexico and the United States*. Edited by John Bailey and Jorge Chabat, 299–334. La Jolla: Center for U.S.-Mexican Studies/ University of California, San Diego, 2002.

Gates, Henry Louis Jr. *The Signifying Monkey: A Theory of African-American Literary Criticism*. New York: Oxford University Press, 1988.
Giorgi, Gabriel. *Formas comunes: Animalidad, cultura, biopolítica*. Buenos Aires: Eterna Cadencia, 2014.
Glissant, Edouard. *Poetics of Relation*. Translated by Betsy Wing. Ann Arbor: University of Michigan Press, 1997.
Gómez Morín, Manuel. *1915 y otros ensayos*. Mexico City: Cultura, 1927.
González Echevarría, Roberto. *Myth and Archive: A Theory of Latin American Narrative*. Durham, NC: Duke University Press, 1998.
González Rodríguez, Sergio. *The Femicide Machine*. Translated by Michael Parker-Stainback. Los Angeles: Semiotext(e), 2012.
González Rodríguez, Sergio. *Huesos en el desierto*. Barcelona: Anagrama, 2010.
Graff Zivin, Erin. *The Wandering Signifier: Rhetoric of Jewishness in the Latin American Imaginary*. Durham, NC: Duke University Press, 2008.
Gugelberger, George, M., ed. *The Real Thing. Testimonial Discourse and Latin America*. Durham, NC: Duke University Press 1996.
Hanchard, Michael. *Party/Politics: Horizons in Black Political Thought*. New York: Oxford University Press, 2006.
Hannavy, John, ed. *Encyclopedia of Nineteenth Century Photography*. New York: Routledge, 2013.
Hartley, George. *The Abyss of Representation. Marxism and the Postmodern*. Durham, NC: Duke University Press, 2003.
Harvey, David. *The Limits of Capital*. London: Verso, 2007.
Hegel, G. W. F. *The Phenomenology of Spirit*. Translated by A. V. Miller. Oxford: Oxford University Press, 1977.
Heidegger, Martin. *Being and Time*. Translated by John Macquarrie and Edward Robinson. Oxford: Basil Blackwell, [1962] 1978.
Heidegger, Martin. *Being and Time*. Translated by Joan Stambaugh. Albany: State University of New York Press, 1996.
Heidegger, Martin. *Discourse on Thinking*. Translated by M. Anderson and H. Freund. New York: Harper & Row, 1969.
Heidegger, Martin. *Kant and the Problem of Metaphysics*. Translated by Richard Taft. Bloomington: Indiana University Press, 1997.
Heidegger, Martin. "The Origin of the Work of Art." In *Heidegger. Basic Writings*. Translated by David Farrell Krell. New York: HarpersCollins, 1993.
Henighan, Stephen. *Assuming the Light: The Parisian Literary Apprenticeship of Miguel Angel Asturias*. Oxford, UK: Legenda, 1999.
Hershfield, Joanne. *Imagining la Chica Moderna. Women, Nation, and Visual Culture in Mexico 1917–1932*. Durham, NC: Duke University Press, 2008.
Iversen, Margaret. "Indexicality: A Trauma of Signification." In *Photography, Trace, and Trauma*, 17–30. Chicago: University of Chicago Press, 2016.
James, C. L. R. *The Black Jacobins: Toussaint L'Ouverture and the San Domingo Revolution*. New York: Vintage Books, 1989.
Jameson, Fredric. *The Antinomies of Realism*. London: Verso, 2013.
Jameson, Fredric. *The Geo-Political Aesthetic. Cinema and Space in the World System*. Bloomington: Indiana University Press, 1992.

Jameson, Fredric. *Postmodernism or, the Cultural Logic of Late Capitalism*. Durham, NC: Duke University Press, 1993.
Johnson, Randal. "Tupy or non Tupy." In *On Modern Latin American Fiction*. Edited by John King, 39–45. New York: Noonday Press, 1987.
Kane, Adrian Taylor. *Central American Avant-Garde Narrative: Literary Innovation and Cultural Change (1926–1936)*. Amherst, MA: Cambria Press, 2014.
Kant, Immanuel. *Critique of Judgment*. Translated by W. S. Pluhar. Indianapolis, IN: Hacket, 1987.
Kern, Stephen. *The Culture of Time and Space: 1880–1918*. Cambridge, MA: Harvard University Press, 1993.
Kiesel, Theodore. *The Genesis of Heidegger's Being and Time*. Berkeley: University of California Press, 1993.
King, John. *On Modern Latin American Fiction*. New York: Noonday Press, 1987.
Kraniauskas, John. *Capitalism and Its Discontent. Power and Accumulation in Latin-American Culture*. Cardiff: University of Wales Press, 2017.
Kristeva, Julia. *New Maladies of the Soul*. Translated by Ross Guberman. New York: Columbia University Press, 1995.
Kutzinski, Vera. *Sugar's Secrets: Race and the Erotics of Cuban Nationalism*. Charlottesville: University of Virginia Press, 1993.Lacan, Jacques. "Du discours psychanalytique." In *Lacan in Italia/Lacan en Italie (1953–1978)*. Milan: La Salamandra, 1978.
Lacan, Jacques. *Ecrits*. Translated by Bruce Fink. New York: W. W. Norton, 2007.
Lacan, Jacques. *… Or Worse. The Seminar of Jacques Lacan, Book XIX*. Translated by A. R. Price. Cambridge: Polity, 2018.
Lacan, Jacques. "Psychanalyse et médecine. La place de la psychanalyse dans la médecine." Accessed January 18, 2022, https:// reseaupsychologues.eu/Lacan/ Psychanalyse-et-medecine.
Lacan, Jacques. *The Seminar of Jacques Lacan. Book I: Freud Papers on Technique. 1953–1954*. Translated by John Forrester. New York: W. W. Norton, 1995.
Lacan, Jacques. *The Seminar of Jacques Lacan Book 11: The Four Fundamental Concepts of Psychoanalysis*. Edited by Jacques-Alain Miller. Translated by Alan Sheridan. New York: W. W. Norton, 1998.
Lacan, Jacques. *The Seminar of Jacques Lacan. Book III: The Psychoses 1955–1956*. Translated by Russell Grigg. New York: W. W. Norton, 1997.
Lacan, Jacques. *The Seminar of Jacques Lacan, Book VII: The Ethics of Psychoanalysis*. Translated by Dennis Porter. New York: W. W. Norton, 1992.
Lacan, Jacques. *The Seminar of Jacques Lacan, Book X: Anxiety 1962–1963*. Translated by A. Price. Cambridge: Polity Press, 2016.
Lacan, Jacques. *The Seminar of Jacques Lacan. Book XX, Encore. On Feminine Sexuality. The Limits of Love and Knowledge*. Translated by Bruce Fink. New York: W. W. Norton, 1999.
Lacan, Jacques. *The Seminar of Jacques Lacan. Book XXII: RSI, 1974–1975*-unpublished seminar. http://staferla.free.fr/S22/S22.htm.
Lagarde y de los Rios, Marcela. "Preface: Feminist Keys for Understanding Feminicide. Theoretical, Political, and Legal Construction." In *Terrorizing Women: Feminicide in the Américas*. Edited by Rosa-Linda Fregoso and Cynthia Bejarano, xi–xxv. Durham, NC: Duke University Press, 2010.

Lasch, Christopher. *The Culture of Narcissism: American Life in an Age of Diminishing Expectations*. New York: W. W. Norton, [1979] 1991.
Lee, Richard E., and Immanuel Wallerstein. *Overcoming the Two Cultures: Sciences and the Humanities in the Modern World-System*. New York: Routledge, 2016.
Legrás, Horacio. *Culture and Revolution: Violence, Memory, and the Making of Modern Mexico*. Austin: University of Texas Press, 2017.
Lienhard, Martin. *La voz y su huella*. Lima: Horizonte, 1992.
Lloyd, David, and Paul Thomas. *Culture and the State*. New York: Routledge, 1998.
Löwy, Michael. "L'irréalisme critique." *Actuel Marx* 45, no. 1 (2009): 52–65.
Maguire, Emily. *Racial Experiments in Cuban Literature and Ethnography*. Gainsville: University of Press Florida, 2011.
Malamud, Diana. "Una imagen NO vale más que mil palabras." In *Psicoanálisis y cultura*. Edited by Ricardo Mauro, 127–32. Buenos Aires: Lugar, 2017.
Mariátegui, José Carlos. "Populismo literario y estabilización capitalista." *Amauta* no. 28 (1930): 6–9.
Marinello, Juan. *Literatura Hispanoamericana: hombres, meditaciones*. Mexico City: Ediciones de la Universidad Nacional de México, 1937.
Martin, Gerald. "Génesis y trayectoria del texto." In *Hombres de maíz*. Edited by Gerald Martin, 471–505. Madrid: ALLCA XX/Fondo de Cultura Económica, 1996.
Martin, Gerald. "Introducción del coordinador." In *Hombres de maíz*. Edited by Gerald Martin, xxi–xxxiii. Colección Archivos. Madrid: ALLCA XX/Fondo de Cultura Económica, 1996.
Marx, Karl. *Capital: A Critique of Political Economy*. Vol. 1. Translated by Ben Fowkes. New York: Penguin, 1992.
Mbembe, Achille. *Critique of Black Reason*. Translated by Laurent Dubois. Durham, NC: Duke University Press, 2017.
McCauley, Anne. "The Trouble with Photography." In *Photography Theory*. Edited by James Elkins. London: Routledge, 2007.
McGowan, Todd. *The End of Dissatisfaction? Jacques Lacan and the Emerging Society of Enjoyment*. Albany: SUNY Press, 2003.
McGowan, Todd. *The Real Gaze: Film Theory after Lacan*. Buffalo: SUNY Press, 2008.
Millay, Any Nauss. *Voices from the Fuente Viva: The Effect of Orality In Twentieth-Century Spanish American Narrative*. Lewisburg, PA: Bucknell University Press, 2005.
Miller, Jacques-Alain. "Ordinary Psychosis Revisited." *Psychoanalytical Notebooks* 19 (2013).
Monárrez Fragoso, Julia Estela. *Juárez, Trama de una injusticia: Feminicidio sexual sistemático en Ciudad Juárez*. Ciudad Juárez, Mexico: Colegio de la Frontera Norte, 2009.
Monárrez Fragoso, Julia Estela. "The Victims of the Ciudad Juárez Feminicide." In *Terrorizing Women: Feminicide in the Américas*. Edited by Rosa-Linda Fregoso and Cynthia Bejarano. Durham, NC: Duke University Press, 2010.
Monasterios, Elizabeth. "Revisionismos inesperados. La contramarcha vanguardista de Gamaliel Churata y Arturo Borda." *Revista Iberoamericana* 253 (2015): 989–1013.
Monsiváis, Carlos. "When Gender Can't Be Seen amid the Symbols: Women and the Mexican Revolution." In *Sex in Revolution. Gender, Politics and Power in Modern Mexico*. Edited by Jocelyn Olcott, Mary Kay Vaughan, and Gabriela Cano. Durham, NC: Duke University Press, 2010.

Monsiváis, Carlos. "Introduccion." *La estatua de sal* by Salvador Novo. Mexico: Fondo de Cultura Económica, 2008.
Monsiváis, Carlos. "La aparición del subsuelo: Sobre la cultura de la Revolucion Mexicana." *Historias* 8–9 (1985): 150–66.
Montgomery, Harper. "Innovators and Iconoclasts: Six Books on Latin American Modern and Contemporary Art." *Latin American Research Review* 54, no. 4: 1082–9, doi: http://doi.org/10.25222/larr.675.
Montgomery, Harper. *The Mobility of Modernism*. Austin: Texas University Press, 2018.
Moore, Melisa. *En la encrucijada. La literatura y las ciencias sociales en el Perú, lecturas paralelas*. Lima: UNMSM, 2003.
Moore, Robin Dale. *Nationalizing Blackness: Afrocubanismo and Artistic Revolution in Havana, 1920–1940*. Pittsburgh: University of Pittsburgh Press, 1998.
Moraña, Mabel. *Arguedas/Vargas Llosa. Dilemas y Ensamblajes*. Madrid: Iberoamericana Vervuert, 2013.
Moraña, Mabel. *Churata Postcolonial*. Lima: Centro de Estudios Literarios Cornejo Polar, 2015.
Moreiras, Alberto. *El no sujeto de lo político*. Santiago de Chile: Palinodia, 2008.
Moreiras, Alberto. "Introduction: The Conflict in Transculturation." *Literary Cultures of Latin America. A Comparative History*. Vol. III. Edited by Mario Valdés and Djelal Kadir, 129–37. Oxford: Oxford UP, 2004.
Mraz, John. *Photographing the Mexican Revolution: Commitments, Testimonies, Icons*. Austin: University of Texas Press, 2012.
Mulvey, Laura. "Visual Pleasure and Narrative Cinema." *Screen* 16, no. 3 (1975): 6–18.
Neruda, Pablo. *Canto General*. México: Talleres Gráficos de la Nación, 1950.
Newhall, Beaumont. *A History of Photography: From 1839 to the Present*. New York: Museum of Modern Art, 1982.
Nietzsche, Friedrich. *The Will to Power*. Translated by Walter Kaufmann. New York: Viking Press, 1982.
Noble, Andrea. *Photography and Memory in Mexico: Icons of Revolution*. Manchester: Manchester University Press, 2010.
Noble, Andrea. "Zapatistas en Sanborns (1914): Women at the Bar." *History of Photography* 22, no. 4 (1998): 366–70.
Orillo, Winston. "*Todas las Sangres*, gigantesco esfuerzo novelistico de José María Arguedas." *Correo de Lima*, February 25, 1965.
Ortiz, Fernando. "Al lector." *Catauro de cubanismos: apuntes lexicográficos*. Havana: n.p., 1923.
Ortiz, Fernando. *Etnia y sociedad*. Havana: Editorial de Ciencias Sociales, 1993.
Ortiz, Fernando. *Glosario de Afronegrismos*. Havana: Libreria Cervantes, 1924.
Ortiz, Fernando. "The Human Factors of Cubanidad." Translated by João Felipe Gonçalves and Gregory Duff Morton. *Hau: Journal of Ethnographic Theory* 4, no. 3 (2014): 445–80.
Ortiz, Fernando. "Por la integración cubana de blancos y negros." *Estudios Afrocubanos*, Havana (1945–6): 216–29.
Ortiz, Fernando. "Por la integración cubana de blancos y negros." *Ultra* 13, no. 77 (1943): 69–76.
Ortiz, Fernando. *Un catauro de cubanismos*. Havana: Revista Bimestre Cubana, 1923.

Ortiz Monasterio, Pablo. *Mexico. The Revolution and Beyond.* New York: Aperture, 2003.
Palmié, Stephan. *The Cooking of History: How Not to Study Afro-Cuban Religion.* Chicago: University of Chicago Press, 2014.
Palmié, Stephan. *Wizards and Scientists: Explorations in Afro-Cuban Modernity and Tradition.* Durham, NC: Duke University Press, 2002.
Palumbo-Liu, David, Nirvana Tanoukhi, and Bruce Robbins, eds. *Immanuel Wallerstein and the Problem of the World: System, Scale, Culture.* Durham, NC: Duke University Press, 2011.
Pascal, Blaise. *Pensees.* Penguin: New York, 1995.
Patterson, Olando. *Slavery and Social Death: A Comparative Study.* Cambridge, MA: Harvard University Press, 1982.
Perez Firmat, Gustavo. "The Philological Fictions of Fernando Ortiz." *Notebooks in Cultural Analysis* 2 (1985): 190–207.
Poulet, George. "Phenomenology of Reading." *New Literary History* 1, no. 1 (1969): 53–68.
Pratt, Mary Louise. *Imperial Eyes. Studies in Travel Writing and Transculturation.* London: Routledge, 2007.
Prieto, René. *Miguel Angel Asturias's Archeology of Return.* Cambridge: Cambridge University Press, 1993.
Price-Mars, Jean. *Ainsi parla l'oncle: essais d'etnographie.* Edited by Celucien L. Joseph. Port St. Lucie, FL: Hope Outreach, 2016.
Rancière, Jacques. *Aisthesis. Scenes from the Aesthetic Regime of Art.* Translated by Paul Zakir. London: Verso, 2013.
Rancière, Jacques. *The Politics of Literature.* Translated by Julie Rose. London: Polity Press, 2011.
Richman, Michèle. *Sacred Revolutions: Durkheim and the Collège De Sociologie.* Minneapolis: University of Minnesota Press, 2002.
Ricouer, Paul. *Time and Narrative.* Translated by Kathleen McLaughlin and David Pellauer. Chicago: University of Chicago Press, 1984.
Rincón, Carlos. "Nociones surrealistas, concepción del lenguaje y función ideológica-literaria del realismo mágico en Miguel Angel Asturias." In *Hombres de maíz.* Edited by Gerald Martin. Colección Archivos, 695–722. Madrid: ALLCA XX/ Fondo de Cultura Económica, 1996.
Roa Bastos, Augusto. "El texto ausente." In *La obra posterior a* Yo el Supremo, Augusto Roa Bastos, 9–16. Poitiers: Centre de Recherches Latino-Américaines, 1999.
Rochabrún, Guillermo. *¿He vivido en vano? La mesa redonda sobre "Todas las sangres" del 23 de Junio de 1965.* Lima: IEP, 2011.
Rochabrún, Guillermo, ed. *La mesa redonda sobre "Todas las sangres."* Lima: Pontificia Universidad Católitca del Perú, 2000.
Rodríguez-Mangual, Edna. *Lydia Cabrera and the Construction of an Afro-Cuban Cultural Identity.* Chapel Hill: University of North Carolina Press, 2004.
Rosenberg, Fernando. "Cultural Theory and the Avant-Garde." In *The Blackwell Companion to Latin American Culture and Literature.* Edited by Sara Castro-Klaren, 410–25. London: Routledge, 2008.
Rotman, Brian. *Signifying Nothing: The Semiotics of Zero.* Stanford: Stanford University Press, 1987.

Rousseau, Jean-Jacques. *Discourse on the Origin of Inequality*. Translated by Donald A. Cress. Indianapolis, IN: Hackett, 1992.
Rowe, William. "Deseo, escritur.a y fuerzas productivas." In *El zorro de arriba y el zorro de abajo*. Edited by E.-M. Fell, 333–40. Mexico: Colección Archivos, 1992.
Ruisánchez José, Ramón. *La reconciliación. Roberto Bolaño y la literatura de amistad en América latina*. Mexico: UNAM, 2019.
Salzinger, Leslie. *Genders in Production: Making Workers in Mexico's Global Factories*. Berkeley: University of California Press, 2003.
Schmitt, Carl. *The Concept of the Political*. Translated by George Schwab. Chicago: University of Chicago Press, 1996.
Schroeder Rodríguez, Paul. *Latin American Cinema. A Comparative History*. Oakland: University of California Press, 2016.
Schurmann, Reiner. *Heidegger on Being and Acting: From Principles to Anarchy*. Translated by Christine-Marie Gros. Bloomington: Indiana University Press, 1987.
Schutte, Ofelia. "Nietzsche, Mariátegui, and Socialism. A Case of Nietzschean Marxism in Peru." *Social Theory and Practice* 14 (1988): 71–85.
Schwarz, Roberto. *Misplaced Ideas. Essays on Brazilian Culture*. Edited by John Gledson. London: Verso, 1992.
Scott, James. *Seeing Like a State: How Certain Schemes to Improve the Human Condition Have Failed*. New Haven, CT: Yale University Press, 1999.
Segato, Rita Laura. *La guerra contra las mujeres*. Madrid-Buenos Aires: Traficante de Sueños, 2016.
Segato, Rita Laura. "Territory, Sovereignty and Crimes of the Second State: The Writing on the Body of Murdered Women." In *Terrorizing Women*. Edited by Fregoso and Bejarano, 70–91. Durham, NC: Duke University Press, 2010.
Shellhorse, Adam Joseph. *Anti-Literature. The Politics and Limits of Representation in Modern Brazil and Argentina*. Pittsburgh: University of Pittsburgh Press, 2017.
Skocpol, Theda. *States and Social Revolutions: A Comparative Analysis of France, Russia, and China*. Cambridge: Cambridge University Press, 1979.
Sloterdijk, Peter. "Rules for the Human Zoo: A Response to the *Letter on Humanism*." *Environment and Planning D: Society and Space* 27, no. 1 (2009): 12–28.
Soler, Colette. "The Body in the Teaching of Jacques Lacan," https://jcfar.org.uk/wp-content/uploads/2016/03/The-Body-in-the-Teaching-of-Jacques-Lacan-Colette-Soler.pdf.
Solomon-Godeau, Abigail. *Photography at the Dock. Essays on Photographic History, Institutions and Practices*. Minneapolis: University of Minnesota Press, 1991.
Sorlin, Pierre. *Le fils de Nadar: le "siècle" de l'image analogique*. Paris: Nathan, 1997.
Spillers, Hortense J. "Mam's baby, papa's maybe. An American Grammar Book." *Diacritics* 17 no. 2 (1987): 65–81.
Staudt, Kathleen. *Violence and Activism at the Border. Gender, Fear and Everyday Life in Ciudad Juárez*. Austin: University of Texas Press, 2008.
Svampa, Maristella. *Debates latinoamericanos: Indianismo, desarrollo, dependencia y populismo*. Buenos Aires: Edhasa, 2016.
Szarkowski, John. *Photography until Now*. New York: Museum of Modern Art, 1983.
Szwed, John. *Crossovers: Essays on Race, Music, and American Culture*. Philadelphia: University of Pennsylvania Press, 2005.
Toledo Vásquez, Patsilí. *Femicidio/Feminicidio*. Buenos Aires: Ediciones Didot, 2014.

Trouillot, Michel Rolph. *Silencing the Past: Power and the Production of History.* Boston, MA: Beacon Press, 1997.
Valencia, Sayak. *Capitalismo gore.* Madrid: Melusina, 2010.
Vallejo, César. *The Complete Poetry. A Bilingual Edition.* Edited and translated by Clayton Eshleman. Oakland: University of California Press, 2009.
Vargas Llosa, Mario. "Cuatro preguntas a Alejo Carpentier." *Marcha* (Montevideo) III (March 12, 1965): 31–2.
Vargas Llosa, Mario. "Una nueva lectura de *Hombres de maíz*." In *Hombres de maíz.* Edited by Gerald Martin. Colección Archivos, 649–53. Madrid: ALLCA XX/Fondo de Cultura Económica, 1996.
Vaughan, Mary Kay. "Pancho Villa, the Daughters of Mary, and the Modern Woman: Gender in the Long Mexican Revolution." In *Sex in Revolution: Gender, Politics, and Power in Modern Mexico.* Edited by Mary Kay Vaughan, Gabriela Cano, and Jocelyn H. Olcott, 21–32. Durham, NC: Duke University Press, 2007.
Vidal, Hernán. "Introducción." In *Treinta años de estudios literarios/culturales latinoamericanistas en Estados Unidos: Memorias, testimonios, reflexiones críticas,* 9–60. Pittsburgh: Instituto Internacional de Literatura Iberoamericana, 2008.
Villalobos-Ruminot, Sergio. *Heterografías de la violencia. Historia. Nihilismo. Destrucción.* Buenos Aires: La Cebra, 2016.
Vogl, Joseph. *The Specter of Capital.* Translated by Joachim Redner and Robert Savage. Stanford: Stanford University Press, 2015.
Von Uexküll, Jakob. *Mondes animaux et monde humain, suivi de Théorie de la signification.* Translated by Phillipe Müller. Paris: Pocket Collection, 1965.
Von Uexküll, Jakob. *Theoretical Biology.* New York: Harcourt, Brace, 1926.
Warwick Research Collective. *Combined and Uneven Development: Towards a New Theory of World-Literature.* Liverpool: Liverpool University Press, 2015.
Washington Valdez, Diana. *Harvest of Women: Safari in Mexico; the Truth about Mexico's Bloody Border Legacy.* Burbank, CA: Peace at the Border, 2006.
Weber, Max. *The Protestant Ethic and the Spirit of Capitalism.* London: Routledge, 1997.
Weizman, Eyal. *Forensic Architecture: Violence at the Threshold of Detectability.* New York: Zone Books, 2017.
Wilderson, Frank. *Red, Black and White: Cinema and the Structure of U.S. Antagonisms.* Raleigh, NC: Duke University Press, 2010.
Williams, Eric. *Capitalism and Slavery.* Chapel Hill: University of North Carolina Press, 1944.
Wilson, Kathleen. "The Performance of Freedom: Maroons and the Colonial Order in Eighteenth-Century Jamaica and the Atlantic Sound." *The William and Mary Quarterly* 66, no. 1 (2009): 45–86.
Žižek, Slavoj. *Irak. The Borrowed Kettle.* London: Verso, 2004.
Žižek, Slavoj. Zizek - 1986 - Pathological Narcissus as A Socially Mandatory Form of Subjectivity | PDF | Id | Narcissism (scribd.com).

INDEX

Adorno, Theodore 7 n.20, 120
Afro-Cuban culture
   Carpentier and 94
   in the 1920s 88–9
   music 89
   Ortiz Fernando 87 n.23
   religion 90
   Santeria 91
Agamben, Giorgio 38
Althusser, Louis
   interpellation 90–1
   Marx's Darsterllung 129–30
Andrade, Drumond de 11
archive
   Asturias and the Maya Quiché archive 31
   Derrida, Jacques 15 n.44
   Palmié, Stephan on 17 n.48
Asturias Miguel Angel
   archive/archivization, 15, 29
   capitalism 44–5
   environmental conservationism 38–9, 45
   Heidegger, and 29
   modernity and 28–30
   myth 30
   politics of time 46
   Popol Vuh, and 22
   slavery and 42 n.46
   surrealism and 25–6
   symbolic and 32, 34, 37
   Weber's *The Protestan Ethics*, and 42
Arendt Hanna, 116, 155
Arguedas, Jose María
   criticism of formal subsumption 132
   cultural heterogeneity in Peru 113
   "El sueño del pongo" 18
   Huayco 129, 131
   monads in *Todas las sangres* 118, 124, 127, 129
   poetic principles 120
   round table on *Todas las sangres* 113–14
avant-garde
   in Asturias 24–6
   collage as formal principle 4
   crisis of reality in early twenty-century and 23, 27 n.16
   Cubism and 22, 24, 28
   in Latin America 1–11
   surrealism 5, 25–6

Badiou, Alain
   criticism of anti-philosophy 13
   democratic materialism 13 n.36
Barnet, Miguel 83–5
Barthes, Roland
   Camera lucida 52, 53, 62, 63 n.34, 59, 70 n.50
   fascism and language 150
Baucom, Ian 10
Benjamin, Walter 124, 131, 134
Berger, John 66, 74
Beverley, John 14 n.43
Bolaño Roberto (*2666*) 133, 141, 153–5
Bosteels, Bruno 12 n.36
Bowden, Charles 141, 148
Braudel, Fernand 126–7
Brecht, Bertolt 3
Breton, André 15, 24
Birkenmaier, Anke 95 n.41, 98 n.51, 103 n.60
Bolivar Echeverría 73, 75
Buck-Morss, Susan (*Hegel and Haiti*) 107–10
Butler, Judith, 68

Cabrera Lydia
   Césaire, Aimé, and 2
   ethnography and politics 81, 93–4

Firmas (Anaforuanas) 105
El Monte 77–83, 90–3
negritude 83
possession 91–2
testimonio, and 86, 108
Campobello, Nellie 67 n.44
Canales, Claudia 60
capitalism
　Arguedas and 122, 125–7
　Asturias and 44–6
　as epochal principle 122, 126
　Harvey David, on 124
　opacity, and 128
　pathological narcissism, and 143, 147
　subsumption 3, 123
Carpentier, Alejo
　¡Ecué-yamba-O! 94, 107
　Eisenstein, and 98 n.49
　embodiment and 4–5
　Haiti and 96–9
　James, C. L. R. and 97, 99
　The Kingdom of this World 4, 95, 105
Cartier Bresson, Henri 63
Casasola, Agustin 53, 55–6, 65
Castellanos Jorge, and Castellanos Isabel 78, 94 n.39
Castellanos Moya, Horacio
　(*Senselessness*) 16
Caygill, Howard 125
Chakrabarty, Dipesh 82, 84
Chandler, Nahum 9
Chow, Ray 150
Christophe, Henry 100, 104
Cimarronaje (fugitivism) 85–6
Clifford, James 24
Cornejo Polar, Antonio 115, 117, 118, 119
Cuba
　abolition of slavery 86–7
　Partido Independiente de Color 87
　(*See also* Ortiz Fernando, Cabrera, Lydia)

Dayan, Joan 91, 93, 105, 106
De Andrade Mario 3
Debroise Olivier 58, 66
Derrida, Jacques
　"Force of Law" 155
　Specters of Marx 71–2

Dessalines, Jean-Jacques 99, 105
Didi-Huberman, Georges 13 n.37, 17, 58 n.18, 62, 63 n.32, 75
Driver, Alice 148
Dufourmantelle, Anne 148

ethical turn
　literary figuration 12
　politics, and 12

Favre, Henri 119
Feldman, Irina 114, 130
Feminicidio 134, 138–9
Ferrer, Ada 85 n.15, 86, 104
Folgarait, Leonard 62
Foucault, Michel 130
Freud, Sigmund 70 n.51, 72, 88, 135, 144, 146

Giorgi, Gabriel 153
González Echeverría, Roberto 86
Gónzalez Rodríguez, Sergio 133, 135, 139, 140, 141, 148

Haiti, revolution 96, 105
Hartley, George, 125
Harvey, David 124
Hegel/Hegelianism 24, 109–10, 120, 127
Heidegger, Martin
　criticism of presence 71
　death, hermeneutics of 110
　departed vs deceased 153–4
　"The Origin of the Work of Art" 5–6
　worldhood of the world 28–9

Jameson, Fredric
　allegory 129
　criticism of realism 7–8
　literature as a means of knowledge 116, 117, 127
　literary mapping 128
Juárez, Ciudad
　maquilas 141
　spatiality 151
　violence 133–4
　women movements and activism 134, 148, 153

(*See also* González Rodríguez, Segato, Rita Laura)

Kojeve, Alexandre 69
Koren, Daniel 143
Kraniauskas, John 22
Kristeva, Julia 144, 151–2

Lacan, Jacques
   capitalist discourse 147
   castration anxiety 72
   decline of reading function 149
   ethics as relation to the Real 7, 11
   holophrase 149–50
   image 52, 91, 145, 146
   language 32–3, 52, 72
   reality and psychosis 144, 147
   symbolic 32–3
Lagarde y de los Rios 133, 134
Landrián, Nicolás 92 n.32
Lasch, Christopher 143
Leduc Paul 66 n.45
Lee, Richard 115
Lienhard, Martin 21
L'Ouverture, Toussaint 97, 105
Löwy, Michael 7
Lukacs, Georg 7

McGowan, Todd 144
Maguire, Emily 79 n.5
Margolles Teresa 146
Mariátegui, José Carlos 1, 2 n.3, 8, 14
Martin, Gerald 21–2, 33–4, 39, 44, 46
Marx, Karl
   commodity as *ungeheuren* 124–5
   presentation of capital 130
Mbembe, Achille 82 n.9, 104, 110
Merleau-Ponty Name 49
Miller, Jacques-Alain 143–4
Monárrez Fregoso, Julia 135, 136
Monsiváis, Carlos
   criticism of pathriarchy 70
   Mexican photography 52, 65
Moore, Robin 88
Moraña, Mabel 122 n.20
Morerias Alberto 15 n.43
Mraz, John 51

Mulvey Laura 68
Museo de la Tolerancia, Mexico 146

NAFTA 140
nativist avant-garde 2–4, 9–10
neoliberalism, 137–8, 146, 156
Neruda, Pablo 4–5, 17
Newhall, Beaumont 60
Nietzsche, Friedrich 14, 24, 130
Noble, Andrea 64, 65, 69
now-then, temporal structure 9–10, 124

Ortiz Fernando
   Black uprooting and Cuban nation 106
   Carpentier, and 94
   Catauro 106
   Cuban nation 101–3, 104
   Eugenics, and 97
   turn 87 n.23
Osuna, Sabino 66 n.40

Palmié, Stephan 17 n 48, 106, 108, 109
Pérez Firmat, Gustavo 103
photography of the Mexican Revolution
   anxiety in the face of women 67
   attunement 62
   function of appeasement 66–7
   photojournalism and straight photography 53–4
   untimeliness 62
   as Western gaze 60
   women as signifier of the popular, and 65
   women and visual insurgency 68–9
   women and universalism 69
Pratt, Mary Louise 24
Prieto, René 28, 35 n.35, 38
psychotic violence 134–6

Rama, Angel 121 n.19
Rancière, Jacques 13 n.37, 26, 114
realism
   Jameson, Fredric and 8
   Latin America and 6, 117
   Lukacs and 7
   Mariátegui José Carlos, and 8
Ricouer, Paul 9

Rincón, Carlos 44
Roa Bastos, Augusto 17, 27
Rodchenko, Alexander 61
Rosenberg, Fernando 5 n.14
Rotman, Brian 49 n 59
Rousseau, Jean-Jacques 39
Rowe, William 130
Ruisánchez, José Ramón 155

Sans Souci 100, 105
Sartre, Jean Paul 115
Sayak, Valencia 142 nn.33, 34
Schmitt, Carl 87
Schurmann, Reiner 127
Schurman, Reinner 150
Segato, Rita Laura
   notion of second state 142
   psychotic personality 143
   War Against Women 141
sexual violence 134–6
slavery, and crisis of language 104–5
solidarity as political trope 97–8

Solomon Godeau, Abigail 70
Spiller, Hortense 103
Spivak, Gayatri 15
Staudt, Kathleen 134
subaltern studies 14–15
surrealism (*see* avant-garde)

Testimonio 14, 83–5
Trouillot, Rolph, 105

Vallejo, César 11
Vaughan, Mary Kay 64
Vidal, Hernán 18–19
Vogl Joseph 41
Voodoo 107, 111

Wallerstein, Immanuel 115–16
Weizman Eyal 153
Weston, Edward 58, 62

Žižek, Slavoj 143, 145, 147 n.50

www.ingramcontent.com/pod-product-compliance
Lightning Source LLC
Chambersburg PA
CBHW061836300426
44115CB00013B/2404